Drugs, Crime and Public Health

Drugs, Crime and Public Health provides an accessible but critical discussion of recent policy on illicit drugs. Using a comparative approach – centred on the UK, but with insights and complementary data gathered from the USA and other countries – it discusses theoretical perspectives and provides new empirical evidence which challenges prevalent ways of thinking about illicit drugs. It argues that problematic drug use can only be understood in the social context in which it takes place, a context which it shares with other problems of crime and public health. The book demonstrates the social and spatial overlap of these problems, examining the focus of contemporary drug policy on crime reduction. This focus, Alex Stevens contends, has made it less, rather than more, likely that long-term solutions will be produced for drugs, crime and health inequalities. And he concludes, through examining competing visions for the future of drug policy, with an argument for social solutions to these social problems.

Alex Stevens is Professor in Criminal Justice at the University of Kent. He has worked on issues of drugs, crime and health in the voluntary sector, as an academic researcher and as an adviser to the UK government, and has published extensively on these issues.

Drugs, Crime and Public Health

The political economy of drug policy

Alex Stevens

First published 2011
by Routledge
2 Park Square, Milton Park, Abingdon, Oxon, OX14 4RN

Simultaneously published in the USA and Canada
by Routledge
270 Madison Avenue, New York, NY 10016

A GlassHouse book

Routledge is an imprint of the Taylor & Francis Group, an informa business

Typeset in Garamond by
RefineCatch Limited, Bungay, Suffolk
Printed and bound in Great Britain by
CPI Antony Rowe, Chippenham, Wiltshire

British Library Cataloguing in Publication Data
A catalogue record for this book is available
from the British Library

Library of Congress Cataloging in Publication Data
Stevens, Alex.
Drugs, crime, and public health : the political economy of drug policy / Alex Stevens.
p. cm.
Includes bibliographical references.
1. Drug abuse. 2. Drug abuse and crime. 3. Drug abuse—Government policy. 4. Drug control. I. Title.
HV5801.S774 2010
362.29'1561—dc22

2010026399

ISBN10: 0-415-49104-5 (hbk)
ISBN13: 978-0-415-49104-4 (hbk)

ISBN10: 0-203-84416-5 (ebk)
ISBN13: 978-0-203-84416-8 (ebk)

For Jo

Contents

Figures

Tables

Preface

I have observed the harms related to drugs and their control all my working life. I have corresponded with imprisoned British drug smugglers, and advised the families they left behind. I have visited prisons across Europe, all of them struggling to deal with influxes of drug users and of the drugs that they want to use. I have helped set up projects to support people in finding a way out of dependent drug use and into employment. I have interviewed many people whose lives have been damaged by their use of heroin and crack. Several of them have since died. Some have continued a life of petty, persistent offending. Others have turned their lives around with the help of drug treatment services, the love of their families, the support of their peers, through sheer determination or a combination of all four. I have discussed these issues in empty streets, crowded bars, fetid hostels, dilapidated bedsits, poster-strewn waiting rooms, bleak cells, noisy classrooms, windowless lecture halls, plush hotel atria and inside the warren-like corridors of number 10 Downing Street. Throughout this career, I have lived in a British society which cannot live without alcohol, where smoking tobacco still kills over 90,000 people every year, where caffeine is indispensable to office life and where cannabis and illicit stimulants are regularly used by callow teenagers and prospective cabinet ministers. I have been surrounded by drugs and drug talk. I have met some remarkable talkers. I have also heard and read a lot of nonsense. This book is my attempt to create a more adequate analysis. It discusses theoretical perspectives and presents new evidence that can be used to test them. Its aim is to change the way you think about the links between drugs, crime and public health.

At the back of this book, there is a long list of people whose work I have leaned on for both illumination and support. I have also discussed the ideas presented here with colleagues in the International Society for the Study of Drug Policy, the British and European Societies of Criminology and the Common Study Programme in Critical Criminology, with co-investigators and partners in the *QCT Europe, Early Exit* and *Connections* projects, as well as with current and former colleagues at Prisoners Abroad, Cranstoun Drug Services, the European Institute of Social Services and the School of Social

Policy, Sociology and Social Research at the University of Kent. Funding to support the research that informs this book has been provided by the European Commission, the Department of Health, the Economic and Social Research Council, the Barrow Cadbury Trust, RAPt, Phoenix Futures, the UK Drug Policy Commission, the Beckley Foundation, London Probation Service and Kent County Council. A shorter version of the analysis presented in Chapter 4 has been accepted for publication in 2011 by *Journal of Social Policy*. Additional data have been provided by the Ministries of Justice of the UK and the Netherlands, the Home Office and the UK Data Archive at the University of Essex. My thanks go to all, with apologies for any errors or misinterpretations that have entered the analysis.

My largest debt is closer to home. My partner, Jo, has been this book's greatest supporter and its most intelligent critic. She gave me the time and the inspiration to write it. It is to her that this book is dedicated, with love.

Chapter 1

Starting points

Drugs, values and drug policy

The debate on drugs is dominated by one, endlessly recurring argument. Should drugs be legal or prohibited? Proponents in these repetitive discussions often talk as if their position, if only it could be universally accepted, holds the golden key to a future where crime, addiction and drug-related deaths are vastly reduced. The vacuous slogan of the 1998 UN General Assembly Special Session on drugs – 'a drug-free world: we can do it' – is countered by libertarian opponents of prohibition who make no less speculative claims about the benefits of allowing a free market in all psychoactive substances. As has often been noted (e.g. Currie 1993; Young 1971), these blinkered discussions close off consideration of the social issues that are at the root of many of the harms for which drugs and laws have been blamed. In this book, I will argue that these harms are deepened by inequality and that policy on drugs and crime plays a part in producing and reproducing inequality. If we were magically to achieve a drug-free world tomorrow, crime and ill-health would continue. And if a Jericho-like blast from a troop of legalizers could somehow bring the whole edifice of prohibition tumbling down, drugs would still be associated with unnecessary deaths and other harms. These harms would continue to be concentrated amongst the most vulnerable people who have been socially, economically and racially marginalized.

The debate on drugs largely ignores issues of equality, and especially the role of drug policy in reproducing inequality. It diverts our attention away from the social mechanisms that produce social harms. It deepens the gap between rich and poor, powerful and powerless that so hinders our ability to reduce harms and increase freedoms. Part of the problem is the lack of a coherent, justifiable system of values to underpin drug policy. Drug policy emerges from competing ways of thinking about these values. Selective attachments to abstinence conflict with utilitarian arguments for the reduction of the economic burdens of drug use. Enlightenment or religious notions of the need for sober self-regulation come up against the apparently universal human desire for intoxication (Klein 2008). Conservative ideas on individual responsibility and sobriety conflict with liberal discourse on personal fulfilment and freedom of choice (O'Malley 2002). One potential response to these conflicts is to step back and view all of them dispassionately, decrying both the moralism of one position (prohibition) and the attempt at disciplinary control of another (harm reduction). Politicians, drug users and their families do not have that option. They are faced with the urgent need to choose, to act. This chapter will seek to provide a rationally justified basis for these decisions. It will then describe the themes that run through the development of modern drug policy, in order to prepare the way for the arguments of this book.

Drug, harms and rights

Not all the acts that are criminalized are inherently harmful. Homosexuality was once considered a crime. Now it is recognized, by the law at least, as an area of individual freedom. Not all harmful acts are criminalized. Examples include the endangerment of human life and health through unsafe working practices, as well as the destruction of wealth by risky banking decisions. We need a better basis than the criminal law for analysing social harms (Hillyard *et al.* 2005). A previous discussion of the moral basis of drug use and associated harms has argued that criminal laws against drug use are unjustified (Husak 1992). However, it (apparently deliberately) did not provide a justifiable principle on which to base discussion of these rights and harms. This book uses the work of the moral philosopher, Alan Gewirth (1978) to provide a rational basis for defining human needs, and therefore for defining social harm. His argument is a contemporary development of Kant's categorical imperative: 'Act in such a way that you treat humanity, whether in your own person or in the person of any other, always at the same time as an end and never merely as a means to an end' (Kant 1981 [1785]: 36).

Gewirth writes in technical language. At the risk of offending philosophers, I will attempt to lay out the steps of his argument here in relatively simple terms. It rests on the law of non-contradiction. This is one of Aristotle's laws of thought. It states that a proposition and its contradiction cannot both be true. Although many attempts have been made to disprove this law, they have all ended in confusion. This is because the law applies even to attempts to contradict it. Arguments against the law are terminally vulnerable to the question: is your proposition that 'a proposition and its contradiction can both be true' itself true or false? To accept this literally nonsensical proposition would be to allow an infinite proliferation of contradictory meanings. No statement could reliably signify any content, as its opposite could be equally valid. This basic problem means that relativist attempts to rule out any possibility of moral judgement, which rely on contradicting the law of non-contradiction, are fatally flawed. This does not mean that such judgments are simple, or need no basis apart from religion, intuition or individual preference. Rather, it commits us to open discussion of right and wrong on the basis of logical rules to which we are rationally committed, whether we like it or not.

The first principle of Gewirth's argument is that any person who seeks to act must value the necessary conditions of action. Such an agent needs freedom and well-being. As Gewirth (1982: 47) puts it, '[s]ince agents act for purposes they regard as worth pursuing . . . they must, insofar as they are rational, also regard the necessary conditions of such pursuit as necessary goods'. He argues that every agent must accept, on pain of self-contradiction, that she has rights to the necessary conditions of action. The next step is to note that because a person accords these rights to herself (or himself) on the grounds of being an agent, then she (or he) must also, again on pain of self-contradiction, accord these rights to other persons who have the capacity to act towards purposes. Gewirth calls this the 'principle of generic consistency', or PGC. Echoing Kant's categorical imperative, the PGC 'requires of every agent that he accords to his recipients the same rights to freedom and well-being that he necessarily claims for himself' (Ibid: 53). The PGC is a rule of mutual respect. This rule cannot automatically resolve debates about what constitutes harmfulness (these questions are always more difficult in practical examples than in the abstract principles, as will be seen in later chapters), but it provides a useful basis on which to ground definitions of rights, duties and harms.

The PGC sets up a hierarchy of rights that can be useful in deciding which harms are most important. Rights are of greater priority when they are more needful for the creation or maintenance of the freedom and well-being that are necessary for purposive action. On this basis, Gewirth distinguishes three, hierarchical levels of rights: basic; nonsubtractive; and additive. Basic rights refer to an agent's right to the preconditions of agency. These include life, physical integrity and health. Harms to nonsubtractive rights are those harms which reduce, but do not destroy, the agent's capacity for action. Examples include losses by theft, deception, exploitation and defamation. We have additive rights to those conditions and actions which increase our ability to act towards our own purposes.

The PGC therefore also provides a basis for the discussion of whether there is a human right to use drugs. The answer is fairly easy in the case of drugs that are used to save life, or reduce pain. These support basic goods. It is necessary to be alive and to be free from severe pains in order to be able to pursue your purposes. But is there a right to use drugs non-medically?[1] It would be possible to construct an argument that there is no such right. It could consist of two claims. The first is that drug use is inherently harmful to the ability to guide one's conduct rationally. As there exists a right to be protected from harm to our rational capabilities (a basic right), it is also right that institutions exist that protect us from drug use by forbidding it. There is therefore no right to drug use.

There are serious problems with this argument. The first is that drug use is not always harmful to the capacity for rational action. Even if a minority of users becomes dependent on drugs, and others may suffer other forms of cognitive impairment, it seems that the vast majority of people who have ever used illicit drugs have done so without causing damage to their capacity to act towards intended purposes. Indeed, drug use is one of those intended purposes for people who find it pleasurable. Drug use is not always harmful to rationality. As the first claim fails, so the second claim (that institutions based on this claim are justified in forbidding drug use) also fails. So the answer to the question of whether there is a right to drug use appears to be yes. But it is a rather small yes. People may rationally choose to experience the effects of psychoactive substances, even if they have no objective need for them. The ability to do so falls within the category of additive goods. It increases people's capacity to fulfil their own purposes. However, in some circumstances, drug use may cause harms to the rights of others. Again, the hierarchy of rights applies. Drug use, as an additive right, cannot be rationally justified where it leads directly to harm to the basic or nonsubtractive rights of other people. This is why the 'yes' given to the question on the right to use drugs is so small. If my right to use drugs conflicts with your rights to retain your property, or to your own health, then that right to drug use is superseded.

Some proponents of abstinence might argue that, in practice, this rules out the right to drug use. They could argue that drug use inevitably leads to theft (or to higher taxation to pay for treatment and imprisonment of drug users) or other harms to others. But these are matters that can be tested empirically, rather than being left at the level of assumption. And empirically it can be shown that, in very many cases, use of psychoactive substances does not lead to stealing, treatment or harms to others. Even drugs that are considered more dangerous, such as cocaine and heroin, have many users who do not cause or suffer these types of harm (Cohen & Sas 1994; Eisenbach-Stangl *et al.* 2009; Shewan & Dalgarno 2006; Warburton *et al.* 2005a; Zinberg 1984). For these users, drug use expresses their additive rights and does not harm any basic or nonsubtractive rights.

Some forms of drug use, of course, do cause such harms. One example is smoking tobacco in enclosed spaces alongside other people. This has been shown empirically to cause harms, including fatal cancers (Taylor *et al.* 2007). In this case, the expression of an additive right conflicts with the basic right to life of the recipients of this action. The action is therefore wrong, and institutions are justified in taking steps to reduce it (within limits, in line with the hierarchy of rights). There is no right to use drugs in ways that directly inflicts harms to others. Examples of such harms include administering drugs to others against their will, or without fully informing them of the dangers involved.[2]

The right to use drugs is usually backed with a citation of the utilitarian thinker, John Stuart Mill (1974 [1859]). His argument that we should be allowed to do what we want with our own bodies has been attacked on the grounds that he provides no basis for agreement of that principle with others who do not share it (although others have defended him from this accusation [Riley 2006]). Gewirth's approach sidesteps this debate by establishing the argument for the limited right to use drugs on a rationally necessary position – the idea that we must all value the conditions which enable us to act towards purposes.

Drugs, harms and public health: terms for analysis

The limits of this Gewirthian argument are set by the levels of harm that can be directly attributed to drug consumption. It is very difficult, however, to disentangle the harmful effects of drug use from the deleterious consequences of drug control. There is a lot of investment in testing the direct, pharmacological and criminal harms of illicit substances. There are many academic journals stuffed with papers on these subjects. Investment in testing the effects of drug policy is relatively small, especially if we want to look at other areas of policy than the treatment of dependent users (Babor *et al.* 2010). This book will play a part in redressing that balance. It invites readers to go elsewhere[3] if they want to find out more about the detailed histories, pharmacologies and physical effects of particular illicit substances. But please stick with this book if you are interested in the interaction between drug users and policies on drug control, crime, health and welfare. The word 'drugs' will be used a shorthand for those psychoactive substances that are currently prohibited by UN conventions.[4,5] The term drug users will usually refer to people who consume these substances, although many other people, including poor farmers, criminal traffickers and powerful politicians also use drugs for their own purposes. Some use will be made of terms like dependence and addiction. Despite the inclusion of drug dependence in the diagnostic classifications used by doctors and statisticians worldwide, the existence of an identifiable disease of drug addiction, with distinctive causes and symptoms, is still controversial.[6] Drug policy will be discussed as an area of state action where laws, institutional capacities, funding programmes and governmental discourse meet in a 'hybrid of social control and social welfare policies' (Benoit 2003: 288). Health will be used in the sense of 'complete physical, mental and social well-being' (WHO 1946). With these definitions of health and harm, improving public health becomes a question of minimizing threats to well-being in the form of physical, mental and social harms.

There is potential for conflict between some interpretations of public health and the primacy of human rights on which Gewirth – and this book – insists. As Griffith Edwards (2004) and many others have noted, public health campaigners are sometimes tempted to place collective health over the rights of the individual. There are at least three critical perspectives on the promotion of public health. The first is libertarian opposition to any interference in the freedom of individuals to decide what is best for themselves (M. Friedman 1992; Szasz 1975). The second position comes from the tradition of political economy. It is that health agencies, in practice, tend to focus on individual responsibility to change unhealthy activities. Health interventions tend to ignore the wider structural issues, including poverty, inequality and environmental degradation, which influence rates of smoking and other risky behaviours (Marmot & Wilkinson 1999). There is a tendency within this tradition to blame the state for harming drug users in seeking to further its own power (e.g. S. Friedman 1998). A third position builds on the work of Michel Foucault (1998) on 'biopower'. It sees public health as a discipline of control which creates categories and knowledge and so produces the power which regulates individuals and actions (Lupton 1995).

I agree with other writers on the extreme dangers of the libertarian approach to drug use. Allowing a completely free market in all potentially harmful substances would be very likely to increase the mortal and morbid harms of drug use (Inciardi 2008; Transform 2009a). I also avoid the Foucauldian position. It has substantial problems at its own foundations, including its moral relativism and its crypto-normativism[7] (Habermas 1987). It has been criticized for misrepresenting the field of public health (e.g. by Dean 1997). It tends to see all public health initiatives as exercises in disguised coercion. This ignores the fact that many people owe whatever freedom they have (by virtue of being alive) to the existence of public health measures. These programmes can protect people's health by giving them informed choices over their actions. This may represent 'governance through freedom' (O'Malley 2002). To me, and according to the PGC (Gewirth 1996), this is preferable both to governance by force and to no governance at all. So this book will take a political economic approach. It will analyze drug use and control in the context of the social, economic and political arrangements which surround and inform them. It will try to avoid the temptation to pin the blame for all harms on an imaginarily unitary state.

The book focuses on drug policy in the UK (more specifically, England) and other countries with similar levels of economic development, who share a similar position in the chain of drug consumption. Readers from the USA, Australasia and mainland Europe will be able to apply the analyzes it presents to their own national contexts. The book does not discuss the more global harms of drug production and policy. The extreme harms that are associated with US drug policy in Colombia are covered elsewhere (Haugaard *et al.* 2008; Ramírez Cuellar 2005; Stokes 2004), as are the wider issues of drug regulation in Latin America (Latin American Commission on Drugs and Democracy 2009). The Transnational Institute has also provided useful discussions of the problems related to drug production and control in Afghanistan (Jelsma & Kramer 2009) and Burma/Myanmar (Kramer 2009). Across the world, the current systems for drug regulation have contributed to other harms. These include the denial of effective analgesic medication to 80 per cent of the world's population, including millions of people who die in agony every year because they do not have access to opiate painkillers (Human Rights Watch 2009). Readers who are interested in wider global issues may want to add some other books to their reading list (e.g. Buxton 2006; Klein 2008; Mares 2006).

The historical drivers of drug policy

On both sides of the Atlantic, the two main influences on governmental approaches to drugs have been medical and law enforcement agencies. While businessmen have played a quieter (although profitable) role, doctors and police officials have more visibly pressed their claims to expertise on how to solve problems related to the traffic in drugs. They have bolstered the power, prosperity and prestige of their professions. Drug users themselves have rarely had a voice in the debate. The differing stories of how two drugs – opium and cannabis – came to be prohibited in Britain and the USA give some indication of the respective roles of law enforcement and medical agencies in these different contexts. By the middle of the nineteenth century, the use of opium for the relief of pain and the pursuit of pleasure had already been known in England for several centuries (it was mentioned by both Chaucer and Shakespeare). The drug was on open sale in grocers and pharmacies and was marketed in preparations for both adults and children. In the mid-nineteenth century, twenty-five drops of laudanum (a mixture of opium and alcohol) were sold for a penny and about three pounds of opium were consumed each year per 1,000 population. Virginia Berridge has noted that, in England, '[o]pium itself was the opium of the people' (Berridge 1999: 37). She has described how, as the century grew older, the emerging professions of physicians and pharmacists were able to use concerns over drug-related deaths, often related to the use of opium by working class mothers and labourers, to change political attitudes to the drug. These were reflected in the 1868 Pharmacy Act, which for the first time gave pharmacists exclusive control of the most powerful painkiller available.

In the USA, two groups were blamed for the spread of addiction to opiates in the late nineteenth century: doctors and the Chinese. For example, Oliver Wendell Holmes, while Dean of Harvard Medical School, blamed the rising problem of addiction in the western states on 'the constant prescription of opiates by certain physicians' (quoted in Musto 1999: 4). Fear of opiates in the western states was intermingled with fear of the Chinese immigrants who were thought to be their principal users (as fear of cocaine became tangled up with fear of black men in the southern states). The first law controlling opiates was the San Francisco opium ordinance of 1875. This forbade the keeping of opium dens, which were specifically associated with Chinese residents. Many of them had moved to the USA following the impoverishing wars which Britain fought to ensure that opium grown by indentured labourers in India could be legally sold in China (Inglis 1976). They must have been confused by the mixed messages on opium that were being given out by the Western powers.

During this period, Britain's imperial efforts in India were also being financed by taxes on the trade in cannabis. This was despite the finding (which later turned out to be based on flawed statistics – so providing an early warning for students of current debates over the psychotic effects of cannabis) that many cases in India's lunatic asylums were caused by cannabis consumption. As Britain profited from the production of cannabis and opium in India, so the USA sought to profit from banning opium in its Philippine colony, a move which opened the way to trading with the Chinese government and enabled it to claim status as a 'morally superior colonial ruler' (Tyrrell 2008: 539). The continuing dispute between the USA and Britain rumbled through the early international conferences on the control of opium (from Shanghai in 1909 to Geneva in 1925), with the USA favouring the elimination of supply, and the British attempting to reduce interference in Indian commercial interests and so focusing on the reduction of demand. British diplomats argued that reducing supply in one location would only lead to increased production in some other region, so long as drugs had users willing to pay for them. It may not have escaped their notice that these other locations would not have been paying taxes on cannabis to the British state. Political maneuvering by Egyptian and US delegates in Geneva led to the inclusion of cannabis in the international list of controlled narcotics for the first time. It was this, rather than any concern over domestic use of cannabis, which led to its British prohibition in 1928 (Mills 2003).

While the British state tried to stave off regulation of cannabis in order to protect its Indian commercial interests, some American law enforcement officials became obsessed with banning the drug, again with a focus on its use by incomers. From 1915, states in the southwest of the USA passed laws to criminalize marijuana. This was a direct result of fear of immigrants from Mexico. Legislators were not afraid of making this connection clear in pressing for criminalization. One Texas senator appears in the official record as saying '[a]ll Mexicans are crazy, and this stuff [marijuana] is what makes them crazy' (quoted by Bonnie & Whitebread 1974). In 1937, the Federal Government introduced the Marijuana Tax Act, which led to punitive taxation of any trade in the drug. In the congressional hearing on the Act, the American Medical Association (AMA) opposed it on three grounds. The first was that the AMA was opposed to any federal regulation of their business, especially regulation by the Treasury. The second was that the cannabis plant had medicinal uses. And third, the AMA objected to the paucity of evidence that was being used to support the proposed prohibitive tax. This evidence was so slim, that the largest part of the evidence introduced in support of the act came from the study of the effect of marijuana on dogs by a pharmacological specialist on the doping of racehorses. When the congressional committee questioned this specialist, Dr Munch, on the applicability of his research to humans, he admitted that he was no expert on dogs, and had even less knowledge of the effects of the drug on people (Sloman 1998).

Still, the prohibition of marijuana in the USA was accompanied with lurid tales of the insanity and violence that inevitably resulted from its use. Bonnie and Whitebread report that this reputation was secured by the use of marijuana as a defence in high-profile cases of extreme violence. Defendants used the growing reputation of the drug to claim that it led them to commit heinous acts that they would never have committed without it. In one case in New Jersey in 1938, two women accused of murder did not dispute that they were the killers, but argued that marijuana had turned them into monsters. Called to the stand as an expert witness, Dr Munch the horse pharmacologist reported that he had now used marijuana himself, and it had turned him into a bat (Bonnie & Whitebread 1974). The defence was successful in this and other cases, compounding the fearful reputation of drugs for turning people into mad, violent criminals.

Themes and chapters

This short summary of how heroin and cannabis came to be prohibited gives us five themes that will recur throughout this book. The first is the role of national and professional self-interest in the criminalization of drugs and drug users. In the UK, the imperial economy and the medical profession drove the early regulation of opiates. In the USA, the federal government aligned itself, sometimes against the medical profession, with abstentionist moral entrepreneurs in ways that suited law enforcement and diplomatic priorities. The second theme is the association of prohibited drugs with threatening foreigners and with unruly members of the working class, although the emphasis on these two targets has also varied in different countries. Thirdly, we see a focus on drugs as a direct cause of criminality. This focus has historically been given more priority in the USA. Although there were doctors who argued before the British Rolleston committee of 1926 that heroin caused their patients to be criminals – and so should itself be dealt with as a criminal matter – these were prison doctors dealing with working class offenders (Berridge 1999). The committee preferred to follow the advice of other doctors whose patients were middle-class users – often members of their own profession (South 1998). For these doctors, heroin use was a medical issue. And so the British system of heroin maintenance was born (although this system was supervised by the Home Office and always accompanied by law enforcement control of the non-medical use of heroin [Pearson 1991]). A fourth theme, then, is differentiation in the response to the users of psychoactive substances. People who use psychoactive substances have long been regulated on the basis of who they are, not what they take (Duster 1970). From the distinctions made between genteel, iatrogenic American heroin users and the desperate 'junkmen' who scavenged scrapyards to fund their habits in the early twentieth century (Courtwright 2001), to the differential policing of cannabis in contemporary life (see Chapters 6 and 7 on the UK and USA respectively), it has always been the case that drugs have been a useful tool to separate the presumed community of 'law-abiding citizens' from the 'suitable enemies' who are supposed to threaten their well-being (Christie 1986). A final theme is how the available evidence of the effects of drugs – in particular their effect in causing crime – has continually been exaggerated or distorted in order to justify policies which contribute both to the creation of inequality and to the production of harm.

These themes will be explored in more depth throughout the chapters of this book. Chapter 2 will focus on the link between drug-related problems and inequality. It will show that there is nothing natural or inevitable about current levels of inequality. These levels have risen dramatically and produce high levels of harms. They are produced, and can be reduced, by conscious human action. International studies show that drug use occurs throughout society and often does not lead to offending or health damage. The harms associated with drug use, including death, illness and criminal victimization are, in contrast, concentrated in socio-economically deprived areas and groups.

Chapter 3 will focus attention on the concept of drug-related crime. It will examine the exaggeration of the causal effect of drugs in producing crime, with a specific critical focus on Goldstein's (1985) tripartite framework of the drug-crime link. In place of reductionist, empirically inadequate accounts, participation in drug markets and chronic drug use will be viewed sociologically as 'subterranean structuration'. This is a deliberately dense phrase. I hope it will draw attention to the constraints placed on the choices made by the people who have been most affected by the withdrawal of employment in deprived areas. These people are forced to make choices in situations which offer them little hope of pleasure, purpose or respect, no matter how hard they struggle for it.

Chapter 4 examines why the copious evidence of both the harms of inequality and the failures of prohibition have been so often ignored in making drug policy. Through ethnographic observation of the process of policy making in the UK government, it will show there are some genuine efforts to reconcile policy with the available knowledge. Policy making is over-saturated with evidence which is often inconclusive. This process is systematically distorted by the use of evidence to tell stories that boost the status and career prospects of their tellers. Uncertainty is methodically omitted from these stories. They contribute to the creation of policies which do not achieve their declared goals, but do operate to sustain the systematically unequal distribution of power and resources.

In Chapter 5, contemporary English policies on drugs and crime will be used in order to test this approach. It will do this through discourse analysis of three policy cases: the Drug Treatment and Testing Order (DTTO); the

Drugs Act 2005; and the cannabis reclassifications of 2004 and 2009. These cases show the effect on policy outcomes of the ideological process of policy creation. The policies that emerge from this process tend to follow the *modus operandi* of ideology that John Thompson (1990) has identified. Specifically, they legitimize inequalities, they fragment people and drugs into 'domestic' and 'foreign' categories and they reify the use of state coercion to control these threatening outsiders.

Chapter 6 will take the analysis further by testing the practical effects of the policies whose discursive effects are discussed in Chapter 5. It will show that the DTTO helped many drug users to reduce their drug use and offending. It did not lead, as some advocates of 'alternatives to imprisonment' had hoped, to a reduction in the number of people being sent to prison. The use of imprisonment has grown. This rise has been especially rapid for drug law offenders, with particularly severe consequences for people of African heritage and other visible minorities. The large over-representation of black people in drug law arrests, convictions and imprisonments cannot be explained by any evidence that they are more likely to commit drug offences. Its explanation is more likely to include the inequalities of which racism consists. Chapter 6 will also demonstrate the bifurcation in contemporary English drug policy between class A drug suppliers and the majority of drug (i.e. cannabis) users. They now face less formal punishment, but a higher rate of interception and supervision by the state.

Chapter 7 will broaden the analysis to include international perspectives on the effects of drug policy. It will show that the USA, which has been the prime mover of international prohibition, has some of the largest drug-related harms in the world. Many of these harms are self-inflicted, including the costs and pains associated with a policy of mass incarceration. They fall particularly heavily on the people who have been socially and racially marginalized from the achievement of the American dream. It will examine the policy of Sweden, to test whether this provides a stronger case for the effectiveness of prohibition. Competing perspectives will be compared to show that Sweden's relatively low rates of drug-related problems may not, as has been claimed, be the result of a restrictive policy. It will also discuss the example of the Netherlands, which has similar rates of drug-related harms, but a very different policy. It has arrived, through a number of stages, at a policy of 'dynamic harm reduction' which seems to fit its needs. Chapter 7 will also discuss the possibility that the rates of drug-related harms that are experienced by a country are more closely associated with levels of inequality and social support than with the type of drug policy that they pursue.

The final, eighth chapter will summarize the preceding arguments. It will examine proposals that have already been made for improving British drug policy. Through a critical analysis of these proposals, and building on the analysis of the previous chapters, it will propose an agenda for progressive decriminalization. This will aim at the minimization of harm and the maximization of freedom through three strategies: the reduction of social inequalities; the reform of international law; and evidence-dependent steps towards the decriminalization of both drug use and drug supply. The recommendations presented here will be based on the rule of mutual respect to which we are all rationally committed. The most important recommendation will be that we need to keep our minds open as knowledge evolves. If this book encourages readers to see that knowledge in a new light or to create better, more accurate representations of drug-related harms and policies, it will have fulfilled its aim. But if it contributes to radical change in policies, without there being any widespread political movement for reform, it would be disproving its own theoretical perspective on the ideological use of knowledge.

Chapter 2

'Afflictions of inequality'?

The social distribution of drug use, dependence and related harms

Drug problems, like many other ills that afflict modern societies, are problems of inequality. Rates of violence, ill-health and early death are all higher where inequality is greatest (CSDH 2008; Wilkinson & Pickett 2008; Wilkinson 1996; Working Group on Inequalities in Health 1988 [1980]). As countries develop out of generalized poverty towards industrialized affluence, they initially see widespread improvements in health. But, past a certain point, increases in average wealth do not produce any more health benefits. And where inequality is deeper, so is ill health, with the poorest always suffering the most harm. This chapter asks whether drug use and drug dependence belong among the 'afflictions of inequality' that Richard Wilkinson (1996) has identified. It examines the nature of inequality. It presents evidence which suggests that drug use is more equally spread through society than dependence is. It examines the social patterning of the harms that are related to drug use and criticizes narrow, atheoretical analyzes of them. It argues for an understanding of drug use, dependence and harms that incorporates the social contexts of drug use.

The unnatural nature of social inequality

According to a long-dead philosopher, there are two types of inequality (Rousseau 2004 [1754]). The first is physical inequality, between people of different ages, heights and abilities. The second is inequality in wealth and power. Rousseau considered any discussion of whether the first type caused the second to be so absurd as to be only 'fit to be discussed by slaves in the hearing of their masters' (Ibid: 1). He insisted that political inequality was entirely man-made. But inequality is still often discussed as if it is the natural order of things.

The rise of inequality

Inequalities have risen substantially since Rousseau's time, both between and within countries. As shown in Figure 2.1, the Industrial Revolution ushered

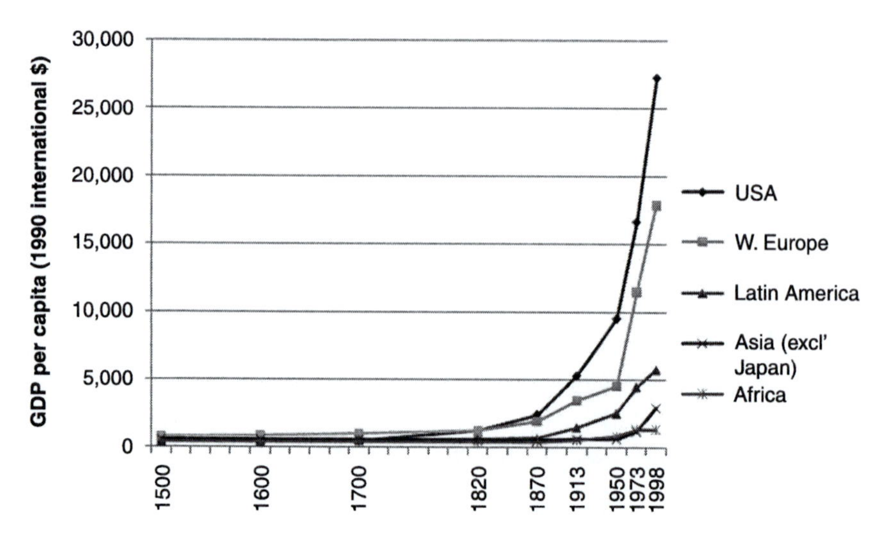

Figure 2.1 Growth in average wealth in five regions, 1500–1998.
(*Source:* using data from Maddison 2001: 264)

in massive increases in wealth in the nations which first experienced it. As Buxton (2006) and others have noted, trade in psychoactive commodities – including tobacco, opium and cannabis – contributed to this Western economic growth. The available figures suggest that between 1820 and 1998, gross domestic product per head (adjusted for purchasing power) increased by a factor of 15 in Western Europe, and 22 in the USA. These massive increases dwarf those achieved by countries of the global South. Average wealth increased by a factor of only nine for Latin America, five for Asia (excluding Japan) and a relatively miniscule three for Africa. It is this global inequality that drives both sides – demand and supply – of the illicit drug market. It provides some people in rich countries with the time and money to enjoy imported substances. It means that some poor farmers in Africa, Asia and Latin America are more likely to avoid destitution by growing cannabis, opium or coca for export than other crops for domestic consumption.

Capitalist industrialization also created increased inequality within the USA and UK until the late nineteenth century. In the first half of the twentieth century, inequality reduced as the voting franchise expanded, trade unions helped to increase wages and welfare systems were created. However, these reductions in inequality were virtually wiped out by significant increases after 1970 (Lindert *et al.* 2000; Schmitt 2009). The depth of various kinds of social inequality has recently been documented by the Hills report in the UK. It showed serious and persistent inequalities between social classes, genders and ethnic groups (Hills *et al.* 2010). Inequality has been seriously affected by a 'fanning out' of income distribution in both US and British society. For example, in the USA between 1990 and 2005, the income of the richest one per cent grew 30 per cent faster than those who were on average (median) incomes. While the very rich got richer, the income of the very poorest has tended to stagnate at levels well below the relative levels of the 1970s (Atkinson 2008). Figure 2.2 illustrates this increasing dispersion in Great Britain. It shows how the people near the top of the income distribution (better paid than 90 per cent of the population) saw their real incomes soar from the mid-1970s onwards. The income of the poorest has bumped along at the bottom, with very little real increase. Another measure of inequality is the Gini coefficient. This measures the difference between the income distribution and perfect equality. The higher the Gini coefficient, the more unequal the country is. In the UK it was at its highest post-war level at 0.36 in 2007/8 (Brewer, Muriel, Phillips *et al.* 2009). In the USA, it was also close to its highest post-war level at 0.47 in 2008 (DeNavas-Walt *et al.* 2009).

In both the UK and the USA, poverty tends to be concentrated in certain areas. The poorest groups have been concentrated in the inner cities by migration (both internal and international), housing policies, the flight of the middle class to the suburbs and the export of manufacturing jobs to countries where the costs and protection of labour are lower. This increasing spatial concentration of poverty has been graphically illustrated for London. By 2000, 15 inner city census tracts had over 50 per cent of their population classified as living in poverty. There had been no areas in London with such high levels in 1980 (Dorling *et al.* 2007). It is these deprived areas which are most affected by the offending of groups of young people who are referred to as gangs (Stevens *et al.* 2009).

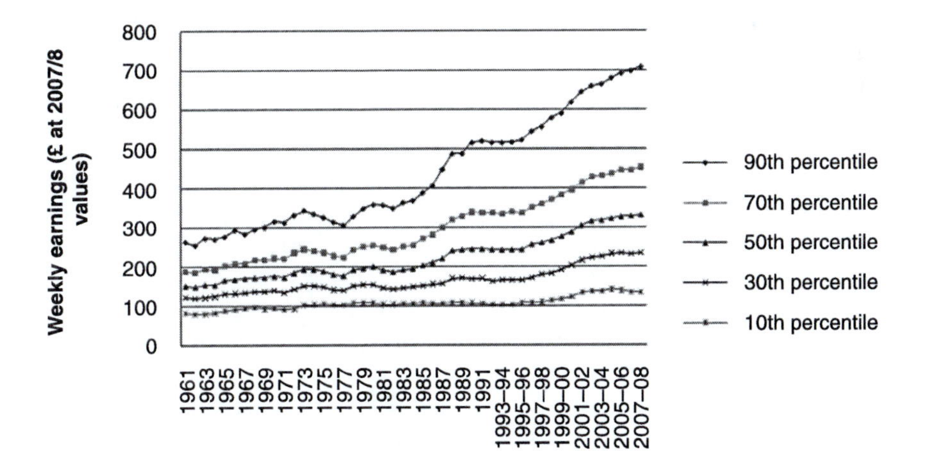

Figure 2.2 Weekly earnings (after housing costs) for people at various percentiles of the British income distribution, 1961–2007/8.

(*Source:* IFS 2009)

The governments of the USA and UK followed radically different policies on the distribution of income during the early years of the twenty-first century. In Britain, the New Labour government at least managed to contain increases in inequality through a mixture of tax credits, increased employment and the introduction of a minimum wage. These were successful in raising the real incomes of the poorest workers and families, although it did not enable them to keep up with the rapid enrichment of the very wealthiest (Brewer, Muriel, Phillips *et al.* 2009). This approach ran out of steam in the mid-2000s. Inequalities in the distribution of pre-tax earnings, and in the receipt of income from investments caused inequality to rise again (Brewer, Muriel & Wren-Lewis 2009). With no significant new policies, the prospect was for an inexorable increase in inequality (Palmer *et al.* 2007), even before the financial crisis hit the debt-ridden markets and threatened the debt-burdened government's ability to do anything more for its most vulnerable citizens. The US Bush administration openly made a virtue of increasing inequality. It continued the duplicitous fantasies of trickle-down Reaganomics[8] by reducing taxation of the rich, cutting welfare entitlements and (until 2008 at least) leaving the federal minimum wage to wither at a level below the market rate for all but the most poorly paid employees. The richest one per cent received 21 per cent of personal incomes in 2005, with the poorest 50 per cent left with only 13 per cent between them (IRS 2006).

Justifying inequality?

These increased and extreme financial inequalities reflect asymmetrical distributions of power. They fuel a wide range of social harms. Many authors are happy to flatter their wealthy patrons by discussing social inequality as if it follows inevitably from bodily inequalities. Economic inequality is often discussed as if it is the natural, inevitable consequence of unequal abilities and the incontrovertible laws of market forces. These justifications are both mistaken and harmful to human well-being.

In the face of developments in the study of human biology, it would be folly to argue that everybody is genetically endowed with equal physical ability and intelligence (even if we must remain sceptical of the attempt to measure intelligence – a notoriously nebulous concept – using such socially constructed measurements as IQ). A review by the American Psychological Association suggested that genetic inheritance accounts for about half the variation in intelligence between individuals (Neisser *et al.* 1996). But, and this is a big but, genetic differences between humans do not explain the distribution of income and wealth. Environments, parenting, peers, social contexts, personal histories and sheer happenstance still count. Indeed, more recent research has found that heritability of intelligence seems to be greater for people who grow up in affluent environments (Harden, Turkheimer & Loehlin 2007; Turkheimer, Haley, Waldron *et al.* 2003). This suggests that, just as increases in wealth are more important for improving the health of poor people than rich people (Wilkinson 1996), so increases in wealth are more important in enabling people to reach their genetic potential in deprived than in affluent environments. And even if intelligence (or any other personality trait) is heritable, that does not mean it is directly inherited. It is only in the environments of supportive families and societies that we can use our genetic inheritance to develop our abilities. Take away sufficient nourishment, emotional care and educative stimulation, and the girl with the smartest genes in the world is not going to reach the top of the career ladder (especially if that ladder is shortened by discrimination). This is exactly what inequality has done to millions of people. Inequality could not be justified by categorizing people into biologically arbitrary groups (such as races or nationalities) even if these groups did differ in their average abilities. Only a racist society would make decisions on where a person could live, what work she should do or what income she should receive by making decisions on the basis of the average of the group she has been assigned to, rather than her individual qualities (Chomsky 1973).[9]

The idea that genetic differences between humans justify the vast inequalities that separate us is an example of 'epistemological violence' (Teo 2008). It results from unjustified speculations about group differences, such as the idea that poor people have poorer health because they are less intelligent.[10] These unsupported, but ideologically useful, conjectures have been used to justify inequalities that have caused massive harm, through exclusion, discrimination and physical violence.

The economic justification for inequality is also based on ideology rather than evidence. The most prominent economic defender of inequality is the Austrian guru of Margaret Thatcher and countless other right-wing politicians: Freidrich August von Hayek. He claimed that inequality arises spontaneously from the market, which is a product, not of conscious design, but of accidental, cultural evolution. This claim is demonstrably false. The market is not spontaneous (Le Grand 1991; Tilly 2003). It is created, maintained and exported worldwide through powerful institutions, including the World Trade Organization, the International Monetary Fund, the World Bank, influential universities, thinktanks and advisers (Sapir 2002). While it may be true that 'truck and barter' (Smith 1970) takes place in all human societies, the shape that the market takes today – with massive and instantaneous flows of capital and the transfer of wealth and protection from workers to corporations – is a product of decisions taken by powerful people in marble-clad conference rooms.

Hayek also argued that, because inequality occurs naturally, we cannot do anything about it. He ignored the fact that collective human action can have important effects in reducing, as well as creating, inequality. One example is the comparative success of post-war, social democratic, European governments in reducing inequality while maintaining economic growth (Parkin

1972). Another is the effect of state intervention in Organization for Economic Cooperation and Development (OECD) countries in attenuating the effects of more recent increases in inequality in market incomes. Redistributive welfare benefits and tax credits have slowed the increase in inequality in net incomes in many developed countries (OECD 2008).

Inequality does not result directly from our genetic make-up or a free market. On the contrary, it arises from conscious action by those people who have the power to ensure that wealth continues to accrue to them, their families and their friends. There are several mechanisms by which wealthy people can do this (Tilly 2003). They include hoarding opportunities by deliberately restricting labour market opportunities to members of closed networks. Inequality between nations is partly maintained by excluding foreign citizens from the highest-paying labour markets. Entry to the highest professions within countries is often reserved, by complex systems of patronage and exclusion, for people who most closely resemble the existing professionals. For example, the top echelons of the legal, media and financial professions in the UK are still occupied mostly by expensively educated men (The Panel on Fair Access to the Professions 2009). Other mechanisms by which inequality is created and maintained include 'emulation', or the transposition of existing hierarchies into new social fields, and 'adaptation', or the 'elaboration of daily routines . . . on the basis of categorically unequal structures' (e.g. mutual aid, political influence, courtship, information gathering) (Tilly 1998: 10). These processes result in the 'bunching' (Tilly 2003: 31) of inequalities according to categories such as race, gender, nationality and religion.

High levels of social inequality are not natural. They are created by human action. As we shall see later, drug policy plays its part in both reproducing these inequalities and masking their unnatural nature.

Equality in drug use?

Illicit drugs are often thought of as something that poor people do. Certainly, it is socially marginalized groups who have most often been targeted by efforts to punish drug users, dealers and producers (Buchanan & Young 2000; Donoghue 2002). But is this concentration of repression justified by rates of drug use that are higher in deprived communities than in wealthy ones?

The immediate answer to this question is: how would we know? Drug use is illegal, widely stigmatized and hidden. We have no direct indicators of who is and who is not using drugs. The indirect indicators available to us are all flawed. Police records of drug offences and seizures are next to useless in determining the number or distribution of drug users. They record police and customs practices, not the activities of drug users. Interesting developments have recently been made in testing for the presence of drugs in municipal sewage (Frost & Griffiths 2008). This may indicate the quantity of drugs that is passing through urine (or being flushed down the toilet when the police come to call), but it cannot tell us much about who is using these drugs. We are left, therefore, with research methods that rely on people's willingness to discuss drug use. We might not expect people to be any more honest when answering questions about drug use than they are when discussing their sexual practices. And we have no easy way for drug surveys – as we do for sex surveys, with their continual discrepancy between male and female reports of the number of past sexual partners[11] – to test the validity of reports. We can be confident that such surveys usually miss out some of the most vulnerable members of society, including the homeless and prisoners. Some surveys, including the ones used below do use techniques to encourage honest reporting. For example, they allow the interviewee to fill in their own responses discreetly on a computer. Such methods can boost validity (Thornberry & Krohn 2000), but should not make us see the resulting data with anything less than a healthy dose of scepticism.

Clutching this scepticism closely to us, what do we see if we look at the results of these surveys? In general, we find three trends in the distribution of reported drug use. The first is that the experience of drug use seems to be relatively widespread. Over a third of adults in England and Wales, and about a half in the USA, report that they have ever used an illicit drug. Table 2.1 also shows us that many fewer people have used drugs recently than have ever used drugs. Most people who tried a drug in the past reported that they have not done so recently. If we believe their reports, this suggests that drugs, for the vast majority of users, do not lead to dependence, or even regular use. The third general trend is that illicit drug use is apparently more prevalent in the USA than in England and Wales.

Our scepticism towards these findings can be reduced a little by the fact that they triangulate well with other types of research, and with what passes for common knowledge in the social circuits of people who have used drugs. When seeking interviewees to discuss use of drugs in qualitative studies, several researchers have found it fairly easy to find people with some experience (supporting the finding that drug use at some point in life is fairly widespread). They have often found that drug use is an experimental or

Table 2.1 Prevalence of self-reported illicit drug use in USA and UK

	USA (18 or older)	*England & Wales (16–59 year olds)*
Proportion ever used drugs	49%	37%
Proportion used drugs in last year	14%	10%
Proportion used drugs in last month	8%	6%
Source	SAMHSA 2008	Hoare 2009
Data refers to	2008	2008/9

transitory phase that people go through when they are young (Pudney 2002). Researchers and journalists have been able to find drug users at every strata of society, from royal families to the street homeless, from prominent politicians to investment bankers, from soldiers to record-breaking Olympian swimmers. Even studies of heroin – the drug which is most firmly associated with poverty in the media and public imagination – have found users throughout the social distribution (e.g. Eisenbach-Stangl *et al.* 2009; Shewan & Dalgarno 2006; Warburton *et al.* 2005a; Zinberg 1984).

Early studies of drug users concentrated on socially marginalized locations and subcultures (e.g. Becker 1963; Chein *et al.* 1964; Finestone 1957; Preble & Casey 1969; Young 1971). More recent research has tended to argue that drug use has become normalized (Blackman 2004; Parker *et al.* 1998). To say that drug use has been normalized is not to suggest that everybody does it (or should do it). Rather, it implies both that drug use has become widespread and that it has become more socially accepted. Parker and his colleagues found, in their study of young people in the northwest of England, that even those who had not used drugs said that they knew how to get drugs if they wanted them, and that they did not look down on friends who had used drugs. As drug use has become socially accommodated, it has also been integrated into the cultural mainstream. References to drug use are now a common feature of pop, rock and rap songs,[12] as well as the scripts of TV and movie dramas. Drugs and related symbols are often recruited to the task of marketing products by branding pleasure, transgression and intoxication (Blackman 2004; Ferrell *et al.* 2008). Dior's perfume, *Addict*, is presumably marketed at women who have become bored of Yves Saint-Laurent's *Opium*. The Scottish beer *Speedball* had the same name as the injected cocktail of cocaine and heroin. It was promoted with the tagline 'class A strong ale' (Sweney 2009).

The idea of normalization has been criticized for implying that the spread of drugs throughout society is a new phenomenon. Mike Shiner (2009) has shown that, in England and Wales, it is the middle classes who have long made most use of illicit drugs. Historical work in both the US and the UK shows that the use of narcotics was common in every social class in the nineteenth century (Berridge 1999; Courtwright 2001; Davenport-Hines 2001). Drug use is now a common feature of diverse social scenes, including those that are well integrated within mainstream society (Moore 2004). This process of normalization should not, however, make us think that drug use is accepted by all. Some forms of drug use are still heavily stigmatized (Shiner 2009). *Speedball* beer was swiftly banned. Normalization is 'a contingent process that is negotiated by distinct social groups operating in bounded situations' (Measham & Shiner 2009: 502). What is normal for some groups is treated with disdain and sanction by others.

Inequality in drug problems?

These groups are not necessarily bounded by traditional sociological categories. In the study in the northwest of England (Parker *et al.* 1998), there were no significant differences in drug use between gender, socio-economic or ethnic groups. This finding is limited by being based on a small age group in a specific part of England.

Testing the distribution of drug use and dependence

There is data available from a larger dataset which covers the whole of England. The Survey of Psychiatric Morbidity (SPM) is a large-scale survey of individuals living in private households, involving interviews with over 8,800 people, aged between 16 and 74, living in England, Wales and Scotland in 2000. It had an 80 per cent response rate. The official report of this survey (Singleton *et al.* 2001) gives details of the sampling and data collection methods. I have reanalyzed the data (available from the UK Data Archive at the University of Essex) to examine the links between reports of drug use, drug dependence and deprivation. The indicators of socio-economic deprivation that were used in this analysis and their prevalence in this dataset are shown in Table 2.2.

Respondents to the SPM used a computer to self-complete questions on use and dependence on the most commonly used illicit drugs in the UK. The computer programme asked respondents about their drug use and indicators of drug dependence.[13]

Exclusion of members of the armed forces, of people aged over 44 and of

Table 2.2 Indicators of deprivation used in the analysis of SPM data

Type of deprivation	*Measurement*	*Prevalence*
Low income	Respondents asked to state their gross personal income and placed in this group if their income is less than 60 per cent of the national median personal income for 2000 (DWP 2001).	37.30%
Social renter	Respondents asked to describe their type of tenure, then put in this group if they are in social housing (i.e. renting from local authority or housing association)	17.80%
Unemployment	Respondents asked about their employment status, then put in this group if not in education or employment.	16.80%
Social class IV or V	Respondents asked their current or most recent occupation, then categorized in social classes IV or V if they have a partly skilled or unskilled occupation.	21.80%
No qualifications	Respondents asked to state their highest qualification, then put in this category if they have no qualifications.	15.20%

people who did not answer questions on drug use and dependence left a dataset of 4,067 respondents. Of these people, 56 per cent were women and 93 per cent reported their ethnic origin as white. The average age of these respondents was 32. Drug use was reported at similar levels by white and black ethnic groups, but at lower levels by people of South Asian origin. As shown in Table 2.3, cannabis was the most popular drug, followed by ecstasy and amphetamine. Reported use of heroin and crack was very rare.

Table 2.4 compares the reported drug use and dependence of the people who reported each indicator of deprivation to the drug use and dependence reported by people who did not report such deprivation. The pattern suggests that drug use itself is not generally more common among socio-economically deprived groups, except for those people who live in social housing. They were significantly more likely to report illicit drug use in the last year. In contrast, people with no educational qualifications were significantly less likely than those with qualifications to report drug use. People who reported each of these indicators of deprivation (except qualifications) were significantly more likely to report indicators of dependence on drugs.

Men were significantly more likely to report both drug use and dependence.

Table 2.3 Proportions of SPM respondents reporting drug use and dependence

Reported last year drug use	Any drug	15.6%
	Cannabis	14.3%
	Amphetamine	3.1%
	Ecstasy	3.0%
	Cocaine	2.9%
	Tranquilizers (non-prescribed)	0.8%
	Heroin	0.2%
	Crack	0.2%
Reported last year drug dependence	Any indicator of dependence on any drug	5.2%

Table 2.4 Drug use and dependence by indicators of deprivation

	Used drugs in last year	*Any indicator of drug dependence in last year*
Income < 60% median v >60% median	*15.8% v 16.7%*	**6.3% v 5.4%****
Social renter v other housing tenure	**18.1% v 15.9%***	**7% v 5.4%***
No qualifications v some qualifications	*11.1% v 17.2%***	**5.9% v 4.6%**
Social class IV or V v other social classes	*15.2% v 16.2%*	**6.7% v 5.3%***
Not in education or employment v active	*14.9% v 16.6%*	**7.9% v 5.3%****

* *p<0.05*, ** *p<0.01*

Bold *text indicates variables for which the indicator of drug use is more common among the more deprived group*

Italic text indicates variables for which the indicator of drug use is less common among the more deprived group

The average age of respondents who reported drug use and dependence was significantly younger than those who did not. And there were significant correlations between these indicators of deprivation.[14] So I used a logistic regression model to test further the links between indicators of deprivation, drug use and drug dependence. The odds ratios shown in Table 2.5 give an estimate of the likelihood of a person who reported a certain indicator of deprivation also reporting drug use or dependence, compared to a person who was not deprived in that way. The model controls for the influence of each of the other variables.

There is at least one counter-intuitive finding. When controlling for the influence of other variables, people with low incomes were about a third *less* likely to report both drug use and dependence than people with incomes over 60 per cent of the national median.[15] People with no qualifications were also less likely to report drug use. Social renters were 20 per cent more likely than people in other types of housing to report drug use, but were not significantly more likely to report drug dependence. People who were not in education or employment were 1.7 times more likely to report drug use than those who were. The biggest difference in reported drug dependence was between people who did or did not have a job. Those who were unemployed were 3.27 times more likely to report drug dependence.

Drug use, dependence and unemployment

This raises the possibility that it is drug dependence which leads to unemployment, rather than unemployment leading to drug dependence. This possibility is pushed by a study that used data from the British Crime Survey (BCS) to argue that people who had used drugs in the past were more likely to be unemployed when they were interviewed (MacDonald & Pudney 2000). The problem with this is that the BCS, like the SPM, is a cross-sectional survey. It

Table 2.5 Odds ratios of drug use and dependence by indicators of deprivation

	Used drugs in last year	*Any drug dependence in last year*
Male	**1.88****	**2.89****
Increasing age	*0.89***	*0.89***
Income < 60% median	*0.61***	*0.67***
Social renter	**1.2***	
No qualifications	*0.71***	
Social class IV or V		
Not in education or employment	**1.7****	**3.27****

* $p<0.05$, ** $p<0.01$

***Bold** text indicates variables which predict higher likeihoods of drug use or dependence, compared to people who are not in this category.*

Italic text indicates variables which predict lower likelihoods of drug use or dependence does not follow people over time. The fact that some people who used drugs in the past are now unemployed does not prove that it was their drug use that caused their unemployment. Some longitudinal studies have enabled us to examine the temporal order of drug use, unemployment and related factors. They suggest a complex dynamic between drug use and unemployment which evolves over the life course. Hammer carried out two studies on a Norwegian sample. One found that unemployment made young people more likely to join subcultural groups that had higher rates of drug use (Hammer 1992). The other concluded that structural conditions, such as the level of work available, were more important in predicting unemployment than individual variables, like drug use (Hammer 1997). A study in New Zealand found that young people who were unemployed had higher rates of drug use and mental health problems, although most of the factors that predicted these variables were present before school leaving age (Fergusson *et al.* 1997). Problems experienced early in life, including socio-economic disadvantage, contributed to problems during adolescence, including substance use, and then to problems in getting a decent job (Fergusson & Horwood 1998). Fergusson adjusted the analysis to take account of confounding variables across the life-course of his young sample. He found that unemployment led to higher rates of substance use, suicidal thoughts and crime in late adolescence (Fergusson *et al.* 2001). In the most recent study from this sample, he suggested that heavy cannabis use in late adolescence reduces the likelihood of getting a degree and a good job, even when taking account of these confounders (Fergusson & Boden 2008). A short longitudinal study in the USA found that adolescents who do not have positive career aspirations are more likely to get involved with drugs (Skorikov & Vondracek 2007). Young people who grow up in socio-economically deprived urban areas face high levels of family and environmental stress. This is associated with high levels of hopelessness (Landis *et al.* 2007).

So it is young people in deprived areas who are more likely to give up on conventional career aspirations. They become more vulnerable to damaging patterns of drug use, which then reduces their chances of getting a job. Young people with the most problematic childhoods are especially likely to experience these problems. The relationship between drug use and unemployment runs both ways, and is also influenced by other factors. It is not drug use itself, but only the most damaging patterns of drug use that are most closely linked to deprivation. The Longitudinal Study of Young People in England found that it was the poorest fifth of 14 year olds who reported the highest lifetime rates of cannabis use (at 10.3 per cent). By age 16, it was the richest fifth of young people that had the highest rates of reported use (at 24.9 per cent) (Chowdry *et al.* 2009). Early onset drug use is the most risky for later problems (Chen *et al.* 2009). A German longitudinal study found that few of the people who started using cannabis in adolescence moved on to dependent patterns of use. Those who did were more likely to have suffered from socio-economic deprivation, and from the death of a parent before they were 15 (von Sydow *et al.* 2002). These longitudinal studies confirm the suggestion that it is the poor who suffer most from drug problems, even if there are higher levels of drug use amongst wealthier people.

All these surveys can only be suggestive of the link between drug use, dependence and deprivation, as we have to be so sceptical about the reports of drug use on which they rely. They also miss out the most deprived people. Their interviewers do not usually reach prisoners and homeless people. There was a specific survey of psychiatric morbidity amongst British prisoners (Singleton *et al.* 1997). It found that more than half of them reported use of illicit drugs in the year before entering prison and over 40 per cent reported an indicator of drug dependence. Research with a sample of 160 young homeless people in four British cities found that 43 per cent of them had used heroin and 38 per cent had used crack (Wincup *et al.* 2003). These rates are many times higher than those found in the general population. People who are so excluded and deprived that they do not feature in household surveys are the most vulnerable to hazardous patterns of drug use. But we should not ignore the existence of illicit drug use throughout diverse sections of developed societies. This drug use is more likely to develop into dependence in situations of socio-economic deprivation. How does this translate into the distribution of drug-related harms?

Public health harms from drugs

The vast majority of illicit drug use does not lead to any visible damage to the user. The British Crime Survey estimates that around 12 million people in England and Wales have ever used drugs (Hoare 2009). Only a very small proportion of these drug users present problems with drugs to health or criminal justice agencies. But some drug users experience grave harms, including ill-health and death. There are also harms to the people around them. The highest profile is usually given to drug-related crime, which will be examined more closely in the next chapter. There is also significant harm done to the families and children of people who have problems controlling their drug use (Kroll & Taylor 2008), although these harms have often been exaggerated and used to control reproduction and parenting by socially excluded mothers (see Boyd 1999).

Drug-related death

One harm to children that sometimes results from dependent drug use is bereavement through the early death of drug-using parents. Only a minority of the drugs that are currently prohibited are capable of causing immediate death. Cannabis, which accounts for the great majority of illicit drug use, is not one of them. In contrast, opiates can be deadly. They kill by suppressing the instinct to breathe.[16] Users who take a fatal overdose usually die by asphyxiation. Cocaine can also kill. It increases blood pressure and over-stimulates the heart. So it can cause cardiac arrest. This is more likely to happen with the freebase version of cocaine. Smoking crack enables a higher concentration of cocaine to enter the bloodstream more quickly, increasing constriction of the blood vessels and strain on the heart. Taking illicit drugs in combination with each other, and with alcohol, is a common feature of drug-related deaths.

An English study found that drug users who sought treatment had an age-adjusted mortality rate that was six times higher than the general population (Gossop *et al.* 2002). In 2008, there were 2,281 drug-related deaths in the UK – a rate of 3.6 deaths per 100,000 population. This was the highest rate ever recorded. Heroin or morphine was mentioned on 46 per cent of death certificates for such cases, methadone on 20 per cent, diazepam on 18 per cent and cocaine on nine per cent (Davies *et al.* 2009). Rates of drug-related death tend to be higher in Scotland than England; so much higher that they represent a third of the excess in mortality in Scotland over England (Bloor *et al.* 2008). In the USA, a different definition of drug-related death is used, making it hard to compare rates. In 2006, there were 38,396 drug-induced deaths recorded in the USA – a rate of 12.8 deaths per 100,000 population (Xu *et al.* 2009). There has been a sharp rise in such deaths since 1990 (Paulozzi & Annest 2007), with particular increases in deaths associated with pharmaceutical opioid painkillers, like OxyContin (a brand name for oxycodone) and fentanyl. These high and growing death rates point to the failures of both the US and UK models of drug control, although there have been some encouraging signs such as an increase in the average at which drug-related deaths occur in the UK (Davies *et al.* 2009) and a slight decrease in the number of deaths associated with heroin or opium in the USA (Paulozzi & Xi 2008).

Other health harms

Short of death, a wide variety of other health problems are related to use of illicit drugs. HIV is the most notorious. The spread of this blood-borne virus through the sharing of injecting equipment has incited much of the global development of services for drug users (UNAIDS 2001). Currently, it is estimated that approximately three million people worldwide are living with HIV acquired through injecting drug use. This is about 11 per cent of the global number of people living with HIV (Mathers *et al.* 2008). In 2003, 16 per cent of injecting drug users in the USA were estimated to be living with HIV. In the UK this proportion has been estimated at two per cent in 2006 (Ibid). There is a big difference in the contribution of injecting drug use to the HIV epidemic on either side of the Atlantic. It seems that the early and widespread adoption of harm reduction strategies, including needle exchange, in the UK has effectively limited the spread of HIV. Many injecting drug users in the USA, where needle exchange is much less widely available, have paid a high price for the refusal of successive pre-Obama administrations to fund this approach.

Even before HIV began to kill large numbers of drug users, other blood-borne viruses were causing concern. The first programmes enabling drug users to access clean injecting equipment were set up by drug users in Amsterdam to protect themselves and their peers from viral hepatitis (Lane *et al.* 1999). Hepatitis B and C now affect startlingly large proportions of injecting drug users. For example, in Great Britain in 2006, 67 per cent of injecting drug users were estimated to be infected with Hepatitis C (HPA 2008). In the USA, studies in Baltimore, Chicago, Los Angeles and New York City between 1999 and 2004 found prevalences of HCV amongst injecting drug users of between 35 and 65 per cent (Amon *et al.* 2008). This disease, when chronic and untreated, leads to liver cirrhosis at an age around 65 in between a fifth and third of cases, with many people developing liver cancer. Hepatitis C is the cause of almost half of liver transplants in the USA (Humar *et al.* 2007). HCV is harder to prevent through needle exchange than HIV. However, it is treatable. A combination of drugs can halt the progression of the disease and even reduce the viral load so much as to provide an effective cure (NICE 2004, 2006). This treatment can work even with people who continue to inject drugs, but current injectors are often excluded from this therapy. This is presumably because it is thought that they are unlikely to comply with treatment and are vulnerable to reinfection. This may be true for some drug users, but a clinic in East London has shown that it is possible to provide effective treatment to active drug users who have Hepatitis C (Wilkinson 2008).

These harms are serious, and threaten the lives and health of hundreds of thousands of drug users. But we need to keep them in perspective. Even though drug use is associated with a variety of health harms, it is still a relatively small cause of death and ill health when compared to others. Figure 2.3 below shows World Health Organization figures on the proportion of deaths attributable to a variety of risk factors in high income countries. Only 0.5 per cent of mortality was attributable to illicit drug use – an estimated 37,000 deaths. Smoking, high blood pressure, obesity, high cholesterol and physical inactivity each contributed to many more deaths. In the USA, recent research has suggested that poverty itself is the biggest killer. Having an income below twice the poverty line accounted for the loss of more quality adjusted life years than smoking, obesity, or binge drinking (Muennig *et al.* 2009).

The distribution of harms

All these causes of death fall most heavily on the poor in developed nations (Marmot & Wilkinson 1999). And the harms of drug use fall especially

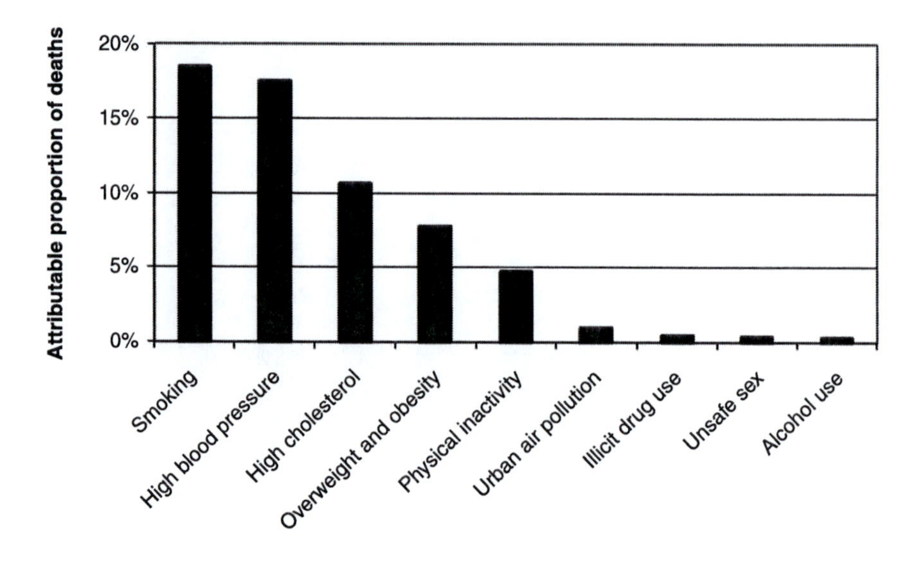

Figure 2.3 Deaths attributable to risk factors in high income countries, 2001.
(*Source:* adapted from Lopez et *al.* 2007)

heavily on poor drug users. Two British reviews of the link between drug problems and socio-economic deprivation found that some people and neighbourhoods are much more vulnerable to drug-related harm than others (ACMD 1998; Shaw *et al.* 2007). These reviews back up the finding that, while recreational drug use is not more prevalent among socially excluded groups, more harmful patterns of drug use are typically reported by people who face socio-economic deprivation of various kinds (see also Coulthard *et al.* 2002; Wadsworth *et al.* 2004).

The huddling together of social problems

Other social problems such as victimization by murder, burglary and robbery, poor health, road traffic accidents and early death also tend to concentrate in deprived areas (Dorling 2006). Drug problems tend to 'huddle together' with social problems to deepen the miseries of those who have been left behind by economic growth (Pearson 1991). For example, analysis of British Crime Survey and census data has found that over half of all property crime is found in the poorest one fifth of communities in England and Wales (Hope 2001). An investigation into drug-related deaths in Scotland found that 42 per cent of those deaths took place in the most deprived neighbourhoods, comprising only 19 per cent of the population (Zador *et al.* 2005). In Australia, the rapid increase in drug-related deaths that followed the increase in the availability of heroin was felt most severely among poorer people. Men who were classified as manual workers were more than twice as likely to die from drugs than those classed as non-manual workers (Najman, Toloo & Williams 2008). A study of over 2,000 such deaths in the census tracts of New York City between 1991 and 1995 also found that they were more likely to occur in areas of high unemployment and low income. These kinds of poverty were the strongest predictor of the number of drug-related deaths, apart from gender (areas with higher proportions of men had higher death rates). Controlling for the influence of other variables, a census tract which had rates of poverty and boarded-up properties higher – and home ownership levels lower – than about five sixths of the city would have had 82 per cent more drug-related deaths than a tract which had a poverty rate no higher than one sixth of the city (calculated from estimates given by Hannon & Cuddy 2006).

Inequality in income is reflected in inequality in a wide range of health measures, not just drug-related harms (CSDH 2008; Ram 2005; Wilkinson 2005). Many studies have observed this social gradient in health. It is particularly severe for mental health, which is especially relevant to the study of drug problems (Friedli 2009). In the UK, a team led by the University of Portsmouth (Asthana *et al.* 2004) reanalyzed the annual Health Survey for England for 1991 to 1997. In common with other researchers in this field, they found that people in lower status occupational groups (e.g. unskilled workers) tend to have higher rates of a variety of illnesses, including angina, stroke, diabetes, deafness and mental illness. They emphasize that, for most diseases, age and sex are more important predictors than social class. The exception is mental health. Social class seems at least as important as age and sex in influencing whether a person will suffer a mental disorder. The study by Stockdale and her colleagues (2007) looked specifically at mental health alongside 'substance abuse' in 60 US communities. They found significant effects of family wealth, low education and social support in predicting who experiences mental health problems. People with smaller savings, who did not complete college or graduate high school and who reported that they had nobody to help, support, or comfort them were more likely to be diagnosed as having a mental health problem.

Datasorauses and social blindness

Such statistical studies give us a lot of information about the distribution of harms. But they tend to share one major failing. They rarely reflect on how this distribution is produced. Cultural and critical criminologists have repeatedly complained that quantitative analysts have allowed their statistical models to blind them to the social realities that underlie the data. Three such critics have used the image of the 'datasoraus' to illustrate their complaint. This is a 'creature with a very small theoretical brain, a huge methodological body, a Byzantine and intricate statistical gut, and a tiny, inconclusive tail wagging mindlessly from database to database' (Ferrell et al. 2008: 169). This monster is emblematic of abstract empiricist studies which refuse to address the implications of their findings in any depth. And so it is for many of the researchers who have studied inequalities in health and drug harms. They use increasingly sophisticated, multivariate techniques to analyze their data. At the end of these analyzes they emerge, clutching log ratios and regression coefficients, too exhausted from thrashing through the statistical trees to glance back at the wood they have just decimated. They focus in on the numbers that their models have given them, rather than considering their application to the real lives of the people from whom they have been extracted. Of course, multivariate models can tell them little about how these people experience their suffering, or how they can be supported to overcome it. Instead, the datasoraus plods on to suggest how a little social engineering could tweak the proximal predictive variables, leaving broader social structures untouched.

Here are just three of many possible examples:

- A team from the University of Texas studied the link between neighbourhood deprivation and health risk behaviours, using data from the US Third National Health and Nutrition Examination (Stimpson *et al.* 2007). They statistically controlled for levels of income and employment and found that people living in more deprived neighbourhoods were more likely to smoke, to have high levels of alcohol use, to be physically inactive and to eat high-fat diets. They briefly discuss the effect of the economic structure in producing stress and in concentrating outlets for unhealthy food in poor neighbourhoods. But they go on to conclude that the solution to inequalities in health is to change the behaviours of those people who live in these places. The idea of reducing the economic inequality that structures these living conditions appears not to have crossed their minds.
- The study of the distribution of drug-related deaths in New York (Hannon & Cuddy 2006) found, as mentioned above, that poverty was important in predicting where these deaths took place. Instead of advocating that efforts be made to reduce poverty levels, Hannon and Cuddy instead argue that efforts should be made to increase home ownership and reduce the numbers of boarded-up properties. They ignore the role of poverty in explaining both the high levels of abandoned properties and people's inability to buy their homes. There seems to be a wilful blindness to the possibility of addressing the causes of poverty, rather than its symptoms.
- Even researchers who combine original data collection and complex analytical techniques with well-developed theory sometimes ignore the policy implications that are staring them in the face. Sampson and Raudenbush (1999) carried out a fascinating study of the link between neighbourhood characteristics and disorder in Chicago. Their researchers

> cruised the streets, videoing what was happening and then viewing the tapes to record any signs of physical or social disorder, including indicators such as syringes on the sidewalk and drug sales in progress. They found – in contradiction to the 'broken windows' theory (Wilson & Kelling 1982) that has formed the basis for 'zero tolerance policing' (Harcourt 2002) – that disorder was not a strong predictor of crime rates. They found that poverty and collective efficacy are both more influential. They recommended taking steps to boost collective efficacy. But they sidestepped the implication that both crime and disorder could be radically affected by reducing the structural disadvantage which their own statistical models told them is so influential.

There are exceptions to this rather depressing rule. For example, a study in Los Angeles examined the social contexts of adolescent mental health problems (Aneshensel & Sucoff 1996). Such problems have been associated in other studies with early onset of substance use and a greater likelihood of dependent use (Clark 2004; Newcomb *et al.* 1997; Williams *et al.* 2004). Aneshensel and Sucoff found that young people in poorer areas were more likely to see their neighbourhoods as threatening and to experience mental health problems. They argue for expansion of the scope of research beyond individual characteristics and their proximal predictors (family, peers, education, etc.) to examine the role of wider social structures in explaining the distribution of mental health problems. Landis *et al.* (2007: 1066) conclude that their study on the effects of stress on adolescent hopelessness 'highlight[s] the importance of public policy efforts to prevent income disparities and segregation so that fewer adolescents are forced to live with the chronic uncontrollable stressors that urban poverty brings'. Similarly, Toby Seddon has reviewed the research on British young people's use of heroin and crack. He finds that socio-economic inequality contributes, through complex pathways, to the unequal distribution of young people's use of these drugs. He argues that policy on drug use should 'move away from a primary focus on individualistic issues . . . towards a more integrated approach which seeks also to tackle inequalities and disadvantage' (Seddon 2008: 242).

The inequality of drug-related harm

Inequality has grown rapidly over the last few centuries and decades. This cannot be explained by pointing to natural inequalities in ability, or by blaming a market which is 'free'. Political and social inequalities are produced by conscious human action, even if the actors are not always fully aware of the consequences they will bring about. Social inequalities are reflected in a wide range of harms to health. The diseases of affluence fall most heavily on the poor in rich nations. Drug use itself does not appear to be one of these diseases. Large proportions of the populations of developed nations have apparently used illicit drugs without much harm to their health, to their education or to their ability to attain high political office. Both drug use and dependence appear to be more common among people with higher incomes, when taking other issues (primarily gender and unemployment) into account. Meanwhile, the most damaging patterns of drug use and their worst consequences are concentrated in deprived neighbourhoods and groups. Too many quantitative studies have shown that inequality is associated with important harms and then failed to draw the logical conclusion that inequality itself should be reduced. Instead, they call on the poor to fix their broken windows and to change their feckless ways.

The lives and values of the wealthy and the poor mingle and merge continually (Young 2007). People throughout society seek purpose and pleasure in their lives, and sometimes use illicit drugs in these pursuits. Blocked from achieving status and wealth by increasing economic inequality, some people find in risky health behaviours a way both to console themselves for their losses and to find meaning in life. The next chapter will explore the theoretical background and the empirical support for a sociological approach that offers a deeper understanding of inequalities in drug use, crime and health harms than is currently offered by the social scientific 'datasorauses'.

Chapter 3

Beyond the tripartite framework

The subterranean structuration of the drug-crime link

As illicit drugs have become more widely used and their users have been found throughout society, it has become harder to maintain that all their users are unproductive moral deviants. The outlawing of drug use has been increasingly based instead on the link between illicit drugs and other types of crime. It has repeatedly been claimed that crime is an inevitable result of drug use and that large proportions of crime are directly caused by drugs. If we could rid our societies of drugs, it is often supposed, then we could also dramatically reduce the crime rate. This argument has spread so widely that the anti-prohibition lobby has turned it against the drug warriors. Its argument is that it is the illegality of drugs that creates the drug-crime link: if illegal drugs cause so much crime, surely the answer must be to legalize and regulate drugs, and so eliminate the related criminality.

This chapter will begin with an analysis of this exaggeration of the scale of drug-related crime. It is usually said that there are three types of link from drugs to crime: psychopharmacological, economic-compulsive and systemic. This chapter will go on to examine this 'tripartite framework' (Goldstein 1985; Goldstein *et al.* 1989). It will argue that – in similar ways to the examinations of health inequalities discussed in the previous chapter – it underemphasizes the importance of the social in determining the scale and distribution of drug-related harms. Looked at closely, the tripartite framework and many of the studies that have inherited its blinkered approach to the drug-crime link fail to match up to the complex social reality that is increasingly visible through the work of sociologists and anthropologists. This chapter then develops an alternative concept of the link between drugs and crime: the idea that both are instances of a process of subterranean structuration. This concept suggests that drug use and offending are linked together by powerful forces of mutual attraction for people who have been relegated to the underside of late modern employment and consumption. People from all walks of life may journey into damaging patterns of drug use. The combination of inequality and consumerism means that the link between drugs and crime is much more likely among people who suffer from relative poverty. If we are to break the drug-crime link, we will need to reduce social inequality.

The exaggeration of drug-related crime

There is a strong link between drug use and crime in many societies. Offending and drug use are often done by the same people in the same places (Bennett *et al.* 2008; Lurigio & Schwartz 1999). The most detailed quantitative studies of this link have shown that drug users tend to offend most frequently during periods of intensive drug use (Anglin & Speckart 1988; Ball *et al.* 1981; Hanlon *et al.* 1990; Johnson *et al.* 1985). However, there has been a tendency to make inflated claims for the amount of crime that is directly related to drug use. UK government policy documents have used an estimate that the annual costs of crime that is directly attributable to drug use are £13.9 billion. The originators of that estimate warned that it was 'exploratory' and should not be part of a 'decision-making model' (Godfrey *et al.* 2002: 8). It suffers many uncertainties (Stevens 2008a). It is based on a selective sample. It uses data from drug users who entered the National Treatment Outcome Research Study (NTORS) (Gossop *et al.* 1998). The Survey of Psychiatric Morbidity suggested that only 17 per cent of people who showed indicators of drug dependence entered any type of day care service in the previous year (Singleton *et al.* 2001). Drug users who enter treatment are likely to be those who have the highest levels of problems with their use, including higher rates of offending. Extrapolating from them to the wider number of people who are estimated to use drugs is therefore likely to exaggerate levels of offending. Also, the NTORS only asked about offences in the previous three months. Godfrey *et al.* (2002) assumed that these people would be offending at the same level all year. Given that offending tends to peak in the months before treatment entry (Gossop *et al.* 2006; McGlothlin *et al.* 1977), this again produces an over-estimate of the amount of crime committed by drug users.

The exaggeration of drug-related crime commonly involves two very questionable assumptions. One is that the link between drugs and crime is directly causal. The other is that this link runs in one direction only: from drugs to crime. These assumptions ignore the possibility that people use drugs due to the opportunities afforded to them by success in criminal endeavours (Burr 1987; Faupel *et al.* 2004). They minimize the role of poverty and inequality in creating the conditions in which some people decide to take part in both crime and drug use. The drug-crime link is a lot more complex than these assumptions allow (Allen 2007; Brochu *et al.* 2002; Faupel *et al.* 2004; Keene 2005; Seddon 2000, 2006).

The case for complexity in the drug-crime link has recently been boosted by a thorough analysis (Bennett & Holloway 2007) of a study that has, ironically, often been used to argue for a simple, economic-compulsive link from drug use to a large proportion of acquisitive crime. The New English and Welsh Arrestee Drug Abuse Monitoring programme (New-ADAM for short) copied its methods from the US ADAM study (Bennett 1998; US Department of Justice 2003). It interviewed 4,645 arrestees at 16 police custody suites between 1999 and 2002. It collected samples for urinanalysis from 92 per cent of them. In total, 69 per cent of those tested were found to be positive for an illicit drug (with 48 per cent positive tests for cannabis, 33 per cent for heroin and 26 per cent for cocaine). This finding has often been used in policy documents to demonstrate that drug use causes a large proportion of crime (e.g. PMSU 2003a). But Bennett and Holloway have repeatedly warned their readers against the assumption of a simple link from drug use to crime. In their books (Bennett & Holloway 2005, 2007), they list several competing explanations, including the idea that crime causes drug use, that both are mutually reinforcing and that both are caused by other factors. Most importantly, they show that there were important distinctions in the links between specific drugs and certain types of crime in their sample. They carry out a logistic regression analysis, including socio-demographic covariates, of the frequency of self-reported offending and drug use. Heroin use was only predictive of a high frequency of shoplifting. Cocaine use was not significantly linked to a high rate of any type of offence. Crack use was only predictive of a high rate of fraud, handling and drug supply (and not robbery, shoplifting, theft or burglary). Bennett and Holloway (2007) conclude from these models that there is no simple drug-crime connection, but multiple drug-crime connections.

However, Bennett and Holloway fail to acknowledge a much wider problem with using the small minority of offenders who are arrested to investigate general relationships between drug use and crime. This approach makes the unsafe assumption that drug users are no more or less likely to be arrested than other offenders. Analysis of data from two British studies shows that arrestees are not representative of all those who commit crimes. Rather, offenders are more likely to be arrested if they are unemployed, of African or Afro-Caribbean ethnicity and – importantly for this analysis – if they also use drugs (McAra & McVie 2005; Stevens 2008a). This over-representation of drug users in criminal justice samples means that figures from arrestees and prisoners should not be extrapolated to the unknown (and unknowable) total number of offenders and offences (Stevens 2007a). They are likely to create over-estimates of the proportion of crime that is committed by drug users.

Also, Bennett and Holloway (2007), along with many other commentators, treat drug use and offending as if they take place in a social vacuum. Their multivariate regression analysis suggests that being male, unemployed, an early school leaver and homeless is more important in predicting the frequency of various types of offending than use of any specific drug, but they leave the sociological implications of their models unexplored. They argue that more research attention should be paid to specific links between individual drugs and certain types of crime. This is true, but we also need to examine more closely the social contexts in which these complex drug-crime links operate. These social contexts are obscured by the predominant framework for analysis.

Testing the tripartite framework

This framework was developed by Paul Goldstein and his colleagues, working in New York City in the 1980s. The original paper presenting this framework (Goldstein 1985) is the most frequently cited research article on drugs and crime.[17] It has become so widely accepted that both academics (e.g. Deitch *et al.* 2000) and policy makers have used it without even referring to its inventor. I have cited it myself in a policy briefing (Stevens, Trace & Bewley-Taylor 2005), making use of the persuasive ease with which it introduces readers to varying perspectives on why drug use seems so closely linked to crime.

One reason for the popularity of this framework is that it offers not just one explanation of the drug-crime link, but three. They are:

1. Psychopharmacological. This link rests on the effect that some psychoactive substances have on the brain in increasing aggression and reducing inhibition.
2. Economic-compulsive. As drug users are compelled to use drugs by their addiction, so they have an economic need to fund their habit by committing crime.
3. Systemic. Illicit drug markets are inherently violent. Traffickers, dealers and users have no recourse to the legal system, and so must resort to violence to regulate their affairs.

Another part of the appeal of this framework must be that it can be used by either side of the prohibition/legalization debate. Prohibitionists, such as James Inciardi (1999), use the psychopharmacological link to argue that any increase in drug use subsequent to legalization would lead to increased crime through the direct effects of these drugs on the brains of their users. Their opponents, like Transform (Rolles 2007), can use the systemic link to argue that the answer to drug-related crime is to take the business out of the hands of violent criminals. The economic-compulsive link is deployed by both sides. One suggests that we should reduce this type of crime by reducing the number of drug users. The other retorts that we should reduce the price of drugs, and so the number of crimes that users have to commit to pay for them (Transform 2009b).

Empirical tests

There are, however, two surprising aspects of the spread of this three-legged approach to the drug-crime link. The first is how rarely it has been tested empirically (MacCoun *et al.* 2003). Apart from Goldstein's own work, I have found three other studies in the USA. I have found no direct tests of the framework in any other country. Inciardi (1990) studied the relationship between crack and violence in a non-random sample of 611 young people in Miami. Their average age was 15. They were very highly criminally involved. Ninety-three per cent of them were crack users. Inciardi found very low rates of psychopharmacological violence, which was reported by only five per cent of his sample. This is rather surprising given the high rate of crack use and Inciardi's later (1999) comments on the inevitability of the psychopharmacological link from crack to violence. There were higher rates of economic-compulsively motivated robberies, many of which were carried out against other crack dealers. Inciardi (1990) concludes that it is particularly deviant young people who are drawn into crack markets. Their involvement with crack then intensifies their criminality.

Menard and Mihalic (2001) used data from nine waves (covering 1976 to 1992) of the US National Youth Survey. This is a more representative sample of the general population than Inciardi's serious young offenders. They found that illicit drug use did not produce psychopharmacological crime in this sample. People who reported committing violent offences were, however, more likely to report high levels of alcohol use immediately prior to committing the offence. Economic-compulsive crime was rare, reported by only about two per cent of drug or alcohol users across the survey waves. People involved in selling drugs, and especially 'hard' drugs, were significantly more likely than others to report violent perpetration and victimization. Menard and Mihalic interpret their findings as suggesting that, apart from systemic, violent crimes by and against drug dealers, the link between drugs and crime may be spurious. There may be other variables which cause both drugs and crime, but with no direct causal link between these two types of behaviour.

The only other published study which explicitly sets out to test the tripartite framework provides a classic example of datasoric[18] thinking (Weiner *et al.* 2005). It uses the rates of drug use reported by Southern California high school students to predict whether they reported committing violent crimes at a follow-up interview five years later. But it uses a statistical model that includes only age, gender and ethnicity as co-variates, with no regard to socio-economic status, educational achievement or a host of other potential mediating factors. Unsurprisingly, given the well-known correlation between drugs and crime, people who used drugs while at high school were more likely to report committing violent crimes at follow-up. In this analysis, violence was significantly influenced by indicators of psychopharmacological motivation (such as whether interviewees stated that they committed crimes while under the influence), but not by indicators of economic-compulsive or systemic offending. Given the inadequacy of the statistical model that was used, we can have little confidence that even the psychopharmacological link was reliably supported.[19] The tripartite framework may have 'intuitive appeal' (Ibid: 1262). But it still has little empirical support.

The misclassification of murder

The second surprising thing about the tripartite framework is how long it has endured. Goldstein and his colleagues used their conceptual framework to analyze murders in New York City in 1988 (Goldstein *et al.* 1989). This was near the height of the crack epidemic, and one of the most violent years in the city's history. Generalizing from the New York of 1988 to drug markets at all other times and places is not to be advised. Since 1988, drug epidemics have come and gone. New York's murder rate has risen, fallen and risen again. But the tripartite framework soldiers on, garnering more citations in the three years from 2005 than it did in the eight years following its original publication.

One of the researchers who worked on the New York studies has twice expressed his astonishment to me that the framework continues to be so influential. And if you read the original articles, you can see why. The first paper on the tripartite framework shows that it was, from the beginning, blind to the possibilities that the link between drugs and crime is explained by anything else than a direct link from drugs to crime (Goldstein 1985). While this first, conceptual paper hedged its bets with words like 'possible' and 'may', it still points only to uni-directional, causal links. Goldstein and his colleagues (1989) then tested the framework by asking New York City police officers to record their impressions of 414 murders. They categorized 53 per cent of these crimes as drug-related. And this idea that drugs cause about half of committed crimes has often been repeated since (e.g. PMSU 2003a; WAG 2008). But we need to look more closely at how this link was established. The role of alcohol was ignored. And it was assumed that some crimes were drug-related even in the absence of any evidence of this motivation. In one case, a 26 year old attempted to rape and then murdered the 56 year old woman who was babysitting his child. This offence was recorded as primarily related to crack, even though the perpetrator was drunk at the time of the offence. He himself attributed it to his use of alcohol. The murder of a crack user whose head was smashed in by a car jack handle was classified as economic-compulsive – not because the killer (who remained undetected) committed the crime to get drugs, but because the victim was assumed (with little evidence) to have been killed in the act of stealing from the killer's car to buy drugs. Another 'bizarre' case was classed as psychopharmacological 'because the perpetrator *believed* that the victim was going to rob him in order to finance a drug habit', even though 'no actual robbery attempt took place' (Ibid: 677, my italics).

Every one of the 'drug-related' murders was categorized as being either psychopharmacological, economic-compulsive or systemic.[20] It was assumed that drug markets are 'normally aggressive' (Ibid: 656). So all murders involving drug users or dealers were classed as systemic where there was no apparent psychopharmacological or economic-compulsive motive. This included 24 'other' cases (representing 15 per cent of all 'systemic' murders) where there was no motive related to the internal working of the drug market. One of them seems to have been more a case of anti-systemic vigilantism rather than systemic violence within the drug market. It involved a 17 year old who shot dead a man who was assumed to be coming to the killer's building to buy crack. Murders were shoehorned into the tripartite categorization, and then used to support the empirical value of the framework, in viciously circular fashion.[21] These classifications do not test the three hypotheses suggested by the tripartite framework. Rather they rest on the prior assumptions that the framework covers every possible instance of homicide where the victim or perpetrator is a drug user, and that drug markets are inherently violent.

Goldstein (1985: 503) wrote that '[s]ystemic violence is normatively embedded in the social and economic networks of drug users and sellers'. It is this assumption that frames the rest of their research, and much subsequent writing on the drug-crime link. So let's look at this assumption in more detail. First of all, can we apply it to all drug users and sellers? As we have seen from the study by Menard and Mihalic (2001), the vast majority of drug users are no more criminal than non-users. So the idea that they are normatively embedded in violence does not stand. As for dealers, it may be true that rates of violent predation and victimization are higher among illicit drug sellers, but two other points are relevant. The first is that many drug sellers shy away from violence. One reason they do so is because it attracts police attention and so is bad for business (Curtis & Wendel 2007). Another is that they simply may not have the heart for it. In a study that emphasized peaceful methods of social control within illicit drug markets, researchers asked a drug dealer in Minneapolis what he was going to do about an acquaintance who had robbed him. He replied, 'fucking nothing, I mean what am I going to do – shoot him?' (Jacques & Wright 2008). Coomber and Maher (2006) studied heroin markets in Sydney and found that they were characterized by peaceful coexistence and even cooperation between dealers (although violence had broken out in the past). The norms of drug users and sellers are not universally violent.

The next problem in Goldstein's assumption is the idea that the 'normative embedding' of systemic violence is specific to the drug market. If it exists, where does this violent attitude to life originate? Sommers and Baskin (1997) interviewed 156 women who were involved in drug selling in New York. They found, as usual, high rates of violence. But following detailed interviews with these women, they concluded that this violence was not caused by their involvement in drug markets. Rather, there was a process of self-selection at work. It was people with the greatest experience and proficiency in violence who were attracted to working in the drug market. And there was also, crucially, a social context to these women's lives. They lived in neighbourhoods that were already affected by high levels of poverty and violence, even before drug epidemics increased the rewards available to the most aggressive residents. Where drug markets are particularly murderous, it may be because law enforcement has driven the more peaceable, risk averse dealers out of the business (Dorn, Murji & South 1992; Klein 2008) in areas with social conditions that are already conducive to violence.

This crucial interaction between drug market and social context is supported by a US study which found that larger drug markets are associated with higher murder rates in poor cities, but not in rich ones (Ousey & Lee 2002). A different study found that murder rates rose fastest between 1982 and 1992 in those US cities which had the highest levels of socio-economic deprivation (Strom & MacDonald 2007). Murder rates have since declined and this has been attributed in large part to the shrinking of the market for crack (Blumstein & Wallman 2000; Bowling 1999). But Ousey and Lee (2007) found that socio-economic conditions were also influential. In cities where socio-economic conditions improved, murder rates tended to decline fastest, even when controlling for indicators of the crack market.

So if violence is indeed 'normatively embedded' in some drug markets, it may not be systemic to the drug market, but rather to the local social structure. Many residents of the areas where the drug-crime link has been found have also been exposed to the 'structural violence' (Wacquant 2007) of social exclusion combined with depressive, abusive or neglectful parenting and heavy-handed policing. It should not be surprising that some of these people reproduce this violence in their dealings with each other. Drugs, in these cases, just add fuel to a fire that was already burning.

Towards a social understanding of inequalities in harm

The people who are most often blamed for drug-related crime are those who fall into the stigmatized category of the problematic drug user, aka the dependent user, the addict, the high harm-causing user, or the junkie. These are people whose identities have, as Mariana Valverde (1998) put it, been 'totalized' by their drug use, whose lives have come to revolve around this central pole (Radcliffe & Stevens 2008). It is difficult to understand why anybody would follow a pattern of behaviour that is so dangerous and shunned. There is a medical explanation which relies on neurobiological models of how people are trapped by their brain chemistry in cycles of self-destructive substance use (The Academy of Medical Sciences 2008; London 2009). But this cannot explain the social distribution of problematic drug use and crime. If the interaction between brain and drug were the only explanation of drug dependence, then we would expect to see it evenly distributed amongst those social groups who have experience of drug use. They would span the entire social range. As we saw in the previous chapter, these harms are not evenly distributed, but concentrated amongst the poor.

Elliott Currie (1993) has listed four models which can help us understand this concentration of some forms of drug use and related harms. The first is the status model. This suggests that drug use and dealing fills a need for status and community for people in places where these are not otherwise available. The second is the coping model. This highlights the use of drugs to relieve the pain and insecurity of life in these disorganized, deprived communities. The third is the structure model, which notes how people who live in these communities are denied the purpose and meaning in their lives that is provided to people in less deprived circumstances by attachment to stable work and families. The fourth is the saturation model. When drugs surround you, when everybody around you is doing it, the decision to use drugs is hardly a decision at all. It is more like going with the flow of what is perceived to be everyday life. Currie summarizes his approach by arguing:

> If we want to understand drug abuse on the mass or endemic level . . . we must begin by recognizing that it is a social phenomenon, not primarily an individual or biochemical one. It emerges, and endures, because in any of several ways it serves to meet human needs that are systematically thwarted by the social and economic structures of the world users live in.
> (Ibid: 122)

Currie's four models are problematic because they might just as well predict higher rates of drug use in deprived communities as they do higher levels of chronic, dependent use. Non-dependent drug use is not necessarily linked to deprivation. People with money often want to buy the pleasures it can bring them. But these models point the way to an explanation of the distribution of drug dependence and crime that combines a focus on the choices of drug users with the influence of social structures.

Subterranean play and structuration in late modernity

David Matza and Gresham Sykes argued that delinquency and bohemianism display the subterranean values of hedonism, disdain for work and the search for adventure (Matza 1961; Matza & Sykes 1961). These values are subterranean because they 'are in conflict or in competition with other deeply held values but . . . are still recognized and accepted by many' (Matza & Sykes 1961: 716). Many of us may only feel or express them in private. People participating in these subterranean traditions do not always reject conventional assumptions, even if they violate them. Matza (1961) gives the example of delinquent youths who recognize the right to private property, but frequently violate it. Jock Young (1971) insisted that conventional and subterranean values are not separate moral regions, but are interlinked. The expression of subterranean values in middle class life is justified by hard work and productivity. The meaning of psychoactive substances for many of their users is to help them pass between production and leisure. As the symbolic roles of coffee and alcohol are, for Joseph Gusfield (1987), to mark the transition into and out of the mode of work respectively, so other substances, such as cannabis and LSD, open the door to a world of subterranean play; a world 'free of the norms of workaday life' (Young 1971: 136). The emphasis of writers like Young, Matza and Sykes on people creating their own activities and meanings from the cultural and material resources that surround them remains vital, and is too often ignored in contemporary criminology (Ferrell *et al.* 2008).

Their emphasis on the interplay of people's choices with their circumstances is echoed in the 'structuration' theory of Anthony Giddens (1979). Giddens argued that all human life involves a recursive link between social structure and people's actions. Actions are constrained by limits of power and resource. People at the top of the social order retain power deliberately in order to be able to satisfy their wants. People at the bottom have to make do with the resources that remain. Struggling within these limitations, they create new social phenomena and relationships. The actions of both powerful and powerless have unintended consequences. Actions, which are chosen by people within the limits they face, may have the unintended effect – as welcome for some people as it is disastrous for others – of reproducing the limits of their actions. Pierre Bourdieu (1998: 27) wrote of participants in hierarchically ordered societies that they 'are all the helpless victims of a mechanism which is nothing but the cumulative effect of their own strategies, engendered and amplified by the logic of competition of everyone against everyone'. Giddens (1979) would insist that people are always aware of at least some of the rules of the game they are playing, and seek to bend them to their own advantage.[22]

These theoretical insights help us to appreciate the way in which people may come to act in ways that damage themselves and their communities. Especially when we realize the ways in which times have changed. Matza and Sykes (1961: 717) observed an increasing emphasis on consumption across society, involving 'a compromise between the Protestant Ethic and a Leisure Ethic'. They argued that delinquency should be viewed as an extension of the leisure ethic of middle-class adults into the lives of adolescents who, in the 1950s and 1960s, could seek excitement, disdain work and consume hedonistically before moving into the world of work and family responsibilities. Two things have changed. The first is that many adolescents are now denied the opportunity to move into a job which enables them to sustain family life. The possibility of work which provides a living wage and an opportunity to win respect has been taken away from many young people growing up in the deindustrialized terrain of late modern society. The second change, according to Zygmunt Bauman (2007), is that we have now become a fully fledged 'society of consumers'. The role of production in structuring society has been taken over by consumption. The Protestant Ethic – which called for hard work, austerity and the deferral of gratification – is dead. The individualized, free-wheeling, high-spending consumer is king. The corporate marketeers and politicians who court his attention will remove any obstacle to his infantile desire to have whatever he wants, when he wants. The countervailing power of trade unions, those outmoded representatives of the producing classes, has been diminished by privatization, globalization and restrictive legislation. The people who used to create national wealth through the strength of their arms and the use of their skills have been relegated to insecure, casually contracted employees to be dispensed with at the drop of a profits warning. Hedonistic consumption is no longer just youthful play, but our principal economic activity. The main aim of the measures taken to rescue our credit-busted economies was, after all, to keep us spending. It used to be just delinquents and the leisure class who were socially recognized for being able to consume without producing (Matza 1961). Now the production-less consumption of the celebrity is a widespread career aspiration. Society rewards or punishes its members in accordance with how well they respond to the call to consume. This becomes 'the paramount stratifying factor and the principal criterion of inclusion and exclusion, as well as guiding the distribution of social esteem and stigma' (Bauman 2007: 53).

The withdrawal of employment, the advance of drug markets

Bauman overstates both the novelty and the extent of this social transformation. Even if the metamorphosis of a society of Calvinistic producers into one of hedonistic consumers has accelerated since the 1960s, Young (1971: 127) had already argued that 'it is during leisure and through the expression of subterranean values that modern man seeks his identity'. Nevertheless, as Tim Strangleman (2007: 100) has noted, 'work still provides structure and meaning in people's lives . . . one only has to look at the obverse of people without work to see the reality of this'. Even if occupational status has become less important in the distribution of esteem, those of us lucky enough to be in stable employment can still look to work to provide us a reasonable income, a modicum of respect and, importantly, a place to spend our time. All these are denied to the unemployed. In earlier sociological discussions of the drug-dependent life, arguments have centred on whether drug use is a 'retreatist' adaptation to failure to live out the American dream (Merton 1938), or an active search for status, meaning and excitement (Preble & Casey 1969). As unemployment and poorly paid, precarious employment have boomed during the upwards redistribution of income from the 1980s onwards, they have expanded the number of people – concentrated in inner cities and poor housing estates – who have little hope of ever getting a job that they value. Geoffrey Pearson (1987a, 1987b) interviewed many of them in the cities of northern England in the early 1980s. What he found for these jobless, working class drugtakers – as Young (1971) had found for his London bohemians – was that their drug use provided a solution to some of the problems that faced them. One crucial problem was how to fill their time. In the absence of a structured routine, they faced a seemingly endless life of purposeless, cashless nothingness. Like Dostoyevsky's (1989 [1864]) nameless underground man, they were denied a place in society, either as producers or valued consumers. They were physically excluded from the hubs of production and consumption. In being described as an 'underclass', they were metaphorically ejected from a society which no longer wanted them, except to scrub toilets, flip burgers and fight wars.

Without employment, they were left with countless hours to fill. As heroin distribution networks spread to their cities from the larger metropolitan centres, they found in drug dependence a way to structure their time. Not only did the daily round of getting out, scoring and using give them a purpose to pursue and a reason to make social connections, it also offered them a certain kind of status. In the post-war heroin epidemics in the USA, researchers observed how heroin users were not necessarily seen as retreatist 'double failures' – failing to achieve respect from either their respectably or their criminally employed neighbours – as Cloward and Ohlin (1960) had portrayed them. In Chicago, heroin use was associated with cool 'cats' in the jazz scene (Hughes *et al.* 1971). In New York, heroin was also cool for 'cats' in search of 'kicks' (Finestone 1957). The performance of prowess and control was central to the subterranean tradition of delinquency that David Matza (1961) identified. The acquisition, ritualized use and mastery of heroin, with its well-known dangers, are ways in which people can transcend the humiliations and limits placed upon them and demonstrate this transcendence to their peers (Katz 1988).

In the British heroin epidemics that succeeded the US model by a good 30 years, Pearson (1987a) observed that it took a fair amount of work for some users to develop a heroin habit. Unemployed young men actively sought entry to the social circles of heroin users by buying drugs *as if* they were dependent. In an ethnographic study of heroin and solvent users in London, Lee O'Bryan (1989) found that introduction into heroin use became a test of machismo among these socially excluded young men. They had to face up to this fearful substance, to show they were 'able to take it'. Mike Collison's study of 80 young men imprisoned in Shropshire in the 1990s also showed how these young men misrecognized the structural constraints that had been placed upon them by the withdrawal of employment. They had fallen for the lie that spectacular consumption of clothes, trainers, alcohol and drugs could lift them above the herd of inadequately dressed 'tramps' who lived in the estates they came from. They spoke of both drug use and crime as things that gave them excitement in an otherwise mundane life. One of them said, 'like drugs, it [crime] opened new doors . . . I was living on the edge all of a sudden' (Collison 1996: 434). Stimulants helped these young men to enjoy crime. Alcohol and tranquilizers helped to reduce the associated anxieties. The underground economy of drug dealing and crime offered a replacement for social structures that had disappeared along with the prospect of industrial employment. The roles it offered and the performances they demanded were congruent with the advancing glorification of hedonistic consumerism.[23]

In some badly hit areas, the illicit drug market has created a social space in which the most vulnerable people can find purpose and company, as well as powerful, passing sensations of comfort, social distinction and excitement. In these deindustrialized zones, many people live with the banality of long-term unemployment. They experience school education as a process of social disqualification, serving only to demonstrate how far they fall short of the ideals to which they are supposed to aspire. Any work available to them tends to be nasty, low-paid and short-term. People have, in their own words, been 'fucked up'. They sometimes go on to 'fuck up' (Allen 2007). Drugs are used in these areas, as elsewhere, to enhance the pleasure of a night out with friends. But they are also used – especially by those people who have been most damaged by abuse, neglect and bereavement – as consolation, to dull the pains of existence and exclusion. The absence of other economic opportunities leaves acquisitive crime and the drug market – also known as 'the belowground illicit drug industry' (Singer 2008: 166) – as principal sources of cash. This market becomes an arena in which people can display their worth, their prowess and their identity. Out of nothing, they can become somebody. In a lifestyle of obtaining and spending money, of using and selling drugs, they can combine the mainstream values of work, success and consumption with the subterranean values of adventure, excitement and hedonism.

Drugs, in these areas, are not just items for play, and are not simple causes of crime. They become objects of exchange and identification. Some people use them in creating their own life story. The story may have several phases, starting with experimentation, moving through an enjoyable period of affordable, euphoric drug use before the money runs out, life structure crumbles and they take on the identity of the 'junkie' (Faupel *et al.* 2004). As they move further into stigmatized and dangerous patterns of drug use, they make it more likely that their exclusion will be confirmed and their life shortened. The only industry that offers them a way out of social oblivion turns into a trap. It becomes an enclosed, criminalized, victimized and unhealthy circuit of people on whom to project fearful fantasies and blame. This is a process of subterranean structuration.[24] Many people engaged in dependent drug use live within heavy constraints that have been imposed upon them. In their struggle against these bonds, they tighten them still further. They reinforce the rules of the game which are so biased against them. They become the supposed proof that the poor are to blame for their own downfall. They justify the state's neglect of their well-being and its control of their activities by refusing to conform to expectations of what a deserving, passive recipient of welfare should be. Socio-economic inequality is translated into morbidity, mortality and criminality by a process (prolonged participation in illegal and damaging drug use) which becomes the justification for even more exclusive practices to be applied.

Social capital and dependence

Some people who do not live in these areas also become dependent on illicit drugs. The pursuit of psychoactive oblivion can be attractive for all sorts of people who need to resolve various existential problems, including the scars of abuse (Whittington 2007), the wounds of racism (Obama 2004), or the plain boredom of living (Cohen & Taylor 1992). The example of Barack Obama's drug use is instructive. In his autobiography he writes that he was at one point headed towards being a junkie, 'the final fatal role of the young would-be black man' (Obama 2004: 141). He used drugs to block out the crisis of identity that he experienced while trying, in the absence of his father's guidance, to reconcile his middle class, mixed race background with a society that wanted him to choose a side. His last two years in high school were marked by use of alcohol and marijuana, as well as cocaine 'when you could afford it' (Ibid: 140). What saved him from the descent into dependence was the guilt that his mother installed in him and the opportunities he had to go to college. A few years later, he was able to find a 'sense of place and purpose' without drugs (Ibid: 288).

Other wealthy drug users have gone further down the path to dependence than President Obama. From autobiographical accounts, this seems to be particularly true of upper class drug users. They are also cursed by underemployment and the consequently empty days which can be filled by dependent drug use. Middle and upper class writers have described how the strong pull of the subterranean dragged them towards crack and heroin (Horsley 2007; Pryor 2003; Self 2006). Seduced by the dirty glamour of William Burroughs (Lee 1953), they indulged heavily in class A drug use, before eventually finding that these substances could not provide the answers to the existential questions they were asking. Will Self describes the realization that he could not follow his early, junk taking, wife slaying idol by being both a writer of declared genius and perpetually stoned. 'When I awoke from this delusion . . . I was appalled to discover that I was not a famous underground writer. Indeed far from being a writer at all, I was simply underground' (Self 2006: 59).

William Pryor (2003: 15) reports that the only thing he learnt at Eton was 'the necessity to go underground to have any contact with life'. However far they fell (or threw themselves) into drug use, none of these relatively wealthy drug users suffered much from enforcement of the laws. Pryor was saved by his family connections from any heavy punishment for his crimes. Self awoke from his delusion in a psychiatric hospital, not a prison. And none reports resorting to shoplifting or domestic burglary to fund their use. The late Sebastian Horsley (2007: 216) wrote, 'I wasn't robbing old ladies on the [crack] pipe, but there was definitely a deterioration in my manners'. They had access to talents, funds and social connections that helped them get through their drug habits. Many drug users, including users of the drugs that are most demonized by the drug-crime link such as cocaine and heroin, are able entirely to avoid dependence and criminality through adhering to rules and routines that rely on other sources of finance, status and love (Shewan & Dalgarno 2006; Warburton *et al.* 2005a). The biographies of working class heroin users, who have less access to the kinds of financial and social capital that are so helpful in preventing and recovering from dependence (Granfield & Cloud 2001), are more likely to include greater physical torments, including spells in prison and on the streets, and much greater recourse to street level crime to fund their drug use (e.g. Johnson 2007; Neale 2002; Whittington 2007).

Examples of subterranean structuration

Inequality creates relative deprivation. People living in deprived neighbourhoods are not only objectively poor, but are acutely aware of their poverty. Their noses are pressed to the shop window that corporate marketeers expose them to every day, simultaneously displaying and withholding the fruits of consumerist cornucopia. Unsurprisingly, this provokes emotions of resentment among those people who have not fully accepted their ascribed social status. Craig Webber (2007) makes the link between Bourdieu (1984) and Runciman (1966) in arguing that this resentment and its effects depend on which reference group people compare themselves to. If people compare themselves to their immediate neighbours, they may accept the status quo and get on with living within the constraints that are placed upon them. However, if they cast their gaze beyond their friends and neighbours, to the images of production-less consumption that are constantly replenished on their screens and billboards, then they experience tension. They may seek to resolve this tension by aggressive acquisition of fetishized products and by seeking networks of peers with whom they can connect through dangerous, stigmatized and exciting behaviours. The combination of inequality and consumerism therefore creates a tendency for some people to combine their drug use with crime.

Empirically, this combination has often been stumbled across, but has less often been recognized. Studies which look at drug use and crime in models which only include individual variables are blind to the social contexts in which the link between these two behaviours is forged. They have presented politicians and the media with the simplistic, direct, causal link from drugs to crime. There have been many studies that have incorporated the social context, but, as Chris Allen (2007) notes, they have been unfairly ignored. There are more recent qualitative and ethnographic studies which have contributed hugely to our understanding of how poverty, space, race and gender intertwine with drugs, crime and ill-health.

The best known is Phillipe Bourgois' (1996) New York ethnography, in which he showed how the crimes he observed were not a simple result of the burgeoning crack market, but a response that some of his neighbours created to the financial, economic, social and racist exclusion that they faced every day on the streets of East Harlem. He describes their actions – which they cobbled together from the cultural resources of patriarchal masculinity and the material resources of guns, money and cocaine – as a form of 'auto-destruction' (Bourgois 1997). In temporarily overcoming social oblivion with their dreams of money and notoriety, they created violent nightmares for themselves and the people around them.

Bourgois describes a specific, local conjuncture of race, class, politics and crack cocaine. But the subterranean link between drugs and crime has been found in very different settings. You cannot get much further from East Harlem, socially if not geographically, than the Swedish provincial city of Norrköping described by Phillip Lalander (2003). Here is a world characterized by relative equality, supportive welfare provision, ethnic homogeneity, peaceful policing, low imprisonment rates and a different drug of choice. But the heroin users that Lalander spoke to also described crime as something they pursued, rather than something they were driven to by pharmacology, economic compulsion or any inherently violent aspect of the drug market. They went shoplifting because they enjoyed it. They rose in drug dealing networks because they already had reputations as competent criminals. And they were chasing drugs, thievery and illegal career progression in lives that were marked, even in the epitomic social democratic welfare system of Sweden (Esping-Anderson 1990), by exclusion from mainstream education and employment. Of course, there were massive differences in life chances in East Harlem and Norrköping. Bourgois' Puerto Rican neighbours were exposed to much deeper levels of income and racial inequality. They experienced frequent police brutality and a form of residential apartheid that was rigidly enforced both by the police (who regularly harassed Bourgois for daring to cross the colour line which segregates New York neighbourhoods) and by the anxieties of his middle-class peers (who refused to follow him across it). But in both environments, the wilder, subterranean underside of late modern capitalism offered a way for young people to seek pleasure, identity and distinction in lives of drugs and crime.

Gender and dependence

The men studied by both Bourgois and Lalander were also full participants in the exclusion and denigration of women. Lalander's male interviewees saw women as weaker and less able to stand the rigours of the heroin-using subculture. Women who used heroin were seen as dirty and undesirable. In East Harlem, men disempowered by the retreat of employment or humiliated at work by female supervisors frequently went beyond the mere expression of sexist attitudes to domestic violence and even rape.

Bourgois and Lalander look at women largely through the lens of their male subjects' views. When women themselves have been the subjects of sociological explorations of problematic drug use, it has been shown that they are neither unwitting victims of circumstance, nor the sole authors of their own destinies (Boyd 1999; Maher 1997; Rosenbaum 1981; Taylor 1993). Both Marsha Rosenbaum and Avril Taylor have argued that women's dependent drug use can be a rational response to the challenges that they face. Their perspective on drug use as career suggests that women are initially attracted to drug use through curiosity at the excitement and danger involved. They create social contacts and a daily routine out of their participation in drug use. But this lifestyle often becomes dangerous, debilitating and unpleasant. Taylor notes that in addition to this public career of female dependent drug users, which is similar to that of men, there is also a private career. Their private sphere is still structured by patriarchal expectations of what it is to be a woman.

In Taylor's (1993) ethnographic study of female, working class, Glaswegian heroin users, she found that these women did not tend to talk of their current drug use as exciting and hedonistic. They did not use drugs to rise above their social constraints to a higher plane of consumption. Instead, they described drug use and the crimes they committed in paying for it as a normal and repetitive part of their daily routine. They used a variety of substances to help them get through days that were otherwise marked by drudgery, depression and domestic violence. The link between chronic drug use and domestic violence has been found in a variety of settings (James *et al.* 2004; Robertson 2007). Men in deindustrialized areas have been deprived of the traditional masculine roles of professional competence and family breadwinning. They may instead perform their masculinity through spectacular consumption and sexism. But the traditional female role, of caring for men and children, still remains. Measham and Shiner (2009) have used the tendency for women to take on adult roles earlier in their lives than men to explain why rates of drug use, which are similar between adolescent males and females, tend to diverge from early adulthood onwards. Motherhood provides an alternative career that 'is always available to women' (Taylor 1993: 155). If women choose this career, they have far less opportunity to develop a lifestyle committed to drugs and crime. It takes time and money to develop a drug habit. These resources are more rarely available to working class mothers. Some women act as 'gangsta bitches' (Maher 1997), or do 'bad girl femininity' (Messerschmidt 1997) in the drug market, but they are still usually excluded from underground money and power. They seek forms of respect and respectability by using the limited resources and connections that are available to them (Laidler & Hunt 2001). Their performances elicit hostile responses from both male and female peers, as well as the police, and may be carried out with some ambivalence by women who know that they have gone well beyond the pale of conventional femininity.

Such patriarchal expectations help to explain why fewer women than men get into drugs and crime.[25] Taylor suggests that when women do go down this path, it is often because the conventional female role for them would mean dependence on men who are violent, spendthrift and poorly housed. The women she got to know were constantly reminded, often by their heroin-using male partners, of their failure to live up to the idealized role of the happy, drug-free mother. They ended up blaming themselves and then using heroin to deaden the pain in a downward spiral of guilt.[26] Some women, then, use drugs and crime to create an escape from situations that they find intolerable. They are often seen as 'doubly polluted' (Ettore 1992: 78), for contaminating their maternal bodies with drugs, and their feminine identity with criminality. Social censure and legal sanctions of female drug-using offenders for betraying their gender can be deepened or mitigated by the effects of racism. In Susan Boyd's (1999) study of drug-using mothers in Vancouver, white women who were able to perform the role of middle class respectability were aware that they were treated far less harshly by police and judges than black or Native American women who were caught for similar crimes.

Drugs and crime as subterranean structuration

Subterranean structuration does not explain every incidence of the drug-crime link. It is no doubt true that some users commit crimes under the influence of illicit substances, that others steal goods to pay for their drug habit and that some murders are committed in order to secure lucrative positions in the drug market. I am, however, claiming, against Goldstein and many of the people who have used his tripartite framework, that these three motivations do not cover every instance of crime that is committed by or against a drug user. They cannot explain the social distribution of drug-related harms. The concept of subterranean structuration is offered here as an explanatory tool that can include these and other motivations, while also helping us to understand why their dramatically damaging consequences are so concentrated amongst the people who have suffered most from deindustrialization and the advance of socio-economic inequality. Currie (1993) pointed towards a social explanation of drug use with his four models of coping, status, structure and saturation. The concept of subterranean structuration enables us to integrate these models with insights from subcultural and cultural criminologists, as well as concepts borrowed from Bourdieu and Giddens, and to apply them more specifically to the most harmful uses of illicit drugs. They help us to avoid two theoretical traps. The first is the belief that either inequality or drug use cause crime deterministically (Katz 1988). The second is that crime is merely a product of free, individual, utility-maximizing choice (Young 2003b). The research reviewed in this chapter shows that people make choices within the constraints that face them. These choices may not be rational in the long run. For some people whose long run looks like it offers very little, they make sense at the time.

The tendency towards the coexistence of drugs and crime is subterranean in that it often occurs in places and people that are considered by the rest of society to be underground. More importantly, it expresses the subterranean values that run under the skin of modern capitalism like blood vessels, bringing the oxygen of excitement and a thirst for consumption to economies that would otherwise collapse in a surfeit of satisfied needs. Without the constant desire for the next big thing, capitalism as we know it could not continue. It survives through the ever-accelerating drive to buy, use and buy again. We are all constantly exposed to this imperative, but many do not have the means to take part in it legally. They did not create this socio-economic structure, but must adapt it to their own needs. Subterranean structuration means that people make use of these values that are hidden just under the surface of late modern capitalism to fashion a life which meets some of their needs for pleasure, status and meaning. Sometimes, the actions which satisfy these needs will involve harmful crimes. But they are not simply caused by the drugs.

This perspective draws on a deep well of criminological work which is too often ignored. Very little has been written in this chapter that would surprise a seasoned sociologist of the drug scene in any Western country.[27] But this knowledge, which has been repeatedly produced, has been consistently ignored. Instead, policy makers, students and the public have been directed towards mono-causal, uni-directional explanations of the drug-crime link. The next three chapters will explore some reasons for this misdirection and the consequences that flow from it. Drugs, and even drug dependence, do not always cause crime. The dedicated pursuit of intoxication can be seen as a flight from life, but it can also be seen as a fight to live a life which is not rigidly defined by the tight constraints of social inequality and immobility. This reaction in turn calls up a repressive complex. The current policy response to drug users overestimates the role of drugs in causing crime. It then uses this exaggeration in attempting to squash such disobedient signs of subterranean life.

Chapter 4

Telling policy stories

Governmental use of evidence and policy on drugs and crime

Previous chapters have explored the wealth of evidence which shows that inequality is associated with a wide range of criminal and health harms. But inequality is often ignored in policy interventions on drugs, crime and health. So this book joins a rising chorus of voices that have complained about governments ignoring the available evidence when they come up with policy solutions (e.g. Barton 2003; Berridge & Thom 1996; Gendreau *et al.* 2002; Naughton 2005; Shepherd 2003, 2007; Stevens 2007b; The Economist 2009; Tonry 2004; Young 2003a).[28] These and other authors have suggested how we might explain this avoidance of the evidence. This chapter attempts to contribute to the development of coherent theory in this area by combining previous theoretical contributions with ethnographic data from a study of the practice of policy making in the UK government. It examines the process of policy making on drugs and crime using data from a six month period of participant observation in the UK civil service. The next chapter will further develop theory through analysis of the policy discourses that have resulted from this process of policy making over a longer period of time.

The policies of the New Labour government, from their origins in the work done while the party was in opposition in the mid-1990s, have made a lot of rhetorical effort to align themselves with certain forms of evidence (e.g. Straw 1996; Straw & Michael 1996). The victorious manifesto for the 1997 election repudiated 'outdated ideology' on its first page, promising to replace it with a concern for 'what works' (Labour Party 1997). There was an initial flush of enthusiasm for 'evidence-based policy', with the establishment of a UK Research Centre for Evidence Based Policy at Queen Mary College in London, and of a related journal, *Evidence and Policy*. However, disillusion soon set in, summed up in the phrase, 'policy-based evidence' (Glees 2005; Stimson 2001; The Economist 2009). This accusatory term suggests that, far from using evidence to inform policy, policy makers seek out evidence to justify the policies that they have already decided upon.

So was evidence based policy making a radical departure in governmental decision making, as Tony Blair would have had us believe? Or was it a cynical attempt to pull the wool over the eyes of a gullible public? This chapter will attempt to provide a more nuanced, critical analysis of how policy makers use evidence on drugs, crime and inequality.

An empirical, ethnographic study of policy making on drugs and crime

The development and testing of theory requires the collection of data which can be compared against theoretical propositions. In the field of policy analysis, this has often been gathered through interviewing policy makers, or interrogating policy documents. While valuable, these approaches are limited in the extent to which they can provide a detailed picture of the actual process of making policy. Tombs has argued, for example, that there is still a 'perplexing silence . . . about the social world of the policy-making process' (Tombs 2003:5).The most powerful method discovered so far by sociologists to gather data from the inside of a social process is to carry out ethnographic, participant observation. Participant observation of the policy making process is rare.[29]

In the summer of 2009, I worked as a policy adviser for six months on a placement, funded by the Economic and Social Research Council, in a policy making section of the UK civil service. The team I worked in had responsibility for advising the highest levels of government about policy on illicit drugs, crime, offender management, anti-social behaviour and youth justice. During these months, I carried out desk research, responded to requests for information, developed policy proposals, represented the section at inter-departmental meetings and external events and generally shared the working life of the team. While carrying out this work, I observed the work of my colleagues and their interactions with other civil servants and with special advisers to ministers. I made fieldnotes as soon as I could after these observations took place. I also interviewed five of the civil servants with whom I had worked at the end of the process. The aim of these interviews was to ask for their reflections on the use of evidence in policy making, which I could then compare with the observations that I had recorded.

Ethnography always involves sensitive questions of ethics and method. I decided to do semi-covert observation. When I started the work, I did not know whether I would learn anything about policy making that was useful to communicate to the outside world. As it became clear to me that I would want to write about the experience, I gradually revealed to members of the team that this was the case, and asked for permission to write up this study from the senior civil servant who was acting as my line manager. I decided not to ask for the informed consent of the other people I observed, for three reasons. One was that it would have been impractical to ask every person I met during my work, whether in fairly large meetings, or in brief chats in corridors, to stop what they were doing while I explained the research, the procedures for protecting their anonymity and so on. The second was that to do so would have created reactivity. I wanted to observe and participate in the work of policy making with the least possible disturbance to the usual process. I feared that announcing that I was doing research would add to the distortion of everyday practice, which was probably already perturbed by my presence as an unusual interloper. Finally, I reasoned that the people I was observing could hardly be described as vulnerable. They are powerful people, with high levels of financial and cultural capital, engaged in work that, while hidden from public view, was carried out on behalf of the public and paid for by the taxpayer. It was possible that revelation of their activities would expose them to difficulties. But I was not looking for embarrassing scoops. I have attempted to shield their identities by not using names or other identifying characteristics, beyond the general subjects they were working on and the type and level of career that they had. This approach was approved by my university's internal ethics committee.

Methodologically, ethnography can provide a picture of only a limited range of reality. I cannot claim that the data I obtained is representative of the entire body of British civil servants, let alone of other actors (inside and outside government) who play a part in making policy. But I hope that it reveals at least some of the mechanisms that characterize this process. Doing participant observation does not provide access to an entirely unmediated world of 'real' experience. While working alongside civil servants, I was not completely one of them. I share the predominantly white, male, middle-class background of the section and team I was working in. But I felt considerably older than many of my colleagues. Fast-tracked civil servants, it became apparent, are expected to be taking on higher responsibilities than my relatively lowly level of policy advice by the time they hit their forties. I also had the curious status of an academic specialist in some of the areas on which I was working. This was unusual, as was occasionally mentioned by my civil service colleagues. During one field visit, a colleague joked to the person we were meeting, 'Alex is our resident academic – he's read things'.

By participating in the use of evidence for policy purposes, and in discussing and observing this process with people who do it every day, I was able to gather data that we can use to develop and test theory in this area. Theoretically, this is hardly uncharted territory. It would have been wasteful to ignore all the previous attempts to explain the evidence-policy link by limiting myself to the development of theory from the data alone (Glaser & Strauss 1967). So I decided to follow Layder's (1998) approach of 'adaptive coding' to analyze this data. This involved generating a list of provisional codes from my previous work in this area (Stevens 2007b) and from the existing literature. This included the sophisticated pluralist approaches of Weiss (1977, 1999), Dunn (1993), Gans (1971), Sabatier and Jenkins-Smith (1993), Nutley *et al.* (2002) and John (1998); the 'post-foundationalist' approaches of Hajer (1993, 1995) and Valentine (2009); and contributions from critical theory, including the work of Therborn (1980), Thompson (1990), Bourdieu (2000) and Habermas (1984, 2002).

As I coded the fieldnotes and interview transcripts, using QSR Nvivo software, I highlighted observations and quotes that related to these provisional codes, as well as generated new codes as other concepts emerged from the data. With initial coding complete, I then went through the codes and their content to reconsider, reorganize and reformulate the analysis to which the coding contributed. This process resulted in the identification of nine key themes, which are discussed below.

Commitment to the use of evidence

My observations and discussions with civil servants suggested that they are not very different from academics, at least to the extent that they have to display competence in the use of scientific reason in order to win reputations which lead to personal and professional status and reward (Bourdieu 2000). The civil servants I worked with were highly committed to the use of evidence. One of them told me, 'it's the job of officials to tell truth to power'. Evidence was ever-present in the development, discussion and presentation of the policies whose construction I observed. So the first casualty of my fieldwork analysis was the idea that evidence is absent from policy making; that drug policy, for example, is 'evidence-free' (The Economist 2009). As for the policy makers that Weiss (1977) interviewed, civil servants thought it proper to use evidence. One of my interviewees told me, 'evidence is a prerequisite for policy'. Another said, 'evidence should be the basis for options we put to ministers . . . evidence-based policy is part of the way that we work'. So we need to examine how this part of the work operates. Weiss' interviewees and mine were also able to report instances where evidence had been used to justify existing policy rather than to develop wholly rational interventions. So how do we explain this gap between the normative commitment to the use of evidence and these policy outcomes?

The oversaturation of evidence in policy

The UK government, through its managerialist attempts to control and incentivize the performance of public sector actors, operates a massive exercise in the collection and storage of data. It employs large numbers of professional analysts, whose job it is to sift this information to answer questions that are asked by ministers and by their own policy making colleagues. The results of these analyzes are regularly reviewed, not only by politicians in Parliament and its various committees, but by the internal hierarchies of the civil service. Still, vast areas of government databases remain untouched by the human brain. Cuts imposed after the Gershon review of public sector efficiency (Gershon 2004) led to a reduction in the internal analytical resources available to contribute to policy on drugs and crime. The remaining analysts simply do not have the time to make full use of the data collected by discontinued studies, such as the Arrestee Survey or the Offending Crime and Justice Survey, let alone ongoing data collection exercises, including the British Crime Survey, the National Drug Treatment Monitoring System (and its outcrop, the Treatment Outcomes Profile), the Offender Index, the NOMIS database of prisoners, the remaining databases of probation offenders, OASYS, ASSET and the thousands of forms filled out on offenders going through the drug interventions and prolific and priority offender programmes.

The many reports that do result from analysis of these datasets have to jostle for attention with a host of other evidence sources. In coding my fieldnotes, I counted 15 types of evidence source that were entered into policy debates. In addition to internally collected government data and externally produced academic analysis, the list included opinion polls, reports by think-tanks (e.g. ippr, Policy Exchange, Centre for Social Justice, etc.) and from management consultancies, previous policy papers produced by various parts of the civil service, independent inquiries, reports of the inspectorates of police and prisons, internal and externally commissioned evaluations of policy initiatives and various kinds of reports from abroad (e.g. reports of the US Center for Court Innovation), press reports, television programmes (examples from HBO's *The Wire* were mentioned several times), personal experience and opinion. Information from parliamentary debates and committees was conspicuously absent from this list. Evidence was often sought through Google searches.[30]

There is a massive amount of information that is available for use in policy discussions. This does not mean that policy problems can be resolved simply by referring to the evidence. The available evidence was often weak and contradictory. Rigorous research studies (and especially controlled evaluations of interventions) are expensive, lengthy and rare in the fields of illicit drugs and criminal justice (Shepherd 2003). It sometimes took hours of searching before an item of information that was eventually useful was found. But the rapidly diminishing rate of return to the investment in time searching through Google provides an incentive not to search rigorously.

In my work, I also realized that very little academic research was directly relevant to the questions I was asked to answer. A colleague told me, when I asked him how he looks for evidence when working on a new policy, about:

> a depressingly similar pattern where you look for the best – usually quantitative – data you can find, and then, as you work through the policy problem you establish that there is not the best evidence that you want and you work your way down until, at the end, you're left with the odd case study, something which was kind of half evaluated, some anecdotal information and then what you can garner through a few field visits.

Thousands of articles and books have been written on the policy areas on which he works. The ignoring of these academic outputs can be partly explained by the 'unsuitabilities' of social science research for use in evidence that Gans (1971) highlighted. The questions that policy makers tend to ask include what should be done in practice; how will it work; what will the effects be; how much will it cost; will there be any adverse consequences; and on whom will they fall? Very little of the evidence that is available to policy makers – including only a very small minority of academic papers – provides conclusive answers to such questions. In using evidence, policy makers therefore have to pick and choose from the available evidence. Evidence becomes a solute in the oversaturated solution of policy problems. There is more evidence than can be absorbed, so some is taken in for use and some is not. The problem with this naturalistic metaphor is that it cannot illuminate the role of human agency. From my observations, the key to understanding this process is to pay attention to the way people use evidence in forming human relationships, and so to the process of telling policy stories.

Intra-government relations

The job of policy making civil servants is to develop proposals that are accepted as government policy. In order to do this job, they have to persuade other people, within and outside government, that their proposals are worth acting on. Other writers have concentrated on the relations between government and external actors (Hajer 1993; Sabatier & Jenkins-Smith 1993). During my fieldwork, the most important influences on policy acceptance that I observed were the relations between people within government. The state is not the neutral arbiter between opposing policy proposals that is presented in Dunn's (1993) 'jurisprudential' model of policy arguments. It is the source of many of these ideas. The daily life of policy makers is spent in discussion and argument with other actors within the state.

Government policies on drugs, crime and health tend to cut across the responsibilities of several government departments (e.g. Home Office, Ministry of Justice, Department of Health, HM Treasury, Department for Communities and Local Government). The Prime Minister is also obviously interested. So to achieve acceptance, policy proposals have to be agreed by a wide range of senior civil servants, special advisers and, eventually, ministers. I observed determined efforts to ensure that these agreements would favour the proposals that my team was working on. The focus of these efforts was often on the 'narrative' of a particular proposal. For example, discussions at several meetings between colleagues and senior advisers focused on the drug strategy (Home Office 2008b). It was felt that the government was vulnerable to the charge that it had wasted money on expanding drug treatment services. So pressure was brought to bear on the National Treatment Agency to 'improve the narrative' on the effect of drug treatment in reducing wider social harms (e.g. crime), which it duly attempted to do (NTA 2009b). Not all of these discussions were about narrative. At one of these meetings I observed a senior adviser requesting that the NTA ensure that services were in place in case drug problems increased in the areas worst affected by the recession. On this occasion he said, 'we don't have to talk about it, we just have to do it'. But the issue of narrative was a constant theme in the creation of new policies, echoing Maarten Hajer's (1995) insistence on the importance of 'story-telling' in influencing which policy proposals will be taken up.

In working up policy documents, colleagues would examine – often in very great detail – the internal coherence of drafts and the way in which they led the reader to the conclusion that the suggested policy was the only alternative that made sense. One example that I worked on was a document which presented a new crime strategy. In order to demonstrate that urgent action was necessary, I was asked to draft a short section that would lay out the scale of the problem (in money terms) and the recent trends in its development. I found it difficult to be precise, given the very wide uncertainties that are acknowledged in the academic literature on the topic, but I produced a summary of the available evidence. This became the focus for weeks of refinement, inter-departmental argument and iterative revision. In a way that I experienced as alienating in the Marxist sense, I immediately lost control of the product of my labour. The document was passed between many colleagues in my team and others which had an interest in the policy area for their comments and revisions. The caveats that I had inserted on the uncertainties in the literature were quickly removed. Whenever the document came back to me, with more questions in the accompanying email, I would try and reinsert some of them.

When the document that resulted from this repetitive process was sent to the analytical section of another department, a fierce email exchange broke out. The other department's analyst was very concerned at some of the estimates that we had used, as they might conflict with what his unit had published in the field. At this point, my colleague Phillip sent him a placatory email, assuring him the figures – which he had denuded of accompanying caveats – were reliable, as they had been produced by an academic criminologist (i.e. me). This attempt to justify the figures on the basis of academic authority rather than their evidential status failed when I insisted that I would not have included the figures without caveats in any academic publication. Phillip told me, 'we have to strike a balance. We don't want to overclaim, but we need to sell the policy'. In the end, we used a headline estimate which had no supporting evidence, but had previously been published in a government report. Some of the caveats were eventually included, but placed in an annex at the back of the published document.

This episode exemplifies how evidence is used as a tool for persuasion (to 'sell the policy') within government, as well as in relations between government, the public and other agencies. An even more striking example was reported to me of a high level meeting where an extremely senior civil servant had used the promising results of an evaluation of a particular scheme. The evaluation itself was not particularly rigorous. It had no control group, but did show – in common with many other interventions on drugs and crime – that people who are intervened with at the peak of their problems tend to get better after this intervention. This lack of methodological rigour did not prevent the use of the evaluation, alongside an apparently impressive display of charismatic and hierarchical authority by the top civil servant who led the meeting, in persuading a number of departments to make savings from their existing budgets in order to expand the favoured scheme.

From contested norms to monetary facts

Both these examples also point to the use of certain types of evidence to resolve questions of normative value that would otherwise be problematic. I questioned the need to come up with a monetary estimate of the problem I was working on with Phillip. I thought that there was plenty of other evidence of the harms associated with it and of the need to take action on it, and that any certain number would be fictional. But I was told that the lack of a number would make it harder to lay out a persuasive case for action. This McKinseyite utilitarian accountancy was taken to an extreme in a meeting which discussed proposals for making savings (the contemporary euphemism for cuts) in public services. When the question of what would be 'fair' was raised, a colleague who worked in a team of economists declared 'fairness can't be measured. It's irrelevant'.

If all policy problems and their solutions could be simply translated into a cost or benefit in pounds sterling, then this would greatly simplify the process of making policy. Of course, this hope is illusory and my colleague's comment on fairness was completely wrong. Normative decisions on values – including fairness, justice, compassion, freedom and all the other ethical standards which we judge our actions against – are at the heart of government decision making. Numerical measures attempt to resolve a contested question of normative value by turning it into a simple question of financial value, a transaction for which there is no universally agreed rate of exchange.

There was one counter-example given by one of my interviewees, who told me that a senior adviser had explicitly and repeatedly argued for a policy proposal on the basis of a normative commitment to a more humane approach to young offenders. However, the fact that the interviewee described this as unusual and that the proposal was not adopted suggest that discussions of normative value are often marginal to policy discussions.

The control of uncertainty

Both the excision of methodological caveats and the avoidance of normative questions point to the importance of the control of uncertainty. Uncertainty was seen by many of my colleagues as the enemy of policy making. If we are unsure of what the real problem is, and we cannot predict the effects of our actions, then we would not, they suggested, get anything done. My discussion of caveats in the work with Phillip was characterized by our team leader Mike as 'verging on the philosophical'. He evidently saw them as an obstacle to the practical issue of what action to take, right here, right now. Uncertainty, which is – of course – a fundamental feature of knowledge (Bhaskar 1978), threatens to disrupt the narrative of a policy. It was rarely entertained in the policy documents which I saw being 'put up' to special advisers and ministers. Indeed, the very form of these documents denied uncertainty. Many policy documents transmitted between policy making civil servants were in the form of PowerPoint 'packs', stuffed with bullet points, diagrams, short text boxes and simple graphs. None of these permitted lengthy discussion of the uncertain or imprecise nature of the knowledge they presented. 'A good chart', I was told, 'is worth ten pages in words'.

The use of graphs was particularly interesting. In the only induction session that I had, they were referred to as 'killer charts'. We were taught to construct these instruments of persuasion by choosing data carefully and by restricting the number of cases and categories that were shown. The policy implications of the data should be immediately apparent from the graph alone. This last recommendation obviously ignores the common academic criticism that statistics, even where they represent an underlying reality, are socially and selectively constructed (Prior 2003). They cannot (or should not) simply 'speak for themselves'. A graph is a visual representation of the results of that construction, which renders invisible the process of construction. In my subsequent work, many hours would be spent searching for data that could be used to make such graphs, and many discussions were had of how to construct them. I knew I had succeeded in making a 'killer chart' the day that a senior civil servant responded unprompted to a graph that I presented. He used it to argue for more urgent action than his colleagues were currently pursuing. The hours that I spent manipulating that data had not been in vain.

The control of uncertainty strengthens the narrative of a policy document. But it also plays a wider role in structuring the context in which civil servants operate. Douglas (1987) argued that collective styles of thinking come to shape individual beliefs in order 'to satisfy the individual demand for order and coherence' (Ibid: 19), as well as through the transactional maximization of individual utility. The civil service 'thought world' (Ibid) shuns uncertainty. There are understandable, utility maximizing reasons for this.

Bureaucratic competence and the civil service career

Utility has at least two meanings. One general sense is usefulness, as in something that is of use in carrying out a task. Another, more narrowly economic sense is the use that something has for the pursuit of personal goals. For civil servants, the maximization of both types of utility can coincide. If they make themselves useful to the task of creating and carrying out policy, then they are more likely to achieve their own goals of professional advancement. This became clear in discussing the civil service career with my colleagues, and from observing civil servants performing their tasks.

In pubs and bars around Whitehall after working hours, civil servants gather to relax, drink, tell jokes and speculate on the progress of each other's careers. As an uninitiated outsider, colleagues would take the trouble to explain to me the rules that were taken for granted when they discussed who was going for what job. These can be crudely summarized as: do not specialize; do be useful; and do find superior supporters. At the end of the project on which I worked with Phillip, we went out for a celebratory drink. Another colleague explained to me that the last two projects he had worked on had been on the same topic, so it was time to move on. On a web chat page hosted by a government department, I saw a discussion of how long was too long to spend in a job. 'Never less than two years, never more than three' was a typical contribution. Another night, a different colleague (Peter) complained to me that the years he had spent working for a particular public service were useless to him in advancing his career in the government department that manages that public service. 'Specialist experience' he said 'is seen as a positive disadvantage'. I did not stay long enough, or delve deep enough in the civil service to understand why it is seen to be disadvantageous to specialize in any particular subject.[31] The important implication for our analysis is that civil servants feel discouraged from developing specialist knowledge. They are therefore less likely to have the time to develop a thorough knowledge of the evidence base in any particular area, and so are less likely to be able to develop or resist policy proposals on the basis of this evidence. They are incentivized to become what Gendreau *et al.* (2002) pejoratively describe as 'fart catchers': generalists who do not have enough expertise to resist whatever the minister decides will be the latest version of common sense.

Although many civil servants resist this incentivization and so develop a deeper knowledge of their particular area, the specialist knowledge that they are incentivized to develop is not of the outside world. It is of the complex inner workings of Whitehall and its inhabitants. In order to get ahead, civil servants need to get recognized for 'adding value' to the policy process. They do this by creating connections and solving policy problems. They need to combine familiarity with the detail of current policy with dynamism, certainty and a degree of personal charisma. Of course, as in other professions, there are many civil servants who lack these qualities. It is possible to advance through civil service ranks at a slower pace. But rapid advancement, of the type aspired to by my young colleagues, was dependent on building a reputation for usefulness. Older civil servants (i.e. about 40 and above) tended to be seen as representing obstacles to change if they did not jump to the latest policy tune. At one meeting, a civil servant of a certain age made an interesting point about the lack of consensus over the fundamental aims of a particular policy. In the pub after the meeting, he was derided by a colleague for representing an older type of civil servant who gets lost in complexity. In contrast, a young civil servant working with senior advisers was generally admired for her impressive abilities to recall the details of the latest policy proposals and to get them agreed. She was soon promoted to a senior position.

Another female civil servant[32] spoke of her frustration that, despite the formal commitment of the civil service to equality of opportunity, promotion often still depended on personal connections with superiors in the hierarchy. She said, 'it's supposed to be open and equal but it's not. People go for people they know. If you've worked with someone senior, you try and stay in touch with them; they can help you'. This need to develop and maintain connections with more senior people requires that superiors come to think of potential protégés as both useful and reliable. The way to build trust is to provide evidence of trustworthiness. At a team meeting, Mike advised us, 'you can't force them [senior people] to CC you in – it's a question of building a relationship, sending up a couple of notes that they like'. This kind of relationship is not developed by using evidence to ask difficult questions. Another civil servant told me about an incident early in his career. He had been working on a policy that had been based on North American evidence and became a high profile part of the government's 'agenda'. But evidence that it was not working was emerging. He reported that his boss had:

> kind of jokingly said, 'Well you're young. Why don't you suggest we look again at [policy area] and see how far that takes you in your career?' So there are certain areas where officials will self-censor and they won't suggest to ministers to change policy on certain areas even though the evidence suggests it.

The third face of bureaucratic reason

As was noted, policy making civil servants have to make a selection from the huge amount of information that they have at their disposal. As has also been noted, they tend to see uncertainty as an obstacle to the development and agreement of policy proposals. Furthermore, there is a tendency to translate issues of normative value into questions of financial value. And all this must, if civil servants are to contribute to the policy process and to their own career development, be done in a way that produces proposals that are useful to their superiors and can be accepted into government policy. These proposals must therefore fit with the existing narrative of government policy. It must be used to tell a story that is simultaneously about the policy area and about the storyteller.

The discursive categories and solutions that the story draws on will often have been set already by the general thrust of government policy, within the thought world that structures the approach that policy makers take. One such general storyline was the belief in the power of the purchaser/provider split to increase value for money in public services. My fieldwork took place six years after the first Carter review (Carter 2003) had recommended that the provision of services to offenders be split from prison and probation service managers though the creation of a National Offender Management Service (NOMS). This recommendation had been swiftly taken up, but years of delay, confusion and waste have followed (see, for example, National Audit Office 2009).[33] I encountered several civil servants who had bad things to say about NOMS, but nobody who questioned the underlying wisdom of the purchaser/provider split that it is supposed to achieve. So I looked for the evidence that had been used to justify the initial and continued pursuit of this policy. And I could find very little. A minister had replied to a parliamentary question that the rationale was to be found in the original Carter review (Goggins 2005). When I read the section he referred to, I could find only a vague reference to the supposed benefits of quasi-markets, with no evidence provided to demonstrate where they had or could be achieved. When I raised this problem, and some of the academic analysis which questions the worth of quasi-markets in the public sector with Mike, he responded that 'it just feels intuitively right that introducing competition would focus more on cost and quality'.[34]

This faith in the application of private sector logic to public sector problems may seem to be what Sabatier and Jenkins-Smith (1993) would call a 'policy core belief'. It cropped up in many other meetings, where civil servants would present policy dilemmas as a failure in the structure of individual incentives. They would ask how to encourage the private sector to provide solutions to public sector problems. However, in line with Hajer's (1995) critique of Sabatier and Jenkins-Smith, these ideas did not arise solely from the operation of individual belief in bringing like-minded people together in 'advocacy coalitions'. Rather, the use of these expressions suggested to me the transfer and performance of discursive tropes among people who learn how to show both that they belong in this thought world and are worthy of promotion within it.

There is an ideological process of 'subjection-qualification' at work here (Therborn 1980: 17). The currently dominant modes of thought constrain the limits of what civil servants think is possible. By reproducing these limits they qualify themselves to take up and perform their role. In telling policy stories, they signal that they hold appropriate, acceptable beliefs. Through the things that they are told, and the careers they see acted out, civil servants learn that the stories they tell should not include uncertainty, complexity or opposition to the narrative that already dominates a policy field. For example, after I gave my views on the failures of current drug policies in a team meeting (views which none of them had disagreed with), Phillip said 'I'd love to see you say that to a minister. You'd blow their mind!' This jocular remark and the laughter which ensued point to an implicit understanding which goes against my interviewee's comment on telling truth to power. This joke implies that to tell people in power that their current narrative is fundamentally mistaken is (a) never done and (b) impossible to imagine doing, except in the absurd scenario of the joke.[35] A different colleague said on another occasion, 'I think if you always use the evidence [when it conflicts with current policy] then you're always going to be the awkward person that's saying, "The Emperor has no clothes" '. This would not be the way to be recognized for being useful, or to build connections with superiors who can support career progression.

So for policy making civil servants, we can add a third face of the use of reason to the two that Bourdieu (2000: 109) perceived amongst academics. The first face is the use of reason and empirical data to create knowledge. The second is the use of this performance of rational aptitude in order to show that one is worthy of respect and status. Civil servants do both these things, but there is also a third face of bureaucratic reason. It is the performance of only certain sections of the range of rationally justifiable positions in order to win the type of respect and personal connections that are necessary to achieve higher status.[36] Acceptable positions to perform are those which reinforce rather than challenge the fundamental assumptions and tropes of current policy narratives.

The silent silencing of inequality

The analysis so far suggests that there is a surfeit of – mostly inconclusive – evidence and a distaste for uncertainty, complexity and contradiction within policy making circles. It suggests that civil servants learn to avoid such problematic features when they construct policy stories. This does not mean that they deliberately avoid, neglect or misuse evidence. But they are influenced in their use of evidence by the constraints of a particular thought world, whose limits they reproduce in their turn. Civil servants in the corridors of power, just like drug users in deprived areas, take part in the 'structuration' (Giddens 1979) of their social world.

So let us test this emerging theory against a particular instance of the use of evidence on inequality in policy – or rather its non-use. As Lukes (1974) noted, power also operates by excluding certain ideas and possibilities from those that are considered in taking political action. Professor Richard Wilkinson was invited to give a presentation at a seminar held in the very grand rooms of the Admiralty in September 2009. Surrounded by portraits of long-dead naval grandees and an audience of senior policy makers from the Home Office, Cabinet Office, Prime Minister's office, the Department of Health and others, he summarized the findings of *The Spirit Level* (Wilkinson & Pickett 2008). This book lends itself well to PowerPoint presentation. It is, for instance, brim full of 'killer charts'. These scatterplots have two axes and a manageably small selection of cases of nations and US states. They all show a clearly diagonal line of best fit, demonstrating that greater levels of inequality are associated with a very wide range of social problems, including mortality, morbidity, mental illness, obesity, poor educational performance, teenage pregnancy, imprisonment, drug use and murder (see Chapters 2 and 7). Professor Wilkinson ran through his slides, explaining as he went that there are very good reasons to think that these associations are not just correlative; inequality causes these ills through various mechanisms. He competently dismissed alternative explanations that were put to him by some of his audience. The very senior civil servants who took the roles of chair and discussant of the seminar both said that they found the presentation 'compelling' and 'convincing'.

The next morning, fascinated by the reaction to this presentation, I made my only attempt to start off one of the email discussions that occasionally broke out amongst colleagues. I sent an email, attaching a paper that Wilkinson uses on inequality and social trust (Rothstein & Uslaner 2005), and asking colleagues what policy proposals would make an appropriate response to this evidence. The result was a tumbleweed-blowing silence.

Just as this electronic silence began, the civil servant who worked opposite me sat down at his desk. He asked if the previous evening's seminar had been any good. When I told him that Wilkinson had argued that inequality causes virtually all social problems, he answered 'didn't we already know that'. I replied, 'if we know it already, why aren't we doing anything about it?' The response was, again, silence. Here we see the downfall of the enlightenment model of the use of evidence in policy (Weiss 1977). This model, simply stated, suggests that evidence affects policy indirectly by influencing the climate of opinion in which policy decisions are made. The problem is that, at this level of simplicity, it assumes that all evidence has a chance of influencing policy (Stevens 2007). It misses a mechanism to explain why some evidence content is consistently ignored. In this example, we can see that evidence of the harmful effects of inequality – which is so comprehensively presented in Wilkinson's work and a host of other sources – has informed the people who play a significant role in making policy. They do not dispute that inequality is directly harmful. Indeed they claim this is something they already know. But this knowledge has consistently failed to make a significant impact on policy making in the fields of drugs and crime. These policy areas retain the influence of individualistic and stigmatizing viewpoints which blame the poor for the harms that they suffer (Cook 2006; Grover 2008; Young & Matthews 2003).

The causal effect of inequality is consistently ignored when it comes to creating policies in this area. When I tried to insert it in a meeting where my team discussed what the government could do to reduce rates of violent crime, I was told that 'the Gini coefficient is not a policy lever that we can pull'. So the search went on for programmes that could 'keep a lid' on the effects of inequality, rather than doing anything to address its causes.

Totemic toughness

While inequality has, in the phrase of Thomas Mathiesen (2004), been 'silently silenced', the search continues for policies to shout about that are tough. On my very first day of fieldwork, I took part in a meeting which discussed what else the government could do – beyond final warnings, referral orders, anti-social behaviour contracts and orders, penalty notices for disorder, juvenile curfews, parenting orders, nurse-family partnerships, family intervention projects and the various other forms of 'naughty step' to which the government has tried to send this country's unruly children and their parents (Gelsthorpe & Burney 2007) – to reduce 'incivility' by young people. 'We need', the meeting was told, 'to come up with tough, totemic policies.'

This need to make a totem of toughness was consistently referred to throughout my fieldwork. Pressure was applied from the most senior levels to create policies that would signal the government's willingness to be nasty to bad people.[37] At one meeting, the prime source of these pressures emphasized the need to keep coming up with 'totemic' policies on crime and disorder, because of the high 'political salience' of these issues.[38] When I questioned him on whether the government played a role in inflating the political salience of crime by its own campaigning on the issue (as has been suggested by Carlen [2008] amongst others), he answered that what ministers say does influence the climate of opinion in which the public (and judges) think about sentencing and the criminal justice system. But he repeated his claim that there is a real need to expand the range of government intervention to reduce justified public fears. This is not the place to engage in debate between the idealist and realist wings of criminology on the basis of public fears about crime. But I do want to draw attention to this revealing use of the phrase 'totemic'.

A totem, according to anthropologists following Lévi-Strauss (1964), is a cultural symbol that is used to provide a metaphorical representation of collective identity. Totems are central to the stories that cultures tell themselves about who they are. The transfer of this metaphor from the study of remote tribes to the everyday language of civil servants working on drugs and crime is quite remarkable. Its application to toughness is even more so. The phrase 'totemic' was often used alongside the word 'tough', and never mentioned in the context of reducing poverty or inequality. The use of this term reveals the central, symbolic thrust of government policies on crime and drugs. It tells us about the stories that civil servants have been encouraged to tell. These stories are most likely to find favour when they tell us that we are a robust and unforgiving people, which is divided between a group of law-abiding innocents who are worthy of protection and support, and a group of threatening outsiders who are worthy of little but material exclusion and symbolic expurgation. At that early meeting on incivility, one of the civil servants said, 'we know who we're talking about. It's not the public school-kids waiting at the bus stop, it's those other kids'. Totemic toughness applies only to the visible, poor and excluded social groups who have been so consistently 'othered' in contemporary crime policy (Young 2007) and who have long been the targets of drug control (Christie 1986; Helmer 1975).

The reduction of inequality is not seen as totemic in this thought style, and so is kept out of the forms of political communication that seek to express who we are. Increasing the penal control of offenders, drug users and other threatening miscreants is, on the other hand, seen as central to the reflection that the government provides of its populace.

Evidence for ideological policy stories

In telling these stories about the policy process, I have shown that there are inherent difficulties in providing and using evidence on policy issues. These include the vast amount, the indeterminacy and the lengthy timescales of academic research and other evidence. Such difficulties are often seen as a principal cause of the failure to base policy on evidence (Nutley & Davies 2000; Nutley *et al.* 2002; Valentine 2009). But the problem lies deeper than this. The data presented in this chapter suggests that governmental communication on policy issues is 'systematically distorted' (Habermas 2002).[39] It does not have to involve deliberate falsehood or explicit manipulation of the evidence in order to count as ideological, in the sense that it supports systematically asymmetrical relations of power (Thompson 1990). The exercise of power and the desire of policy makers for the maintenance and enhancement of their own status short-circuits the thorough use of the available evidence, in what I have described (following Bourdieu) as the operation of the third face of bureaucratic reason. This chapter has shown how social interactions at the interpersonal level contribute to this distortion. The next chapter will show how the sum total of these small-scale interactions leads to the silencing, not only of inequality, but of other discourses (such as the demand for liberalization of drug laws) that threaten the smooth reproduction of the social order in which these policy makers achieve and perform their positions.

These stories do not tell us all we need to know about the policy process. They cannot, for example, explain policy change, as would need to be done by a comprehensive theory of policy formation (John 1998). Six months is too short a time to analyze policy change, which typically takes place in cycles as long as a decade (Sabatier & Jenkins-Smith 1993). A longer timescale and additional methods would be necessary to add an explanation of policy change to the insights developed here. Chapter five will examine English drug policy over a longer timescale.

Faith in the ideal of evidence-based policy dies hard. An eminent scientist with long experience of advising policy makers has recently said that 'nobody rational could possibly want a government based on any other type of policy-making' (Blakemore, quoted by Doward *et al.* 2009). This ethnographic analysis of the process of making policy suggests that holders of this faith may have to wait a while to see the ascension of their preferred method of policy making. It has shown that there is little conclusive evidence available for policy makers in the vast mass of information that is available to them. A certain group of policy makers choose some of this information as evidence to tell stories. They select evidence that fits with the stories that have previously constructed their unquestioned concept of public value. This arises ideologically from the extant distribution of power which structures their capability to take part in policy decisions. They use evidence to tell stories that are likely to be accepted within a thought world that favours certainty over accuracy and action over contradiction. They attempt to transform issues of ethical value into questions of financial value. They usually display a utilitarian lack of normative engagement with ideas on the fundamental aims of public policy on crime and drugs, leaving the pursuit of bureaucratic competence and career advancement as primary goals. The stories they tell, and the evidence they use in telling them, are biased towards the rationalization and reification of the uneven balance of power that constitutes the British state. These stories therefore ultimately support the consolidation of power in the hands of the people who already hold it. Civil servants are not likely to select evidence which challenges the unequal status quo for use in telling these policy stories. This makes their policy making an intensely ideological activity, not in the sense that it uses the kind of political doctrine that Tony Blair explicitly rejected, but because it reinforces the asymmetrical relationships of power which he did so little to challenge. According to this analysis, the answer to the question of how policy makers use evidence might have been predicted by Giddens (1979). It is that they use evidence by the rules of a game of which they are at least partially aware and which leads them to reproduce the ideological legitimation of the unequal distribution of power.

Chapter 5

The ideology of exclusion

Cases in English drug policy

The previous chapter looked at the process of policy making. It suggested that the copious evidence of the link between inequality and drug-related harms is unlikely to fit the ideological use of evidence that characterizes this process. This chapter will take a look at some of the products of this process. Instead of participant observation of the daily lives of policy makers, it will use discourse analysis of the products of their labours. More specifically, it will follow the recommendations of John Thompson (1990) on the use of 'argumentative analysis'. Thompson rejects accounts of government action which reduce the state to the role of a mere instrument of a ruling class. He argues that this view ignores the way in which the state responds to the demands and interests of other social groups. He proposes instead an approach to analyze the contest for power and for control of meaning that underlies the policies that governments create. He recommends that we:

> break up the discursive corpus into sets of claims or assertions organized around certain topics or themes, and then . . . map out the relations between these claims and topics in terms of certain logical, or quasi-logical operators (implication, contradiction, presupposition, exclusion, etc.).
>
> (Ibid: 289)

The 'discursive corpus' that we examine here will be the laws and legislative initiatives that were introduced in England by the Labour government after 1997. As we have seen, these policies have often been criticized for their apparent irrationality and for failing to use the evidence that is available. The last chapter showed that policy makers do not ignore evidence. But it did suggest that they make selective use of it. This chapter will show how discursive 'logical operators' – and especially the idea of excluding certain substances and their users – have been influential in diverting drug policy from a more fully rational use of evidence.

Ideology and evidence in drug policy

The process of making policy is ideological, in that it serves to sustain existing asymmetries in power. The products of policy making are also ideological to the extent that they are symbolic forms that support and maintain such inequality. Thompson (Ibid) identifies five *modus operandi* through which ideological forms serve to sustain inequalities in power. They are:

- Legitimation (rationalizing power inequalities and presenting them as being in the interests of all)
- Dissimulation (concealing, denying or obscuring power inequalities)
- Unification (the creation of false unity)
- Fragmentation (the creation of threatening outsider groups)
- Reification (the presentation of current arrangements as ever-lasting and inevitable, and as having arisen without conscious agency).

Hypothetically, these *modus operandi* will affect the use of evidence in drug policy. Of course, as was mentioned in the last chapter, there are other, competing hypotheses on the link of evidence to policy. One is the idea of a direct, linear link from evidence to policy which is often presented in politicians' references to 'evidence-based policy'. This rarely operates, even in fields like medicine where its use is most widely promoted (Black 2001). Another is the view, described earlier as the enlightenment model (Weiss 1977), that evidence seeps into policy by a process of gradual assimilation. Research evidence may not have direct effects on policy, but it will inform the climate in which decisions are made and the knowledge that policy makers use in these decisions. As noted in the previous chapter, this model does not include issues of power in the filtering process through which evidence passes into policy and so does not predict systematic bias in the use of evidence. Yet another hypothesis – which does include issues of power – is the political/tactical model (Young *et al.* 2002). This suggests that interest groups, rather than using all the available evidence, make tactical use of that evidence which suits their political needs. Its notion of politics is pluralistic. It does not predict that policy will systematically sustain social inequality.

These hypotheses can be tested through close examination of the actual use of evidence in drug policy. This chapter will look at three examples of such uses. The first is the creation of the Drug Treatment and Testing Order (DTTO). The second is the Drugs Act 2005. The third is the debate over the classification of drugs. These examples provide three case studies of how evidence is used in drug policy. They cannot generally prove or refute hypotheses, but can provide valuable information in their testing and refinement (Yin 1994).

Evidence-based policy and the Drug Treatment and Testing Order

In 1998, the Crime and Disorder Act created the DTTO. It gave the courts powers to order offenders to enter treatment, with regular drug testing and court review. The DTTO was targeted on persistent, acquisitive offenders (e.g. shoplifters and thieves) who were assessed to be dependent on illicit drugs. These offenders had to give their consent to enter treatment in order to get a DTTO, so it can be seen as an example of quasi-compulsory treatment (Stevens, McSweeney, van Ooyen *et al.* 2005). The DTTO replaced the Section 1A(6) order of the 1991 Criminal Justice Act. This was the first English legal provision for court-ordered treatment of drug dependent (rather than mentally ill) offenders (Collison 1993), but it was little used (Barton 2003; Hearnden 2000). The DTTO was replaced in its turn in April 2005 by the Drug Rehabilitation Requirement (DRR), which shares many features of the DTTO (McSweeney *et al.* 2007). Policy innovations which link drug testing, treatment and compulsion through the criminal justice system have multiplied since 1998 (Duke 2006), and the DTTO can serve as an exemplary prototype for such measures.

In order to analyze the policy discourse around the DTTO, the evidence on drugs, crime and treatment that was available to policy makers was analyzed (Stevens, Berto, Heckmann *et al.* 2005). Then, policy documents (including policy reports, white papers, legislative bills, parliamentary debates and probation and Home Office circulars) which referred to the DTTO were retrieved and analyzed, again using the approach of 'adaptive coding' (Layder 1998), and QSR Nvivo software as a tool for analysis. Codes for items of evidence were developed from previous literature in the field and from the actual use of evidence in the documents. This coding enabled analysis of the 'quasi-logical' operation of discursive inclusion, opposition and exclusion that structured the argument for the DTTO (Thompson, 1990).

Evidence available for use

In summary, the international review of the literature on drugs, crime and treatment found that:

- There is a consistent correlation between drug use and elevated rates of offending. However, there is no consensus in the literature (despite the frequent citations of the 'tripartite' framework) that there is a simple, causal connection from drug use to offending. Rather, there are multiple connections between drug use, other influences (e.g. socio-demographics and inequality) and offending. As we saw in Chapter 3, there are references, in the literature, to the complexity of this link and to its interaction with drug prohibition and socio-economic deprivation.

- There is consensus that treatment leads to reduction in drug use and offending (Prendergast *et al.* 2002; UNODC 2002). This was also the main finding of the UK government-funded National Treatment Outcome Research Study (NTORS) (Gossop *et al.* 2003).
- However, there was much less consensus on the effectiveness of court-ordered drug treatment. The early studies of US drug courts tended to report that they were effective in reducing offending and drug use (Goldkamp 1994; Peters & Murrin 2000; Tauber 1993). However, these reports relied on selection bias to produce their findings (Nolan 2001): they tended to compare only those offenders who completed treatment to those who did not, violating established methodological guidelines and proving only that 'the successes succeed and the failures fail' (Goldkamp *et al.* 2001: 32). More recent, methodologically rigorous research – which was not available at the time of the original DTTO policy debates – does suggest that drug courts have an impact in reducing offending (GAO 2005). At the time of the DTTO's creation, however, results from international research, including studies in Germany (Egg 1993; Projektgruppe Rauschmittelfragen 1991), were less promising.

Evidence used

Compared to the research literature in this field, the political debates around the creation of the DTTO were remarkably consensual, with no political party or lobby group posing strong opposition to it. The policy debate included the following codes:

- *Evidence-based policy*. Participants in the debate often referred to the need to base policy on evidence, and even congratulated their political opponents on their use of evidence. As will be shown below, this rhetorical commitment was not followed through in practice.
- The threat of *drug-driven crime*. Repeated references were made to the high proportions of crime that were related to drugs. Estimates ranged from a fifth (Bishop of Oxford 1997) to 70 per cent (Jowell 1997). They tended to settle on around half of crime being caused by drugs. The cause that was mentioned or assumed was Goldstein's (1985) 'economic-compulsive' link: the idea that drug users are driven to seek money to feed their addiction and commit crimes in order to do so.
- *Treatment outcome*. Reference was made to studies on the effects of drug treatment (e.g. the NTORS study). But this was always in the context of how treatment can provide benefits to those who were not actually experiencing it – by reducing crime. There was rarely any reference to individual need for treatment or its effects on other aspects of people's lives (such as their health or their social integration). This positioning of treatment as being primarily an issue of protection of the public from the

costs and victimizations imposed on them by drug users fits with the wish to appear tough.

- *Toughness*. The consultation paper which introduced Labour policy on the DTTO referred to it as 'a new, much more rigorous approach to the drug related offender' (Straw 1996: 7). Not a more effective approach, but a more 'rigorous' one. This presentation of the DTTO as tough continued in parliamentary debates. When there was opposition from the Conservative party, it tended to be on the grounds that the DTTO was not tough enough.
- *Drug court*. As policy makers sought a solution to drug-driven crime, they turned their gaze westward. They found the model of the drug court, which was rapidly spreading through the USA. It was imported to the UK by Justin Russell, who can be seen as a prime policy entrepreneur of the DTTO. He was a policy officer for the Labour party who became a special adviser on drugs and crime in the Cabinet Office. In a report of his Harkness Fellowship to the USA (Russell 1994), he repeated positive findings from drug courts in Dade County, Miami and Oakland, California, while not acknowledging the selection bias that limited the validity of these findings. The drug court model informed Labour Policy and was referred to as a successful prototype in the policy discourse by both Labour and opposition politicians.
- DTTO as *the answer to drugs and crime*. The discourse around the DTTO constructed a discrete problem, 'drug driven' crime. It then constructed the DTTO as a solution to this problem from the emerging evidence that treatment was effective in cutting crime, and especially the promise of the uncritical early reports from the drug court movement. The DTTO was not presented as one of a possible range of solutions to drug-related crime, but as the single necessary answer. When challenged on drugs and crime in political debates, Labour ministers tended to mention the DTTO and nothing else. While in opposition, they had included poverty, unemployment, poor education, lack of facilities and homelessness as causes of crime that had to be addressed (Straw & Michael 1996). But these issues were completely absent from debate around the DTTO.

In analysis of the policy discourse, it became evident that there was a separate category of empty codes. These were categories and concepts that were present in the literature review on drugs, crime and treatment, but which were notably absent from the political discourse which surrounded the DTTO. These included:

- The link of inequality to drugs and crime.
- The failure of drug prohibition to end drug use.
- Criticisms of evidence-based policy.

- Connections between drugs and crime other than the economic-compulsive link.

The lack of attention to these ideas cannot have been because they were not visible to the participants in the discourse. For example, ideas on the failure of prohibition are regularly raised in drug policy debates, if only to be batted away as a signal of how tough and uncompromising politicians intend to be in pursuing the scourge of drugs. Neither can this inattention be explained on scientific grounds. There is no consensus in the community of researchers who study drug policy that, for example, the sole link between drugs and crime is economic-compulsive. So the selective filtering of ideas and evidence in this policy discourse tends to refute again the ideas of a linear or 'enlightened' link from evidence to policy. This leaves the political/tactical and the ideological models offering potential explanations. Both have purchase here. For example, the competition over which party had the toughest policy on drugs can be seen as an extension of the political manoeuvring initiated by Tony Blair's famous promise to be doubly tough on both crime and its causes.

However, these political tactics have ideological consequences. The desire to appear tough necessitates the identification of a group on whom to be tough. In this case, this group was formed of 'drug-driven' criminals. Focusing on the drug-crime link provided a means of fulfilling Blair's double promise, but in a way that prioritized one supposed cause of crime over others. And it was a cause that required no challenge to existing inequalities. It reinforced the symbolic, imaginary 'fragmentation' between abstinent law-abiders and drug-consuming predators. The filtering out of inequality of education, employment, income and housing in explaining crime played a role in 'dissimulating' the existence of such inequalities. The use of criminal justice responses to the complex problems of dependent drug users also helps to 'legitimate' these inequalities. The proposed solution to them is the projection of unequal power on to the bodies of those who suffer most from these problems. And this solution is presented, not as a partial, politicized response, but as the natural outcome of the disinterested use of evidence.

Evidence for legislation and the Drugs Act 2005

The Strategy Unit (formerly the Prime Minister's Strategy Unit, or PMSU) is a part of the Cabinet Office whose website[40] claims that it has 'a strong emphasis on analysis and evidence, allowing issues to be addressed from first principles'. In June 2003, it presented two reports to the cabinet on drug policy. They were based on the work of a team led by former BBC Director General John Birt. He had been brought in to lead on 'blue skies thinking' for Tony Blair. The reports were kept secret for two years, but were eventually dragged into the public domain. They summarized the available evidence on drug problems (PMSU 2003a) and recommended policy responses to them

(PMSU 2003b). Some of this work informed the legislation introduced in the form of the Drugs Act 2005.

This episode again offers a route through which to follow evidence as it makes its way into drug policy, and see to what is selected in, and what is selected out. The aim of Birt's first report was 'to identify the mix of policies which will substantially reduce the harms caused by drugs to users and others' (PMSU, 2003a: 1). As shown in Chapter 2, there were some serious harms that could have been selected. They included drug-related deaths, infectious diseases, crime and harms to children.

It is instructive to see which of these harms were emphasized in the PMSU report. This was produced, in typical civil service style, in the form of a PowerPoint pack (PMSU 2003a). Out of 105 slides, twelve are on crime. One covers both HIV and hepatitis. The slide on drug-related death is used to show how much more dangerous heroin is than other drugs, rather than to highlight drug-related death as a significant problem. And harm to children is mentioned under one bullet point on one slide. One slide gives a simple breakdown of the estimated annual costs of drug-related harms. It claims that the health-related costs of heroin and crack use are £5 billion per year (of which deaths account for £1 billion and costs to the NHS another billion). But this is dwarfed by the estimated cost of 'drug-motivated crime', which is stated to represent 56 per cent of all crime. The source of this estimate is given as 'team analysis' using data from the New-ADAM study. As shown in Chapter 3, there are several reasons why this study should not have been used to estimate drug-attributable proportions of crime. Some of them were included by its authors in their reports of its findings. Interestingly, this phase 1 report also devoted several pages to demonstrating how drug prohibition has failed to prevent the availability of illicit substances. It stated that government interventions in the drug trade are 'a cost of business, rather than a substantive threat to the industry's viability' (Ibid: 94).

Filtering and costing of harms

So, at this first stage of evidence selection, we see a filtering out of significant harms to drug users and their children, in favour of a focus on drug-motivated crime (as was also seen in the DTTO policy discourse). We also see, from the perspective of a unit that prides itself on looking at issues from first principles, evidence of the failure of prohibition to reduce drug use. The next stage of selection is to see what policy responses were suggested in response to this selection of evidence in the phase two report. This report stated that '[m]ost heroin and crack use results from deprivation and is often an escape from multiple difficulties in users' lives' (PMSU 2003b: 15). But the solutions it suggested did not include reducing poverty. They rather provide an extreme example of the idea that treatment and penal responses to drug use can be entirely compatible (see Mascini & Houtman 2006). Expansion of heroin prescription should, it argues, be accompanied by the criminalization of unprescribed heroin use (it is possession, not use that is currently a crime). This proposal is presented as a solution to the failure of treatment services to 'grip' a high enough proportion of 'high harm causing users' ('HHCUs') (PMSU 2003b). Arrestees who showed up as positive for heroin in a compulsory drug test would face a 'drug treatment and registration order'. This would enable the state to keep watch over these troublesome renegades while allowing them to end their status as outlaw drug users by entering carefully monitored heroin or methadone treatment. Some have argued that existing harm reduction practices – including substitution treatment and drug consumption rooms – represent disciplinary, governmental surveillance (Bancroft 2009; Bourgois 2000). But at least drug users have some choice over whether to use these services (O'Malley 2008). The Birt recommendations explicitly turn treatment into a mechanism of coercive state control. The report itself recognizes that its proposals risk breaching the European Convention on Human Rights. It does nothing to address the harms of drug control, even though it states that drug seizures are useful only in 'handling perception' (PMSU 2003b: 87). It makes massive claims for the potential cost savings to be achieved by rapid, radical change. It estimated that the full set of the 'transformational' changes that it proposed would save £8 billion per year. These savings would all be in the form of reduced crime costs. These estimates are based on the inflated estimates of the crime that is directly caused by drug use and grand, untested assumptions about the effect of the proposed policy in reducing it (see Chapter 3 and Stevens 2007a, 2008a). A further process of transformation and selection has therefore occurred. The question of normative value judgments on the use and harms of drugs has been translated into a financial cost-benefit equation. The costs and harms of death, infectious disease and child neglect have been selected out. The exaggerated harm of 'drug-motivated crime' has been selected in.

Translation of evidence into law

The next major development in drug policy following these PMSU reports was the passing of the Drugs Act 2005. It created a list of new crimes and aggravating circumstances to existing offences. These included:

- Possession and supply of unprocessed psilocybin mushrooms (which were put in class A, alongside heroin and cocaine).
- Dealing near schools.
- Presumption of supply for certain amounts.
- Using people aged under 18 as drug couriers.
- Refusing a drug test at arrest.
- Refusing to be assessed for treatment.
- Refusing intimate searches and X-rays.

Some have dismissed the 2005 Act simply as a vote-raising gimmick. One MP described it as 'pre-election window dressing' (Carmichael 2005). While the first four of these listed measures can be seen simply as non-evidence based efforts to appear tough on drugs and drug dealers, the last three show continuity with the recommendations of the Birt report. They fit with his advocacy of increased identification and 'capture' of drug users at arrest in order to 'grip' them in treatment. These legal innovations paved the way for the subsequent 'tough choices' programme, which made use of the provisions on compulsory testing and assessment of drug-using arrestees to force people into contact with treatment services.

At this stage of selection, the failures of prohibition, of harms to drug users and the consequences of inequality were again filtered out in favour of measures which increased the identification and coercion of heroin and crack users. Again, there is a focus on policies which are both politically advantageous to their proposers in the short-term and have longer-term ideological consequences in 'fragmentation', 'unification' and 'legitimation'. The increase in coerced treatment of heroin users worked ideologically. It reified the distinction between domestic and foreign drugs. It fragmented drug users into a group of relatively benign recreational users and a threatening group of 'HHCUs'. However, the more radical proposals were not fully adopted as government policy. The idea of the 'drug treatment and registration order' for heroin use had apparently been forgotten by the time I was ethnographically observing the creation of drug policies within government in 2009 (see Chapter 4). This suggests that there are limits to the extent with which ideology can impact policy. Whether these limits are set by countervailing evidence, concern for human rights or by governmental inertia remains as a question for further study.

Drug harms and the classification of 'foreign' drugs

The Misuse of Drugs Act 1971 created a schedule of drugs that are classified into class A, B or C, depending on how harmful they appear to be. The Act stated that the government can make changes to this classification. It has to consult the Advisory Council on the Misuse of Drugs (ACMD), although it does not have to follow its recommendations.

Two reclassifications and a sacking

The contemporary story of drug classification runs from 2002 right up the time of writing of this chapter (Autumn 2009). It covers the two reclassifications of cannabis, the refusal to reclassify ecstasy and ends, for the moment, with the sacking of Professor David Nutt from his position as Chair of the ACMD. Charlie Lloyd (2008) has provided a useful description of the government's clumsy footwork on cannabis. The short version of this story is that, following recommendations by the Police Foundation (Independent Inquiry into the Misuse of Drugs Act 1971 2000) and a successful pilot of cannabis warnings in Lambeth (PRS 2002), the then Home Secretary, David Blunkett, told the Home Affairs Select Committee (2002) that he would ask the ACMD to review the classification of cannabis. The ACMD (2002) reported that cannabis was not as harmful as other drugs in class B, such as amphetamine sulphate. Blunkett accepted their recommendation and reclassification to class C came into force in January 2004. This step was controversial, and has since been repeatedly discussed. With the general election in 2005 looming, the decision was referred back to the ACMD. Once the election was out of the way, the ACMD recommended that cannabis stay in class C and this recommendation was followed. After Gordon Brown's accession to the premiership, and with another possible (postponed) general election in the offing, the decision was referred for a third time to the ACMD. The Council stood by its recommendation to keep the drug in class C, but was ignored by the government, which placed cannabis back in class B from January 2009.

The story on ecstasy is simpler. The ACMD was criticized for its failure to review the classification of MDMA by a parliamentary committee (House of Commons Science and Technology Committee 2006). In 2008, it carried out a review, and found that ecstasy is less harmful than other drugs in class A (like heroin and cocaine). So the Committee recommended that it be placed in class B (ACMD 2008a). The Home Secretary, Jacqui Smith, refused to follow this advice. The justification given for this was that the risks of ecstasy were not yet clear, that downward classification might increase use and the government has to 'err on the side of caution' (Campbell 2008). Later, after he had treated a patient who was suffering from a head injury which occurred while horse-riding, Professor Nutt published an academic editorial which showed that, per episode, using ecstasy is less dangerous than equestrianism (Nutt 2009c). This provoked Ms Smith into phoning Nutt as he treated another patient, and demanding that he apologize for this finding, which she found to be offensive to families who had suffered from ecstasy use (Nutt 2009b).

The story of drug classification subsequently fell off the front pages for the next few months, only to be placed back on the news agenda by Alan Johnson, who replaced Jacqui Smith as Home Secretary in the summer of 2009. In October 2009, a lecture which Professor Nutt had given three months earlier was published (Nutt 2009a). He gave it at King's College London, in his capacity as Professor of Psychopharmacology at Imperial College. He showed slides from his lecture to the Home Office in advance. However, Mr Johnson took offence at some comments that were made in the press release that promoted the lecture and decided to demand Nutt's resignation from the ACMD (Johnson 2009). This was the cue for much controversy, with five resignations by other members of the ACMD and public spats between government ministers (Summers *et al.* 2009). Johnson accused Nutt of confusing the public about drug policy. He said that independent advisers could either enter the political arena or oppose government policy, but could not do both.[41] This statement effectively turns nominally independent scientists into highly qualified spin doctors, only permitted to publicize and defend their findings if they happen to concur with the government line of the day. Nutt in turn accused Johnson of creating an excuse to rid himself of his turbulent adviser (DDN 2009).

Analyzing the cannabis kerfuffle

These controversies provide rich material for discourse analysis. Let us limit ourselves to the case of cannabis. Three main arguments were deployed in calling for re-reclassification from class C to class B: the effect of cannabis on human (especially adolescent mental) health; the strength of available forms of cannabis; and the effect of classification in 'sending signals' that reduce drug use.

Cannabis harms

It has become increasingly clear in recent years that cannabis is not harmless to human health. These harms were acknowledged in the ACMD's original report, which stated that '[c]annabis is not a harmless substance and its use unquestionably poses risks both to individual health and to society' (ACMD 2002: 12). This has been acknowledged by those who argue for regulated legal availability of cannabis (under strict controls) (Room *et al.* 2010). There is evidence from a variety of sources of a significant association with schizophrenia, especially in making the condition more severe for those who already suffer from it (Arseneault *et al.* 2004; D'Souza 2007; McLaren *et al.* 2010; Semple *et al.* 2005). The role of cannabis in causing schizophrenia is more controversial, with ongoing debate on how to explain the statistical association between cannabis and schizophreniform disorders. A much-publicized article in *The Lancet* claimed that use of cannabis increased the risk of such disorders by 40 per cent (Moore *et al.* 2007). There is also some evidence of association between cannabis use and increased risks of cancer, heart disease and accidental injury or death (e.g. while driving, although the role of alcohol in combination with cannabis is important here) (Hall 2008a). Much less attention has been paid to emerging evidence that cannabis use may not be a major cause of cancer (Hashibe *et al.* 2006) and may even reduce some forms of cancer (Liang *et al.* 2009).

Cannabis potency

Advocates of re-reclassification frequently referred to the increasing strength of the most commonly used strains of cannabis, with specific reference to 'skunk' (a poorly defined term often applied to forms of strong, dried, sinsemilla cannabis[42]). The available figures should be treated with extreme caution, as they are based on the small proportion of cannabis that is seized by the police. There is no reason to expect them to collect a random sample. Recent data from the Forensic Science Service suggests that the average potency of seized samples of sinsemilla increased from six per cent in 1995 to a peak of 14 per cent in 2005 and then decreased to 10 per cent in 2007 (White 2008). Claims of very steep increases in cannabis potency (e.g. the claim that the increase is by a factor of 25 [Owen 2007]) turn out to be vastly exaggerated.

There is evidence for the claims that skunk is more commonly used than it was in the past, with one report that sinsemilla accounted for over 80 per cent of seizures by sampled police services in early 2008 (Hardwick & King 2008).[43] Less well reported is the effect of law enforcement efforts (combined with consumer preferences for stronger strains) in changing the English cannabis market. This market used to be dominated by cannabis resin from North Africa (primarily Morocco). As the Moroccan government and European countries have successfully clamped down on the production and transit of hashish, the market share of domestically grown sinsemilla has risen. Similar unintended, adverse effects of drug law enforcement in increasing the drug's potency have also been seen in Canada and the USA (Bouchard 2004; Kleiman 1989).

Sending signals

The third major argument that was made for cannabis re-reclassification is that it sends a signal that cannabis is harmful. For example, the Centre for Social Justice's report on addictions argued that cannabis should be in class B in order to 'send a clear message about its potential for individual and social harm' (Gyngell 2007: 111). Such use of drug policy to send signals was specifically criticized by the House of Commons Science and Technology Committee (2006). It stated that the drug classification system should be based on objective measures of harm, rather than on a wish to communicate with the public. There is no evidence that such telegraphic use of the criminal law has any deterrent effect on potential drug users. The evidence rather suggests the opposite. Cannabis use declined after reclassification to class C (Hales *et al.* 2009; Hoare 2009).

The cannabis policy argument

The first two of these arguments were examined in some detail in the ACMD's third review of the evidence on cannabis (ACMD 2008b). It recognizes the evidence on health harms, and specifically the link to psychosis and schizophrenia. However, it notes that reported cases of cannabis poisoning have been falling, as have the numbers of people diagnosed as schizophrenic, even during the years when cannabis use was increasing and skunk was taking a larger share of the market (see Degenhardt *et al.* 2003; Frisher, Crome, Martino *et al.* 2009). It also remarks – with reference to *The Lancet* article on cannabis and psychosis – that much of the apparent link disappears when confounding variables are taken into account. The ACMD avoids commenting on the issue of using classification to send messages. But it does point out that an opinion poll carried out in early 2008 showed that 96 per cent of people still knew that cannabis was illegal and that only 24 per cent wanted the penalties for possession to be increased, with 67 per cent wanting them unchanged or abolished.

The Home Office and Labour Party both issued press releases attempting to justify the decision to ignore the ACMD's advice to keep cannabis in class C. They both referred to a 'crackdown' on cannabis, with repeated use of words like 'tough', 'strong' and 'robust' (and much less frequent use of 'health', which is what the debate is supposed to be about) (Home Office 2008c; Labour Party 2008). The Home Office bragged that this reclassification means 'more robust enforcement', 'tackling cannabis farms', increasing sentences for some cannabis dealers, curtailing the sale of cannabis paraphernalia and 'refreshing our public information message'. Of itself, the move back to class B meant nothing more than the (rarely enforced) maximum prison sentence for possession being increased from two years to five. But the press release makes clear that reclassification is about more than just the legal details that await cannabis users who are unlucky enough to end up in court.

The various policy moves on cannabis provide another interesting test of the competing hypotheses on the use of evidence in policy. The original reclassification to class C could be seen as an example of the enlightenment hypothesis in practice. Over many years, the gradual accumulation of evidence on the relative harms of cannabis and other drugs (combined perhaps with increasing personal knowledge of the drug among politicians and their advisers) led eventually to a rational, evidence-based change in policy, even if this was undermined by changes to the Police and Criminal Evidence Act which meant that cannabis possession was still an arrestable offence, and by increasing the maximum sentence for supplying class C drugs to 14 years – the same as for class B. These addenda to the reclassification hint at the problems of the enlightenment approach. It cannot account for the influence of powerful lobby groups (in this case, the police) in diluting the impact of evidence on policy. Nor can it explain the increase in maximum supply sentences. If cannabis is less harmful than was thought when it was placed in class B, why make punishment for supply the same as for class B, even while downgrading its possession? The answer can be given by the political/tactical hypothesis. The increase in sentencing for class C supply was presented as another instance of the government being tough on drug dealers[44], a tactical move which had the effect of guarding the government's right flank against attacks for being soft on drugs and of publicizing the government's totemically tough stance.

Of course, the enlightenment hypothesis cannot explain the re-reclassification back to class B. The available evidence has been distilled by the ACMD three times, but is still not strong enough to persuade the government. The political/tactical hypothesis seems much more persuasive in this case, with the government responding politically to tactical attacks made on them by various right-wing newspapers and columnists. The *Daily Mail* and *Daily Telegraph* provided particularly egregious examples of the misuse of evidence in public discourse.[45] The British Social Attitudes survey showed that the proportion of the public who support the criminalization of cannabis had dropped to about four in ten in 2001. It was back up to 54 per cent by 2007. The government was apparently more in tune with changes in public opinion than with expert, ACMD advice (Bailey *et al.* 2010).

Evidence, ideology and the cannabis debate

Mark Monaghan (2008) interviewed 24 key policy actors involved in the debates around cannabis classification in 2006 and 2007. He divides them into radical, rational and conservative perspectives. He shows how actors from each of these perspectives used evidence tactically to support their pre-existing beliefs. They tended to highlight elements of the evidence that were most favourable to their cause. Cannabis 'conservatives', for example, focused on the evidence on health effects, while ignoring the lack of evidence that classification can reduce these harms. 'Radicals', on the other hand, tended to emphasize that latter part of the evidence-base and decried drug prohibition as 'evidence-free'. 'Rationalists' supported the ACMD's position (several interviewees were ACMD members) and focused on the relatively lower harms of cannabis, compared to other drugs, while not challenging the legal framework within which classification operates. Monaghan argues that the use of evidence depends, for people from each of these perspectives, on what counts *as* evidence.

This reminds us of the need to consider issues of ideology and power when looking at the use of evidence. Some groups in the debate have more power to determine what evidence will be considered, and what will be ignored. In this debate, it was the conservative perspective which eventually prevailed. This fits with a longer pattern of using evidence of drug-related harms to bolster unequal power arrangements. Nils Christie has written that there are valid reasons for attempting to limit the use of some psychoactive substances. But these reasons cannot explain the forms that such attempts have actually taken. The war on drugs, he argues, is also a war on those characteristics that have been associated with drug use. It is primarily young, unemployed men who have been targeted as 'suitable enemies' in this war (Christie 1986, 2000). As shown in the first chapter, the control of psychoactive substances has long made a distinction between drugs that are seen as 'domestic' (e.g. tea, coffee and alcohol) and those that are seen as 'foreign' (e.g. the derivatives of coca and opium) (Harris 2005). These have also been described as 'my' drugs and 'your' drugs (Carnwath & Smith 2002). These distinctions mark the boundary between the substances that are seen as acceptable in polite society, and those which are to be pushed to the marginalized fringe, along with their users.

Products of the cannabis plant have traditionally been placed in the latter category, but the 2004 reclassification, justified in part by the savings in police time from not having to do the paperwork on a drug of which use had become widespread, suggested that cannabis might be crossing the border to become a domestic drug which would not mark its users out as criminals. Cannabis was becoming one of 'my' drugs. Jacqui Smith and several other prominent politicians and commentators have admitted to using it in the past. In order to justify continuing the criminalization of current cannabis users, while absolving these past users, the strength and mental health effects of 'skunk' have been exaggerated in order to separate it from the forms of cannabis that these powerful people took in their youths. Here we have a clear example of the selective use of evidence in creating a narrative about drugs and the policy response to them. It is a story which separates out 'responsible' from 'flawed' consumers (Bauman 2007) by setting up a false distinction between 'my' regretted but harmless use of cannabis and 'your' reckless, dangerous use of skunk. So (in a similar way to the DTTO and PMSU drug policy discourses) it contributes to ideological 'fragmentation' by identifying a group of people who are threateningly different and justifying their expurgation and punishment.

Continuity and change in drug policy

This chapter has covered a period of 12 years: 1997 to 2009. According to Sabatier and Jenkins-Smith (2003), this should be enough time to perceive the process of policy change. But English drug policy has shown a large degree of continuity over this period, and even longer (Barton 2003; MacGregor 2009). Two main strands of the current approach precede the Labour government that arrived in 1997. The focus on harm reduction, that has been little mentioned in political discussions, but has been carried on and expanded in actual practice, dates back to the Thatcher government. Advocates of harm reduction were able to use the governmental view of AIDS as a public health emergency, which prevailed between 1986 and 1987, to win governmental support for the measures that they had long been advocating (Berridge & Strong 1991). The subsequent expansion of needle exchange, outreach services and opiate substitution treatment succeeded in limiting the spread of infection (Stimson 1995). Their effects can still be seen in the internationally low rates of HIV among British drug users, despite relatively high rates of problematic drug use (EMCDDA 2009a) and recent increases in these rates (HPA 2008).

A second major strand of the current approach is the use of partnerships to lead local action on drug issues and then requiring them to achieve targets set by central government. The concept of the multi-agency drug action team was introduced in the Major government's strategy, *Tackling Drugs Together* (Lord President of the Council and Leader of the House of Commons *et al.* 1995). South (1998) attributed this development to a Thatcherite desire that drug control in the public sector should ape the managerialist, performance-measured management style of the private sector. The multi-agency, centrally accountable approach has been retained and extended in subsequent strategies under Labour (Home Office 2008b; President of the Council 1998). The government has used the available evidence on the effectiveness of drug treatment to justify increasing investment in opiate substitution treatment. After years of delay (Duke 2003), it has expanded this treatment to prisons under the Integrated Drug Treatment System.[46] It has introduced initiatives, like the Drug Interventions Programme (see next chapter), which have a weaker evidence base, but fit more closely with the desire to be tough. Instead of substantial change between governments, there has been a process of continuity and intensification.

The next chapter will show some of the effects of this intensification, and the bifurcatory response to drug users that it has involved. Here, it is worth attempting to add a perspective on policy change to the explanations of policy formation that have been presented in this chapter and the last. Other writers have ascribed policy change to the use of 'policy windows' (Kingdon 1984) through which to insert research into policy (Lenton 2008). The perception of AIDS as an emergency created a window through which harm reduction measures entered central government policy although – as Berridge and Strong (1991) note – this window closed once the perceived threat of AIDS receded. Policy windows often occur around changes of government. But the English drug policy example shows that elections, even when they lead to a change in the governing party, do not necessarily lead to substantial policy change. This can be explained by the shared, ideological narrative held by both Conservative and Labour governments, who have both insisted that drugs are an external threat to the health and security of the nation, and in so doing have taken attention and resources away from the problem of inequality.

Another reason for policy change is emphasized by Sabatier and Jenkins-Smith's (1993) 'advocacy coalition framework' (ACF). It is that events that are external to the policy process can shift the beliefs that animate advocacy coalitions and so lead to changes in the policies they bring to power. This helps to explain, for example, the radical change that happened in drug policy in Britain and some other countries as the threat of AIDS changed the relative priority given to health and criminal justice responses to drug users (Kübler

2001). But as Kübler suggests, the ACF needs the addition of an explanation of the resources that various actors in the debate bring to it. And it needs an explanation of how external events come to shape actions within the policy debate. Here again we turn to Hajer's (1995) emphasis on storytelling. It is by linking external events to issues that are important to people who hold power that these external events come to change the policies they support. This means that the coalitions that affect policy are not just about advocacy, but about discourse. They vie to control the interpretation that is put on to objective events that occur outside the policy debate. The spread of HIV and AIDS was not a discursive, but an objective event. But it could only affect policy once it had been interpreted in ways that led to the institutionalization of certain discourses and practices. The interpretation placed on HIV was that it posed a threat, not just to drug users, but to the whole population (ACMD 1988). This justified the shift to health as a priority in the late 1980s (MacGregor 1998). As it has become clear that injecting drug users do not pose a significant threat of infection to society as a whole, other narratives, and particularly the idea that drugs cause crime, have gained influence in the policy debate (Stevens 2007a).

Evidence and ideological exclusion

In the previous chapter, I analyzed the process of policy making. I suggested that evidence is used selectively to tell policy stories. There are genuine attempts to reconcile government policy with the best available knowledge of reality. And these attempts may, as will be shown in the next chapter, lead to good outcomes for some drug users. But these attempts, I argued, are distorted by the uneven distribution of power within and around the state. In this chapter, we can see the cumulative effect of these distortions on drug policy. They result in policies that support a certain view of the world – a view which is held by the people who have most power to transform their view into action. This view is both divisive and exclusive. It divides psychoactive substances into categories which are either accepted as safe, 'domestic' drugs, or reviled as threatening, 'foreign' drugs. And it divides drug users into an indulged, forgivable group of people – who may once have dabbled with illicit substances, but who now feel suitably ashamed of themselves – and a recalcitrant, dangerous group of 'suitable enemies'. This division forms the basis for the penal exclusion of some of the people who use drugs. As will be shown in the next chapter, it is the people who already gain least from the unequal distribution of power and resources who suffer most from the ideologically selective use of evidence.

Drug policy is not the product of a linear or even-handedly enlightened process of using evidence to improve society. There is use of evidence, but some types of evidence are more likely to be used than others. The influence of political/tactical concerns is visible, especially in the timing of some drug policy events, such as the pre-election Drugs Act 2005. But the political consensus between the two main political parties on issues such as the 2009 re-reclassification of cannabis, and the subsequent sacking of Professor Nutt, suggests there is something deeper going on. Drug policy is not only influenced by short-term political manoeuvres. It is also affected by the use of drug policy as an ideological tool. Once again, this does not mean that all the evidence used to support current policies is false. Nor does it mean that drug policy is determined by a particular political doctrine. It means that groups who hold an unequal share of the power to determine their own and other people's life chances use drug policy to justify this inequality. They use it to tell stories about who is worthy of full citizenship. Their selective use of evidence supports the idea that 'foreign' drugs threaten our safety and security. They construct drugs and their users as scapegoats for the ills of a 'broken' society (Gyngell 2007). They draw attention away from the rise in inequality and the destabilization of vulnerable communities that have been caused by their pursuit of the fruits of late modern capitalism. This is not the result of a conspiracy to ignore conflicting evidence. It arises from the willingness of people who hold power to listen more attentively to stories which do not challenge that power. If enough such stories are told – without effective contradiction – then they come to be accepted as true by the people who have the resources to translate them into political action.

Chapter 6

The effects of drug policy

Drug policies have symbolic, ideological effects. But they also have immediate effects on the lives of the people who are directly exposed to them. This chapter will analyze some of the effects of the policies whose development has been traced in the previous two chapters. It will avoid generalizations about the effects of entire national drug policies (although they will be risked in the next chapter). Rather, it will be limited to analysing three specific areas of English drug policy that have been mentioned in previous chapters. They are the use of treatment to reduce crime; the continuing use of the criminal justice system as the main tool of drug policy; and the ambivalent policies on cannabis. This chapter will look at drug policy effects under each of these headings in turn, with a specific focus in the middle section on the differential impacts of drug law enforcement on people of Afro-Caribbean origin. It will argue that the material effects of drug policy deepen its discursive impact in justifying and reinforcing inequalities.

Drug treatment as crime reduction

Since 1998, there has been a very large increase in the availability of treatment for drug dependence. The number of people 'in contact with structured drug treatment' in England grew from 88,000 in 1998 to over 207,000 by 2008/9 (NTA 2009a), with another 14,000 people referred to treatment in Wales (WAG 2009). As the English National Treatment Agency's Director has repeatedly told drug treatment workers, this investment has been the result of the government's use of drug treatment as a tool to reduce crime (Hayes 2005, 2006). One specific policy in this area has been the Drug Interventions Programme, known as DIP. Since 2005, some DIP areas have been using the powers that were given by the Drugs Act 2005 to test arrestees for drug use and direct those who test positive to undergo a 'required assessment' at a treatment centre. At the time of writing, this initiative is shepherding over 4,500 people per week into drug treatment (Home Office 2009). Many of them end up on Drug Rehabilitation Requirements (DRRs). These form part of the generic community order that was introduced by the

Criminal Justice Act 2003. They replaced the Drug Treatment and Testing Order (DTTO) in April 2005, but retain many similar features, including a requirement to spend a specified number of hours in drug treatment, for a specified period (between six months and three years). During this time, offenders are also subject to supervision by probation, court review by sentencers and regular drug tests. If they commit new crimes, or fail to comply with the order, they are 'breached'. This involves taking them back to court, where the judge or magistrate can decide to rescind the order and resentence, often to imprisonment, or to impose new conditions.

Crime reduction, maturing out and regression to the mean

The results of DIP are subject to debate. An evaluation was commissioned from the Institute for Criminal Policy Research, but was never published. It was excluded from a summary that the Home Office (2008a) produced of research on DIP. Its authors wrote a critical article about the use made by the Home Office of externally commissioned research, but defended the right of civil servants to challenge the methodology of such studies (Hough & Turnbull 2006). A later analysis – which has not yet been fully peer reviewed and published – compared offenders in one region who did or did not go through DIP (McSweeney 2009). The results on effects are inconclusive. There were reductions in offending by people who went through the programme. However, offenders who did not go through DIP also reduced their offending. The difference in reoffending between the two groups was not large enough to make the programme cost-effective in this analysis. In the meanwhile, the Home Office had carried out its own review. This study examined the rates of offending by 7,727 offenders before and after they were in contact with DIP, with no comparison group. It found that the volume of offending by these offenders fell by 26 per cent in the six months following their identification by DIP (Skodbo *et al.* 2007). However, without a control group, it is impossible to tell whether this reduction was caused by the programme. It may have been caused by offenders moving down from peaks in their offending. This process of 'maturing out' may have happened without DIP involvement.

Home Office civil servants have also used figures on general reductions in crime to suggest that DIP is having a distinct effect. For example, they have argued that there has been a 32 per cent reduction in acquisitive crime since the introduction of DIP in 2003 (Home Office 2009). The problem with this claim is that, as far as we know, crime was falling faster in the period between 1995 and 2003 (before the introduction of DIP) than it has done since, so it is difficult to perceive a separate DIP effect (see Figure 6.1). A different attempt to demonstrate the effect of DIP involves the claim that crime has fallen fastest in areas which have had the most intensive intervention from DIP (Ibid). But these areas were chosen precisely because they had a higher rate of crime. In a period when crime rates are generally falling, the phenomenon of

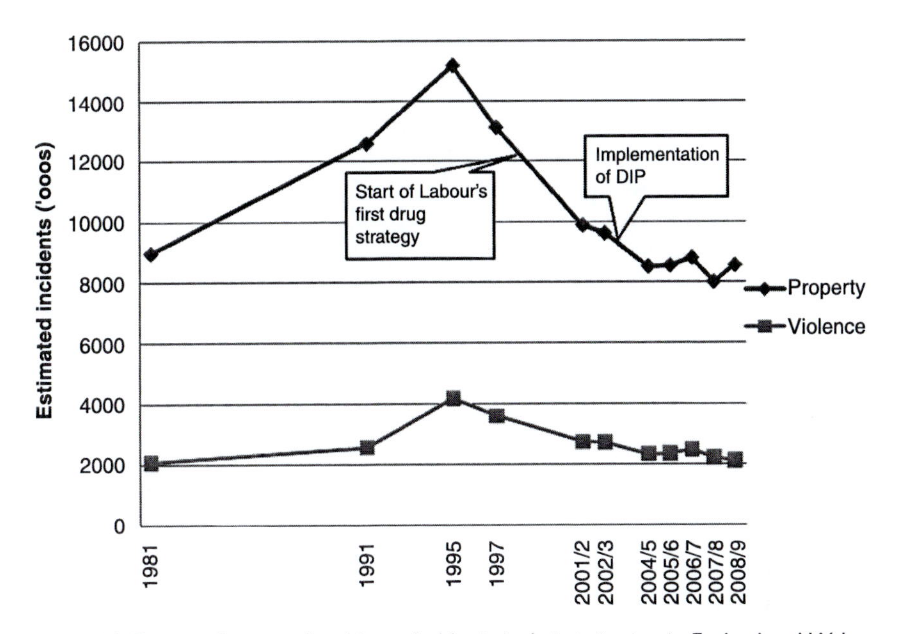

Figure 6.1 Estimated personal and household criminal victimization in England and Wales, 1981–2008/9.

(*Source:* Walker *et al.* 2009)

regression to the mean[47] would be expected to lead to faster reductions in the higher crime areas, whether they had DIP intervention or not. None of these objections mean that DIP has had no effect. They just show that, despite its claims, the Home Office has not yet been able to demonstrate that DIP has reduced crime.

Effects of the DTTO

A similar problem with the lack of control groups challenged the early evaluation of the DTTO. A pilot involving three sites, but no comparison group, started in October of 1998. Results were mixed. A large proportion of the orders were revoked before completion (from 40 per cent in Croydon to 60 per cent in Gloucestershire). A large proportion of the urine tests carried out on offenders were positive (42 per cent for opiates, 45 per cent for cocaine). However, for those who stayed on the order, there were significant reductions in drug use and offending (Turnbull *et al.* 2000). The lack of a comparison group, and the failure to follow-up people who did not complete the programme make it very difficult to ascribe these reductions to the DTTO intervention. Follow-up results showed that the rate of recidivism from the pilot DTTOs was similar to that for other community sentences

(Hough *et al.* 2003), as in Ian Hearnden's (2000) study of the previous 1(A)6 probation orders with conditions to attend treatment.

It is very difficult to find an adequate comparison group for people who go through court-ordered drug treatment. There have been randomized trials of drug courts in the USA (GAO 2005), but no British court has so far allowed randomization of drug-involved offenders to receive a DTTO/DRR or other intervention. However, it is possible to compare court-ordered drug treatment to drug treatment that is undertaken 'voluntarily'.[48] There is convincing evidence that the types of drug treatment that are provided to people on DTTO/DRRs do have positive effects in reducing crime and drug use (Babor *et al.* 2010; Prendergast *et al.* 2002; UNODC & WHO 2008). Therefore, if people who enter such treatment through the courts have similar outcomes to those who enter through other routes, then this would support the hypothesis that court-ordered drug treatment is effective in reducing drug use and crime, at least at the individual level. From 2002 to 2005, I led the QCT Europe project. The project set out to test this hypothesis in England and four other European countries (Austria, Germany, Italy and Switzerland). The results for the whole European sample are presented elsewhere (Schaub *et al.* 2010). Here, we will concentrate on the findings for the English sample, some of which have also been published in the *British Journal of Criminology* (McSweeney *et al.* 2007).

In England, we interviewed 157 people who entered drug treatment during the six months from June 2003. Eighty-nine of them entered treatment under a DTTO and 68 entered 'voluntarily'. Their average age was 31. The form of treatment they entered was mostly structured day care. This usually involved five days a week attendance at a treatment centre. Most members of the sample were also given a methadone prescription to help them stop using illicit heroin. We used various research instruments, including the European Addiction Severity Index (Kokkevi & Hartgers 1995), to ask them about their health, their drug use and their offending. They were generally a highly vulnerable, highly criminal group, with greater levels of risk among the DTTO group. Table 6.1 shows that there were high levels of self-reported use of heroin and crack. These levels were significantly higher in the DTTO group than the 'volunteers'. Thirty-two per cent of the DTTO group and

Table 6.1 Nature and extent of drug use during the last 30 days at treatment entry

	DTTO	*'voluntary'*
Mean number of days using heroin (n=138)*	25.0	19.3
Mean number of days using crack (n=122)*	19.8	7.4
Mean reported monthly spend on drugs (n=156)*	£3,579	£1,059
Mean days injecting drugs (n=105)*	19.4	10.5
Mean EuropASI drug use score (n=156)*	0.216	0.151

Statistical significance of differences between groups tested by T-test:* ($p<0.001$)

13 per cent of the 'volunteers' reported being homeless at the start of treatment. Both groups had generally low levels of education, employment and physical health. The 'volunteers' were significantly more likely than the DTTO group to report mental health problems, with 53 per cent of the total sample reporting that they had ever experienced severe depression. Sixty-four per cent of the respondents stated that they had been the victim of a crime at some point during the last 12 months (see Stevens *et al.* 2007). When it came to their own crimes, the DTTO group, unsurprisingly, reported a higher level of offending than the 'volunteers'. We asked them about offences they had committed in the past 30 days.[49] Table 6.2 shows the results. It again suggests that many problematic drug users finance their drug use through crime, and that shoplifting is more common than burglary in this group.

So the sample seems fairly typical of the people who enter drug treatment in England. They have similar ages, drug use patterns, rates of offending, mental health and other problems to those found by larger studies, such as the National Treatment Outcome Research Study (NTORS) (Gossop *et al.* 1998) and the Drug Treatment Outcome Research Study (DTORS) (Jones *et al.* 2007).

In common with the results of DTORS and NTORS, we observed large reductions in drug use and offending among our sample (see Figures 6.2 and 6.3). More specifically, these falls were not larger in the 'voluntary' than the DTTO group. Indeed, the reductions were larger in the DTTO group, due to the higher levels at intake.

As shown in the shrinking size of the sample (n) over the three follow-up phases of the QCT Europe study, we were unable to follow up many members of the sample. This creates the possibility that the evident reductions in average levels of drug use and offending were caused by the most frequent users and offenders leaving the sample. In order to check for this effect, we repeated the analysis using the technique of last observation carried forward. Missing values for a person who has not been contacted at follow-up were replaced with the value from the last interview with them. This provides a

Table 6.2 Nature and extent of reported offending during the last 30 days at treatment entry

	DTTO	*'voluntary'*
Mean number of days involved in any crime (n=157)*	22.8	8.4
Mean number of days involved in shoplifting and other minor property crime (n=122)*	18.1	8.1
Mean number of days involved in burglary (n=79)*	5.0	0.04
Mean number of days involved in drug dealing/trafficking offences (n=66)*	11.1	0.46

Statistical significance of differences between groups tested by T-test: * ($p<0.001$)

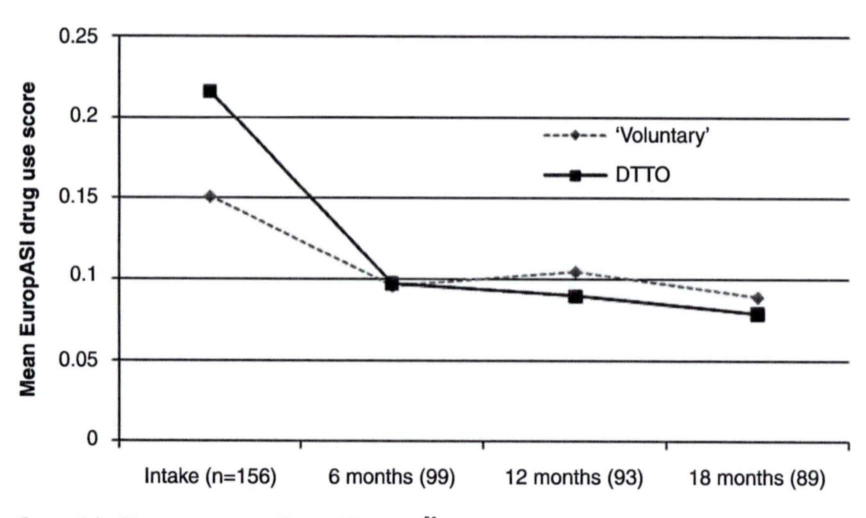

Figure 6.2 Changes in mean EuropASI score[50] from intake to 18 month follow-up.

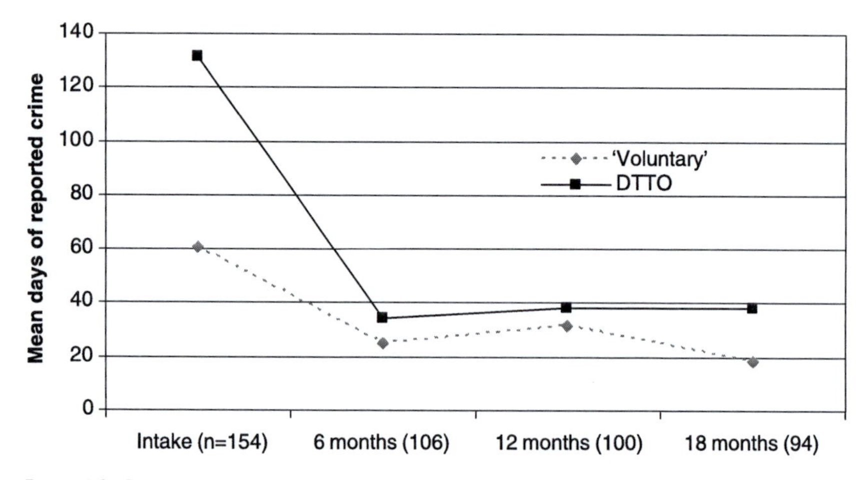

Figure 6.3 Changes in mean days of reported crime in previous six months.

conservative estimate of the effect of treatment. This analysis also showed significant reductions in drug use and offending in the six months following treatment entry.

The QCT Europe study was not a randomized controlled trial. It cannot prove that the observed reductions in drug use and offending were caused by the treatment. It is possible that maturing out and regression to the mean contributed to the observed reductions in both groups. But, if we are confident of the research that suggests that drug treatment is effective in reducing drug use and offending, then the QCT Europe results suggest that court-ordered treatment under a DTTO was no less effective than 'voluntary' treatment.

The study has also produced useful findings about the criminal victimization of dependent drug users (Stevens *et al.* 2007), the link between motivation and coercion in quasi-compulsory treatment (Stevens *et al.* 2006), influences on treatment engagement (Stevens 2008b), the processes of court review and drug testing (McSweeney *et al.* 2008) and the conditions which enable or hinder the development of dependent drug users' commitments to change (Oeuvray *et al.* in preparation). It is important here to focus on the wider effects of the policy on DTTO/DRRs. As noted in the last chapter, in 1997 and 1998, government ministers, including George Howarth and Mike O'Brien, were presenting the DTTO as *the* answer to the drug-crime link. Challenged in Parliament on what they were doing about drugs and crime, they mentioned the DTTO and no other measure (Commons Hansard Debates 1997a, 1997b; O'Brien 1998). Twelve years later, the government is still discussing this link and addressing it through new, ever tougher means. Even if DTTOs and DRRs have been successful in reducing the offending of many of the people who have gone through them, they have certainly not succeeded in breaking the associative link between drugs and crime.

Effects on crime and net-widening

The original 'policy entrepreneur' behind the DTTO advised drug treatment agencies to emphasize the drug-crime link in order to win more investment in their services (Russell 1994). This has worked in expanding the scale of drug treatment. However, Russell warned that the very large number of offenders – compared to the relatively tiny number who are caught by the police and are therefore eligible to be ordered into treatment by the court – would mean that court-ordered drug treatment would be unlikely to make a significant dent in overall crime rates. This warning has been ignored. The Home Office is still claiming that overall crime rates can be significantly reduced by ordering more captured drug users into treatment.

Some advocates of court-ordered drug treatment have seen it as offering a means to reduce the use of imprisonment. In Europe, for example, the European Union *Action Plan on Drugs* and the Council of Europe's *Recommendation R(99)2 (concerning prison overcrowding and population inflation)* have endorsed the use of drug treatment as an 'alternative to imprisonment'. However, the data from England and Wales suggests that court-ordered drug treatment has been used as an adjunct and not an alternative to imprisonment (see Figure 6.4). In 2007, over 12,000 people were sentenced to non-custodial drug treatment, compared to fewer than 2,000 in 1995. The figures for new prison sentences were 91,740 and 89,173 respectively. Increasing the annual number of sentences to treatment alternatives by over 10,000 appears to have had no effect at all on the use of imprisonment, and this happened during a period of falling crime rates.

So there has been a large expansion in the use of both 'voluntary' and

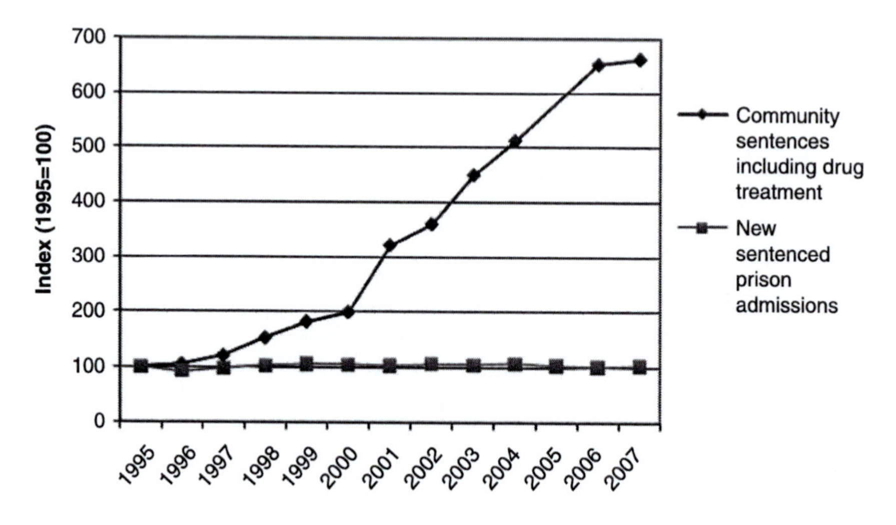

Figure 6.4 Trends in the use of imprisonment and drug treatment 'alternatives' in England and Wales 1995–2007.

(*Source:* calculated from figures given by Ministry of Justice 2009b; RDS NOMS 2007)

'quasi-compulsory' drug treatment since 1998, mostly involving opiate substitution treatment with structured day care, for those who enter treatment through the courts. The increase in investment and coercion has been justified by putative effects in reducing crime (Home Office 2009; NTA 2009b). This has fitted the policy narrative that drugs and their users, and not inequality and poverty, are to blame for crime. Many people who have gone through the expanded treatment system have reduced their drug use (Jones *et al.* 2009; Marsden *et al.* 2009). There have been encouraging reductions in the numbers of adults presenting for drug treatment to general practitioners (Frisher *et al.* 2009) and in young people seeking treatment for crack and heroin use (Campbell 2009a). But these reductions should not be seen uncritically as a direct result of government policy (Stevens & Reuter 2009). Given the general lack of evidence of the effect of drug policy on drug use (Reuter & Stevens 2007), they may well reflect declines in the 'epidemics' of crack and heroin (Caulkins *et al.* 2004).

While the government has been focusing on using drug treatment to reduce crime through expanding opiate substitution and day care, rates of drug-related deaths have increased, as have rates of HIV among injecting drug users. These worrying trends have largely been hidden under a welter of criticism of the failure to wean more people off opiates altogether (e.g. Easton 2008; Gyngell 2007, 2009). Such criticisms informed the development of the most recent drug strategy (Home Office 2008b), which promised to focus more on enabling drug users to move out of treatment. However, the performance management systems that drive local drug action partnerships to prioritize crime reduction remain in place and agencies are struggling to implement the new proposals (McGrail & MacKintosh 2009). These plans still do too little to address the rates of death and infection among people who continue to use drugs. And they do nothing to address the deep-seated poverty that creates the conditions in which drug problems flourish.

The differential impact of drug law enforcement

The deliberately inflicted pains of drug control have usually fallen most heavily on the poor and on visible minorities. As noted in the introduction to this book, the development of drug controls can be partly explained by the fear of immigration and the desire to control the activities of people who are seen as threatening to the ethnic and cultural mainstream. The racial imbalance in drug law enforcement continues to this day. African Americans are three times more likely to be arrested and ten times more likely to be imprisoned for drug offences than white Americans, despite the absence of evidence of higher rates of drug use or dealing (Beatty *et al.* 2007; King 2008; Tonry & Melewski 2008). This disparity is more visible in the USA than in the UK. Racial inequalities are starker in America, where social inequality is deeper and wars (both civil and cultural) have been fought over the legacy of slavery. In the UK, issues of racial conflict and discrimination have been less publicly visible. Jock Young (1971) had criticized the current Misuse of Drugs Act, when it was still just a bill, on the grounds that it would lead to differential impacts on young, black people. A report for the Commission for Racial Equality (Hood 1992) found that such fears were justified. People of Afro-Caribbean origin were massively over-represented in the prison population compared to their presence in the general population. Police targeting of black people for dealing cannabis was found to be a 'substantial factor influencing the number of black persons in the prison population' (Ibid: 181).

Concern about discrimination in the criminal justice system led to the setting up of standard systems for ethnic monitoring. The statistics produced by these systems have many drawbacks. Data are not available for every entrant into the criminal justice system. Data on ethnicity were only recorded for 22 per cent of those tried at Magistrates' Courts in 2007, and for 81 per cent of those tried at Crown Courts (Riley *et al.* 2009). Human biology and anthropology do not show the clear genetic or behavioural distinctions that are suggested by dividing people into distinct ethnic groups (Graves 2004; Smith 2009). Some classifications are more arbitrary than others. For example, the monitoring statistics place Irish people, north and south Europeans together with white Britons in the white group. They place people whose families moved from the Caribbean alongside people of more recent African origin in the black group. Nevertheless, these statistics enable us to check for disparities between the ethnic groups that are included.

Ethnic disparities in drug law enforcement

Figure 6.5 shows the disparities at each stage of the criminal justice system, as they apply to people placed in the white and black groups. It shows that people recorded as black are more likely than those recorded as white to be included at each of these stages of the criminal justice system for drug offences. Less than two in a thousand white people were arrested for drug offences in 2007/8, compared with over ten in a thousand black people. In terms of imprisonment, the rates vary from 0.1 in a thousand white people to 1.1 in a thousand black people. This means that black people in England and Wales are 6.1 times more likely to be arrested and 11.4 times more likely to be imprisoned for drug offences than white people. Black people were also 9.2 times more likely to be stopped and searched for drug offences. This differential enforcement of drug laws contributes substantially to the over-representation of black people in prison in England and Wales. On 30 June 2008, 25 per cent of the people serving sentences for drug offences were of African or Caribbean origin, although only 2.2 per cent of the population aged over 10 are estimated to be of this ethnic group (Riley *et al.* 2009).

The graph concentrates on the difference between white and black ethnic groups because it is these differences that are largest. People classified as Asian are two times more likely to be arrested and 3.1 times more likely to be imprisoned than white people for drug offences. The equivalent ratios for people classified as 'other' are 2.1 and 6.2.

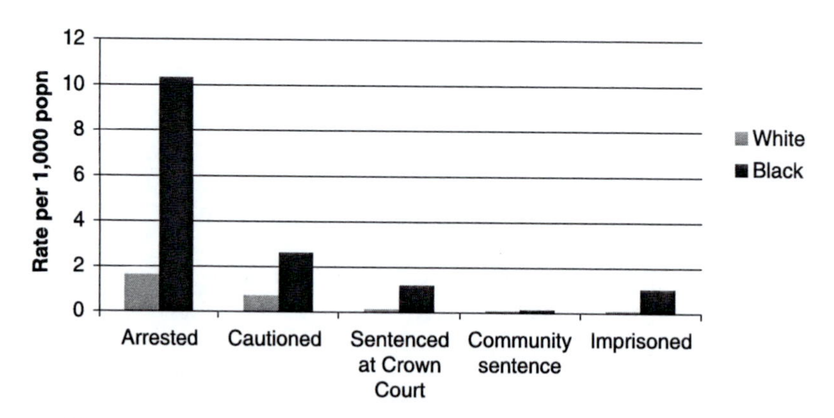

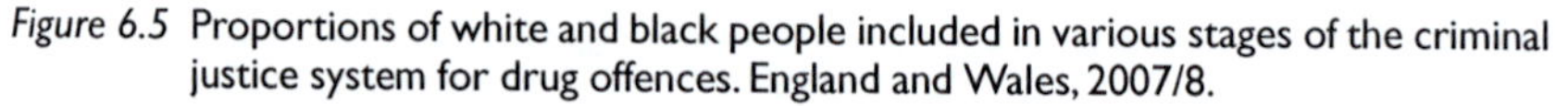
Figure 6.5 Proportions of white and black people included in various stages of the criminal justice system for drug offences. England and Wales, 2007/8.

(*Source:* calculated from figures given by Riley *et al.* 2009)

Disparities in drug use and dealing?

There is ongoing debate about the causes of this apparent discrimination. The most convenient explanation for the criminal justice agencies would be that they are simply responding to higher rates of drug offences in the various ethnic groups. Unfortunately for these agencies, the available data do not support this explanation. The British Crime Survey results on drug use have not been reported by ethnic group for several years, but the data from 2001/2 suggested that black people are no more likely than white people to report using illicit drugs, and that black people have a lower rate of use of class A drugs (Aust & Smith 2003). There is more recent data on drug use, dealing, arrest and self-defined ethnicity from the Offending Crime and Justice Survey (OCJS). This is a household survey of about 5,000 people aged 10 to 25. Figure 6.6 below shows results from the 2004 sweep of this survey.

Statistics from household surveys also have drawbacks. They miss out people, such as students, prisoners and the homeless, who may be most likely to be using and dealing drugs. And they rely on people to report honestly on hidden and stigmatized activities (even if confidentiality is guaranteed and supported by the use of computer-assisted interviewing). There is the potential for differential validity, if some ethnic groups are less likely to report drug use and dealing that has actually occurred than others (Bowling & Phillips 2002). Some of the ethnic groups in the OCJS are small (there were only 48 black people who answered questions about drug use), so it may not provide a reliable picture of drug use in the wider population. But the available figures, with all their limitations, do suggest that drug use and dealing are more prevalent in white than in other ethnic groups.

Reliable data on drug dealing is obviously hard to find, as dealers are

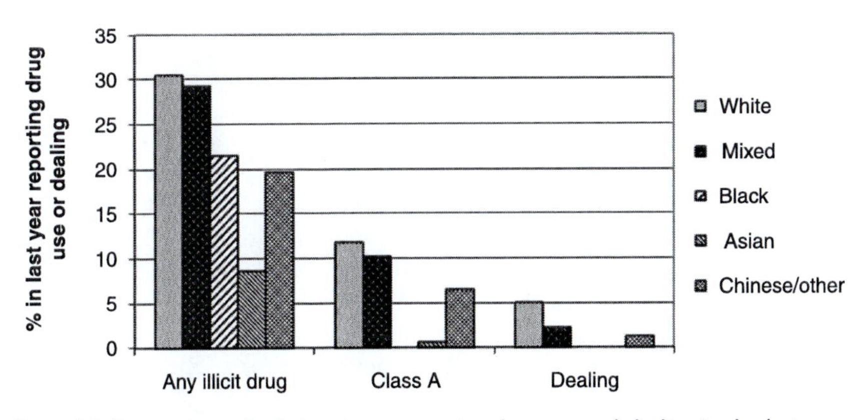

Figure 6.6 Percentages of ethnic groups reporting drug use and dealing in the last year. England and Wales, 2004.

(*Source:* secondary analysis of OCJS raw data[51]).

necessarily discreet in advertising their activities. However, there is some data to add to the OCJS from the National Treatment Outcome Research study. This found that nearly a third of the drug users who entered treatment at its selected sites in 1995 reported selling drugs in the previous three months. There were no significant differences between drug users of different ethnicities in their reporting of drug selling (Gossop *et al.* 2000). There is also data from the New-ADAM study. Of the interviewed arrestees, eight per cent were black and 79 per cent were white. White arrestees were significantly more likely than those from other ethnic groups to report both drug use and drug dealing (Bennett & Holloway 2007). Again, we need to be cautious about the results of this study because of its non-random sampling of both arrestees and offenders.

Race, racism and inequality

It seems unlikely, from the limited available evidence, that the ethnic disparities in drug law enforcement are the result of differences in ethnic patterns of drug use and dealing (see also Mills 2009). So is it about discrimination? There are several ways in which the police may discriminate against ethnic minorities (Reiner 2000). The form that is most akin to racism is 'categorical discrimination', in which people are treated differently because of their membership of a certain group, regardless of the relation of this group to crime. Given that nearly one in five people are apparently willing to admit being prejudiced towards members of ethnic minorities (Stonewall 2003), it would be surprising if police services managed to avoid employing people who hold negative attitudes towards black people. Several studies have found that some such attitudes are held at all levels of the police (Bowling & Phillips 2007).

If there is racism in the police, then we need to ask why that is. Is it that people who hold racist attitudes are more likely to join the police (Colman & Gorman 1982)? Or is it that they share a prejudicial view of black people that is common across British society? Whether this view comes in the form of error-strewn analyzes of biological differences in intelligence (Fischer *et al.* 1996; Herrnstein & Murray 1994), or in claims that black culture (and specifically black fathers) are to blame for crime (David Cameron, as quoted by Wintour *et al.* 2008), it ignores the history (and present) of violent subordination and exploitation of black people by white people. The use of economic and coercive power against black people is visible from the slave trade of the seventeenth and eighteenth centuries, through the importation of Commonwealth citizens to act as cheap labour after the Second World War, to today's tendency to lock up disproportionate numbers of black people, whether in prisons or mental health wards (Care Quality Commission 2010). This exploitation of black people is not just a problem of the criminal justice system. It is embedded within our economic structure. It is one of the reasons why Britain is richer than most other countries, and it also helps to explain why some Britons are so much richer than others. To blame police officers, prosecutors and judges for the effects of these structured inequalities is to hold out a false promise that we can eliminate their worst effects without dealing with their underlying causes.

Racial inequalities in wealth and power also produce differences in the ability of different groups to impose 'strain' on criminal justice agencies, and so avoid their attentions. Strain is the hassle and fear for individual careers and organizational reputations which powerful and well connected offenders are able to inflict on organizations that attempt to scrutinize them (Chambliss 1976). If black people in general are less wealthy and powerful than white people, then they are less able to strain the police and prosecutors. A good example is provided by the case of the Rausings, a very wealthy, white couple who were reported to have been caught in possession of over £2,000 worth of cocaine and some heroin (Camber 2008). They had the wealth to engage lawyers in 'protracted correspondence' (Ibid) with the Crown Prosecution Service. They also had the support of powerful friends, including the Prince of Wales (Lewis 2008). Many people caught with that amount of drugs would have faced imprisonment. The Rausings were given individually tailored conditional cautions. It is less likely that drug offenders with less expensive lawyers and less powerful friends would have benefited from similar treatment. Inequalities between ethnic groups originate in differences in power. Inequalities in the targeting of police resources and in decisions on how to deal with arrestees need not, therefore, arise from direct prejudice. They can come from a realistic assessment of the likely costs and benefits of harming people, given the power they have to bite back. Wider inequalities affect the distribution of this power. They therefore deepen the effect of all the other types of discrimination that black people face.

Confounding race?

The confluence of race and class makes it very hard to examine any 'independent' effect of being black on the likelihood of harsher treatment. Some studies, including one of my own (Flood-Page *et al.* 2000; Stevens 2008a; Waddington *et al.* 2004) have suggested that, although black people are more likely to be stopped and arrested than white people, this difference can be explained (in multivariate analysis) by other variables such as unemployment, being out on the streets and having friends who are in trouble with the police. These statistical analyzes may be of little interest to the people at the sharp end of this process, who accurately perceive that black people are more likely to be arrested for drug offences than white people. For an individual, there is no independent effect of being black. Racism is experienced alongside all the inequalities that go with it. Attempts to isolate the effect of ethnicity in criminal processing risk ignoring the other inequalities that black people face. They 'make a theoretical error by trying to take away the very factors through which race is constituted' (Smith & Smith 1989: 22).

The Hood report (1992) found an independent effect of ethnicity of sentencing severity, even when controlling for other factors. But a later Home Office report (Flood-Page & Mackie 1998) did not. It suggested that differences in sentencing could be entirely explained by factors other than ethnicity. This, alongside an apparent reduction in open expressions of racist attitudes since the 1970s and 1980s (Bowling & Phillips 2002), suggests that, although direct racism in the criminal justice system may be reducing over time, the influences of the other inequalities faced by members of ethnic minorities continue to lead to differential law enforcement. As Bowling and Phillips state:

> [c]riminalisation is the fulcrum of racialised social exclusion; it is where the metaphor of social exclusion is transformed into an explicit, formal social practice and into the personal experience of being literally excluded from society through imprisonment and all that flows from that.
>
> (Ibid: 247)

Drug law enforcement is one of the ways in which this social and racial exclusion is enacted.

Bifurcation in drug law enforcement

In the last chapter, I argued that the concern for public health on English drug policy, which waxed following the AIDS epidemic of the 1980s, has since waned. The discourse that favours criminal justice system responses to drug users has since retaken the lead (see also Stevens 2007a). This is visible in the merging of drug treatment with the criminal justice system, which has occurred through measures such as DTTOs/DRRs and the Drug Interventions Programme. It is also evident in the increased use of police and penal resources to target people who use drugs – and especially black people who use drugs – whether they use them for pleasure or for profit. The available figures suggest that there has been a process of bifurcation. While the government has been talking tough on drugs and imprisoning more and more drug law offenders, it has also been reducing the punishment for the majority of intercepted drug users while simultaneously widening the net of surveillance.

Trends in imprisonment

The most expensive, intensive criminal justice sanction is imprisonment. There has been a substantial increase in the overall prison population of England and Wales, in line with the intensified 'social authoritarianism' that

Joe Sim (2009: 96) describes. A report from the Ministry of Justice (2009c) attributes a large part of the rising prison population to two offence categories: violence and drug offences. Between 1995 and 2007, the number of people sentenced for drug offences rose by 41 per cent and the proportion who received a custodial sentence rose from 17 per cent to 20 per cent. Average sentence lengths for drug offenders have also risen. This has resulted in a rise in the number of people sentenced for drug offences that has been even faster than the rise in the overall prison population. Figure 6.7 shows that between 1996 and 2008, the number of people in prison for drug offences increased by 91 per cent. The increase in the number of people in prison on sentences for other offences was smaller at 53 per cent. Drug offenders made up 16 per cent of the sentenced prison population in June 2008.

In 2008, courts in England and Wales handed out 25,367 years in prison sentences for drug offences (calculated from Ministry of Justice 2009a). If we use a conservative estimate of the current cost of a year in prison at £41,000 (Eagle 2009), assume that prisoners serve half their sentence and exclude the cost of arrest, prosecution, sentencing and post-release supervision, then the annual cost of this use of imprisonment was £520 million. For comparison, total central and devolved government expenditure on drug treatment in England and Wales in 2008/9 was £423 million (NTA 2008; WAG 2008). An internal government report on the 'value for money' of the drug strategy included the cost of treatment but excluded the cost of imprisonment of drug law offenders (Home Office 2007). The government has given itself a highly distorted picture of public expenditure on drug policy.

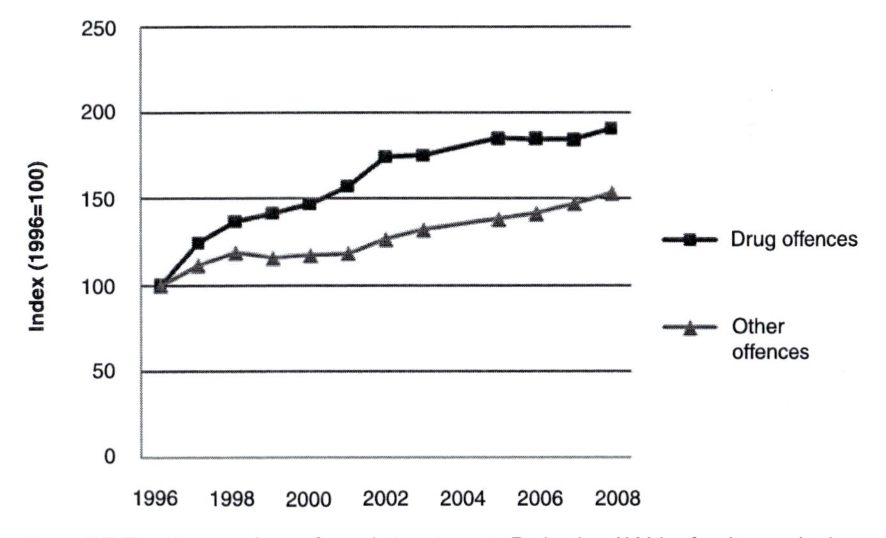

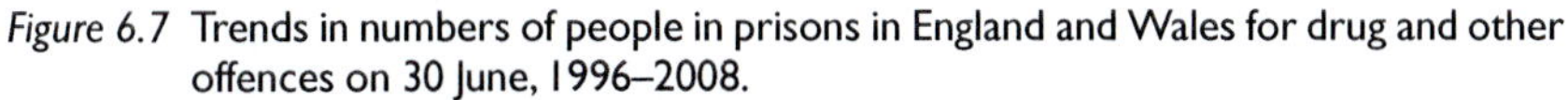
Figure 6.7 Trends in numbers of people in prisons in England and Wales for drug and other offences on 30 June, 1996–2008.

(*Source:* calculated from data provided by Ministry of Justice, Justice Statistics Analytical Services)

The consequences of the rise in imprisonment have fallen heaviest on women, foreign nationals and people of ethnic minority origin, who all face specific pains of imprisonment (Bui 2009b, 2009a; Carlen & Worrall 2004). Between 1996 and 2008, the increase in the number of women in prison sentenced to drug offences was 104 per cent, compared to 90 per cent for men. The increase in foreign nationals imprisoned for these offences was 135 per cent, compared to 23 per cent for British nationals. The increase in the imprisonment for drug offences by ethnicity is shown in Table 6.3 (all these figures are calculated from data provided by Ministry of Justice, Justice Statistics Analytical Services).

The imprisonment of drug suppliers

When we look at the reasons for this rise in the use of imprisonment for drug offenders, we see that it is mostly caused by an increase in the use of imprisonment for traffickers and dealers of class A drugs. Between 1997 and 2008, the number of people sent to prison for class A drug offences rose by 52 per cent. For class B and C drugs combined, it fell by 59 per cent (calculated from figures given by Ward 2009). The increase in the use of imprisonment for class A drug offences fits with the intention of every government, since at least the 1986 Drug Trafficking Offences Act, to come down hard on people who are responsible for the availability of these drugs. Political rhetoric against class A drug traffickers has been effective in increasing the punishments they face. Whether this represents an effective use of public monies is another matter. In early 2009, the government's Sentencing Advisory Panel, drawing on a report that I wrote with Peter Reuter (Reuter & Stevens 2007), argued that there is little evidence to suggest that lengthy sentences for traffickers are effective in restricting the availability of illicit drugs (SAP 2009). In this, they were also echoing the findings of the Prime Minister's Strategy Unit's Birt report on drug policy (PMSU 2003a).

Most of the people who are caught up in this increased use of imprisonment are not the Machiavellian, bling-wearing, Scarface-emulating gangsters

Table 6.3 Breakdown of numbers and trends in convicted offenders in prison for drug offences by ethnic group (at 30th June)

	Number in 2008	*Proportion of total number in 2008*[2]	*Percentage increase since 1996*
White	6,333	58%	59%
Black	2,721	25%	117%
Asian	1,067	10%	345%
Mixed[1]	430	4%	

1 Data not available for 1996
2 Column does not total 100% due to other category and missing data

of drug peddling, rap video legend. Few drug dealers can expect to live a life of consumerist luxury, however hard they wish for it (Hall *et al.* 2008). Rates of pay for street level dealers are often low (Levitt & Venkatesh 2000). Most of the profits end up being spent on quick thrills or an increasing drug habit. The drug dealers I have interviewed (who were, admittedly, so unsuccessful at it that they had had to resort to methadone to sustain their own dependence) tended to express a world-weary cynicism about the trade. They felt no particular shame at supplying potentially lethal drugs to people who were very keen to buy them. They saw dealing as preferable to financing their habits by going out and stealing other people's property. Ending their own use of opiates was not, in their pin-pupilled eyes, a realistic alternative.

My experience of working with imprisoned British drug smugglers, as a caseworker with the charity Prisoners Abroad in the early 1990s, was that most of them were low level, poorly paid employees. Their rarely arrested bosses were making far more money than the couriers stood to gain from their unsuccessful attempts to get drugs into the UK. Many were caught at the ports to the English Channel with a few kilograms of cannabis resin, or a few hundred ecstasy tablets. They were often family men, struggling to pay mortgages or other debts by whatever means they could. Outside prison, they had wives who strived to keep families together in their husband's absence. These families were relatively well off, compared to those of hundreds of women from the Caribbean, Latin America and West Africa who have been arrested in the UK and sentenced to lengthy terms – frequently over twelve years – for their attempts to bring in class A drugs (Heaven & Hudson 2005). Often oblivious to the sentences they face, and to the harms that the drugs they carry can cause, these women come to believe that smuggling offers them a quick route out of harsh, enduring poverty (Green 1991). They leave their children behind, hoping to return in a short while with enough money to start a decent life. For many of them, these dreams are interrupted at Heathrow Airport, where an official pulls them out of the line at customs and conducts an internal examination. From there, it is a long, depressing journey through years spent in HMP Holloway and other prisons, before eventual deportation and the attempt to find out how their children have survived the intervening separation (see Sudbury 2005).

The graphs in this chapter do not just reflect numbers compiled by courts and their clerks. They represent pains that are written on people's minds and bodies. This infliction of pain is not justified by the attempt to reduce the other pains experienced by some drug users and their families, as there is so little evidence that it does anything to reduce them.

Net-widening for cannabis users

In the last chapter, I described the woeful kerfuffle over cannabis classification. Charlie Lloyd has written that this was 'full of sound and fury, signifying nothing' (Lloyd 2008). It is tempting to agree that the 2004 downward classification and simultaneous changes on powers of arrest and formal warnings seemed to be 'self-cancelling' (Warburton *et al.* 2005b: 116), but it is important to examine their actual effects.

Hamish Warburton and his colleagues interviewed 150 serving police officers. Before reclassification, many police officers reported that they would ignore cannabis possession offences. They saw arresting people for small amounts as a waste of time, unless there was another good reason for arrest. These reasons included whether the person was a known offender, whether they failed the 'attitude test' by not being appropriately apologetic, or if in other ways they fitted the 'stereotype' of the sort of person that the police should arrest. Sixty-nine per cent of the officers reported that they had at some point informally avoided arresting a suspect for cannabis possession. So there was a large number of cannabis users who were avoiding any formal action by the police, even when they were caught in possession. This may have had something to do with the fact that half of the interviewed police officers acknowledged that they had themselves used cannabis. These officers were the most likely to use informal disposals for cannabis offences.

On the basis of their interviews, Warburton *et al.* predicted that the 2004 reclassification could lead to one of two paths being followed. There would either be 'net-widening' or 'selective decriminalization' (Ibid: 124). Net-widening would occur if formal warnings were given to people who previously would have had their offences ignored. Selective decriminalization would involve police officers interpreting the downward classification as a licence to ignore a larger number of offences, and expanding their selective discretion by not even issuing formal warnings to people whom they thought did not deserve them.

It is very important to remember that the police retain discretion as to whether to issue a warning. If the offender is caught smoking cannabis in a public place, in an area where there is a 'locally identified problem', or where it is necessary for 'protecting young people', then they can still decide to arrest (ACPO 2009). So they can still use cannabis possession as a reason to arrest the 'usual suspects' (McAra & McVie 2005) for further interrogation. In a follow-up to the Warburton *et al.* (2005b) study, May *et al.* (2007) found that police practice varied between areas. In one of the four sites they studied after the 2004 reclassification, officers continued to arrest cannabis users as a means to disrupt the street market.

Now, in 2010, we can see whether either of Warburton *et al.*'s 2005 predictions came true. Figure 6.8 shows that there was a steep rise in the number of formal warnings given for cannabis after their introduction in 2004. Between 2000 and 2007, the number of people receiving some form of intervention from the criminal justice system for cannabis offences increased by 92 per cent. The net of formal response to cannabis use has indeed expanded. As cannabis use has apparently been falling in this period (Hoare 2009), it is very

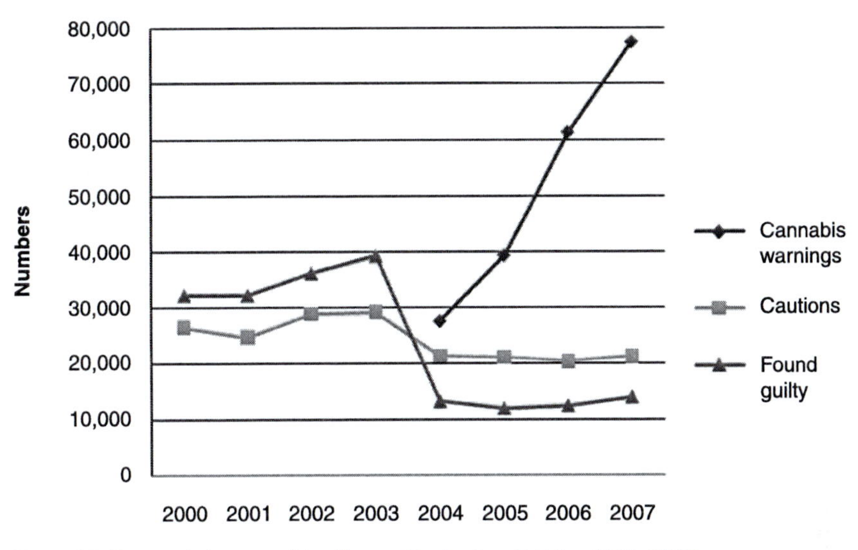

Figure 6.8 Disposals for cannabis offences, England and Wales, 2000–2007.

(*Source:* data provided by Ministry of Justice Office for Analytical Services)

likely that this increase is caused by the police giving formal warnings for offences that would previously have been informally ignored. However, when looking at nets of social control, we need to look at the tightness of the mesh as well as their width (Cohen 1985). The mesh of the cannabis warning is currently very loose indeed. It leads to no action being taken against the offender and does not create a criminal record. In January 2009, guidance was tightened to require the police to issue a penalty notice for disorder (in effect, a fine of £80) if a person who has previously been warned is again found in possession of cannabis. But there was no central system in place for recording warnings, so people could receive them again and again as long as they were not recognized in person.

From 2011, the government has promised that there will be a database (known as PentiP) to record all the people who receive cannabis warnings and penalty notices for disorder. So, even if no direct pain is inflicted on the vast majority of the increasing numbers of people who are formally dealt with for cannabis, they will find themselves subject to more intensive surveillance than has previously been possible. Whether such surveillance will have any effect in reducing drug or other offences is highly debatable.[52]

Formal police contact with cannabis users has been expanded. But most of this contact has very low impact. These developments have led to a situation where a lower proportion of drug users intercepted by the police had any type of obligation placed upon them in England and Wales than in Portugal, where possession of all illicit drugs has been officially decriminalized. In

Portugal (in 2007), 18 per cent of people who had formal contact with the police for drug offences had to pay a fine, undergo treatment or some other restriction of their liberty. In England and Wales (in 2006), this proportion was 15 per cent (EMCDDA 2009b).

If we look at cannabis policy in the wider context of drug policy, we can see that there has been 'selective decriminalization', but not in the way suggested by Warburton *et al.* There has been an increase in the imprisonment of drug offenders. This has particularly affected Asian, black, female and foreign national drug offenders. However, two categories of drug users have been allowed to slip through this expanding net. Repentant users of heroin and crack are encouraged to go into treatment. If they succeed there, then they can avoid the more punitive forms of social control. And users of cannabis – as long as they show a suitably apologetic attitude and do not fit the poor, dishevelled category of 'police property' (Lee 1981) – are simply recorded and allowed to go on their way. This process is highly selective. It again enforces an imaginary fragmentation between the people who use drugs. They are placed in categories that are either guilty of undermining society, and so are penally excluded, or capable of reintegration into the social body, and so given the chance to prove their worth under supervision.

Stan Cohen correctly predicted the development of a 'political ideology which will insist on a rigid bifurcatory and punitive agenda in order to command legitimacy' (Cohen 1985: 234). He saw bifurcation in the development of crime control policies that have both hard and soft ends, which are 'symbiotically related' (Ibid: 99). The hard end is there to deter offenders and reassure the public, while the soft end expands – at lower cost – the number of people who come under the supervisory gaze of the state. As the imprisonment rate has climbed, and arguments over the classification of various drugs have raged, the police have quietly been increasing the number of drug users that they formally intercept, while reducing the proportion that have anything done to them. Both the hard and the soft ends of drug control have expanded.

The bifurcation has been done covertly. Politicians have talked tough on drugs. They have refused to countenance any form of explicit decriminalization. While he was Home Secretary, Charles Clarke (2005) stated that 'I do not believe that decriminalizing drug abuse is the right approach. Indeed, it is the exact opposite of the right approach'. Behind the rhetoric, there has been a formal recognition of the futility of arresting large numbers of drug users. The government has found a way to depenalize the majority of drug use, without openly decriminalizing drug possession. It has done so in a way that has done nothing to challenge the image of drug users as threats to the social order. It has 'fed the wolf' of public punitivity (Green 2009a). Public support for the criminalization of cannabis users appears to have increased (Bailey *et al.* 2010). Some drug users, many of them from the middle classes, have benefited from this bifurcation. Others have not. The use of state powers to control the people whose precarious, risky lives are seen as threatening has again increased the systematically unequal distribution of power between social, ethnic and gender groups which drug policy sustains, both discursively and in its practical effects.

The effects of English drug policy

In advance of the concluding chapter of this book, we can start to draw the threads of the argument together. Drug use is distributed throughout society, but the harms of drug use and control are experienced more frequently by the poor. Crime is one such harm, but it is not caused directly by the drugs. Rather, it often happens alongside problematic drug use in the communities that have been worst affected by globalization and deindustrialization. Policy makers have used the harms related to drug use to tell selective policy stories. These stories emphasize the drug-crime link and minimize the inequality-harm link. The resulting policies have led to increased availability of drug treatment, including treatment of drug users who have committed other crimes. This has had benefits, in terms of reduced drug use and offending, for many people. But the flip-side of the focus on drugs as a criminal problem has been a large increase in the use of the criminal justice system to inflict punishment on people for drug and other offences. This has not been reduced by the increased use of treatment 'alternatives' to prison. First imprisonment of drug offenders soared. Then there was a huge increase in the number of drug users who are formally intercepted by the police. Disproportionate targeting of people of African or Caribbean origins and other visible minorities means that it is they who have suffered most from this bifurcatory expansion of control. Many women and people from other countries have also suffered particular pains in this exercise. This is a sorry picture. Millions of pounds wasted. Thousands of people deliberately harmed. And to what end? Proponents of the criminalization of drug policy argue that it is necessary to reduce drug use and related harms. Before we conclude this argument, we need to test such claims against international evidence. This suggests that drug control policies are not justified by their effects on drug use and related problems. It reinforces the claim that other social arrangements are more important in reducing drug-related harms.

Chapter 7

International perspectives

Does drug policy matter?

Drug policy is inherently international. Drugs are transported across national borders, and so are the measures that are taken to control them. The international framework created by the various UN conventions limits the freedom of signatory states to try different policies, but there is still some 'room for manoeuvre' (Dorn & Jamieson 2000). Different countries have tried different mixtures of penal, public health and other measures to limit the harms associated with drugs. This chapter will attempt to draw some lessons from these various attempts. It will compare the available figures on the effects of drug policies against the aims of reducing drug use and the harms associated with it. Comparison in this area is very tricky. Countries have very different legal and historical contexts. Their indicators are often measured differently. It is important to be alert to the national peculiarities, policies and outcomes (Newburn & Sparks 2004). This chapter will show that through all these specificities, two general propositions stand out. The first is that drug policy appears not to be the most important determinant of drug use or problems, although it can affect the harms related to drug use. The second is that levels of inequality and social support are probably more important in alleviating drug problems than drug policy is.

United States of America: the failure of mass incarceration

The USA has the highest level of income inequality and the lowest level of decommodification[53] in the developed world (Scruggs & Allan 2006). If its citizens cannot pay for basic goods and services through employment, inheritance or crime, then they face a tough struggle to live a decent life. In view of the subterranean structuration of drugs and crime (see Chapter 3), it is not therefore surprising that the USA also has a substantial drug problem. The USA has been the most enthusiastic country in fighting a drug war against its own people, as well as those of other countries. The imbalance between the resources spent on drug law enforcement, as against treatment and prevention, is large and enduring. In the federal drug control budget for fiscal year 2011, for example, $7.6 billion were devoted to law enforcement and interdiction, with $5.6 billion for treatment and prevention (ONDCP 2010). The imbalance in federal funding was in the opposite direction in Richard Nixon's first presidential term. At the beginning of his 'war on drugs', half the drug control budget was devoted to treatment and rehabilitation, with only 30 per cent going to law enforcement. Nixon boosted spending on law enforcement. Under the Reagan administration, drug treatment expenditure shrank while law enforcement funding continued to increase. Demand reduction spending reduced to less than 20 per cent of the federal drug control budget by 1985 (Benoit 2003).

These budgets do not include the enormous costs incurred by the states in imprisoning drug law offenders. There are over two million people imprisoned in the USA. About 360,000 people are there for drug offences. Over seven million people are under correctional supervision (including those on probation or parole). This means that one in every 31 Americans is under some form of penal supervision. Although the rate of expansion is slowing, the US prison population has increased every year since 1972, placing massive burdens on state budgets and inflicting substantial harms on prisoners, their families and their communities.

Alongside the huge growth in imprisonment, there has also been an expansion of less visible punishments, including disenfranchisement, withdrawal of welfare benefits and student loans, restrictions on driving licences and exclusion from a wide range of occupations. The growth in incarceration and these 'invisible punishments' for drug offences have both disproportionately affected women and African and Latino Americans. These are the people who suffered the fastest increases in these forms of penal exclusion in the 1980s and 1990s (Chesney-Lind 2002; Travis 2002). This disproportionate increase has slowed, and then reversed in recent years, especially for African American women. The number of all African Americans in prison has actually fallen since 2002 as the number of people in prison for crack has reduced. But it still leaves a rate of imprisonment which is 6.5 times higher for African American men than white men, and three times higher for African American women (Sabol *et al.* 2009).

Harsh enforcement reduces drug problems?

Other effects of US drug policy are less well publicized. These include the limited availability of harm reduction services. The ban on federal funding of needle exchange programmes, which was only overturned late in 2009, has limited the provision of effective services to people who need them. This has led to unnecessarily high rates of HIV amongst injecting drug users.

The US government claims some success from its efforts. Attention is often drawn, for example, to the fall in levels of drug use amongst high school seniors since 1979 (e.g. Kerlikowske 2009a). A more detailed look at levels of drug use and related problems suggests that the massive expense and harms of the USA's repressive, retributive approach to illicit drugs have not produced good outcomes. Figures 7.1 and 7.2 give international comparisons on rates of drug use and of problematic drug use. They show that the USA has

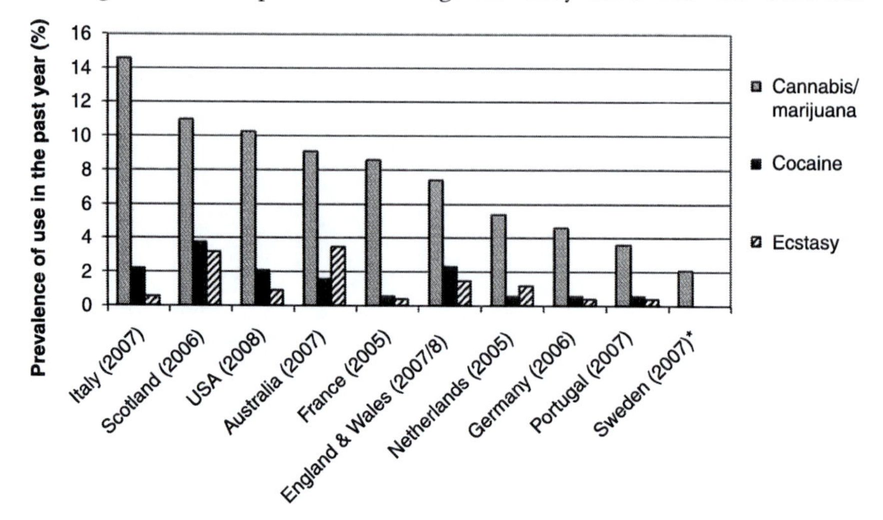

Figure 7.1 Estimated rates of past year drug use reported in national surveys (methods vary).

(*Sources:* EMCDDA 2009a, SAMHSA 2009a, AIHW 2008).
* Data not available for cocaine and ecstasy use in Sweden.

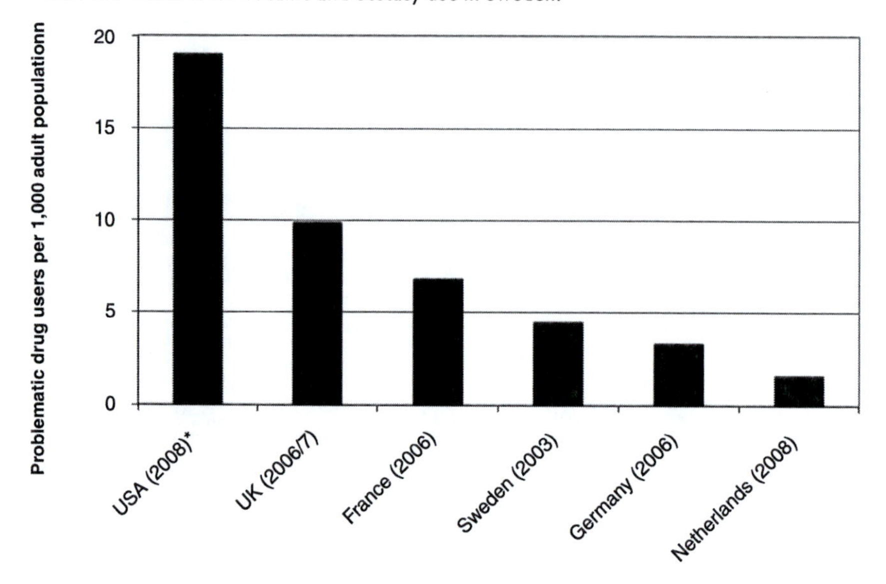

Figure 7.2 Estimated rates of problematic drug use (methods vary).

(*Sources:* EMCDDA 2009a, SAMHSA 2009a, Cruts & Van Laar 2010).
* Estimate of dependent illicit drug users.

internationally high rates of both use and problematic use. If we look at trends in reported use of all illicit drugs (Figure 7.3), we see that there have been fluctuations since the 1979 peak. However, there are various problems with the surveys that have produced these figures and it is more important to look at indicators of harm, rather than indicators of use (Boyum & Reuter 2005).

The Drug Abuse Warning Network (DAWN) collects data on the number of drug-related visits to hospital emergency departments in a sample of US cities. The methods changed in 2003, meaning that DAWN figures after this date are not comparable to those from before. However, Figure 7.4 clearly shows that there was a huge increase in the emergency department visits that

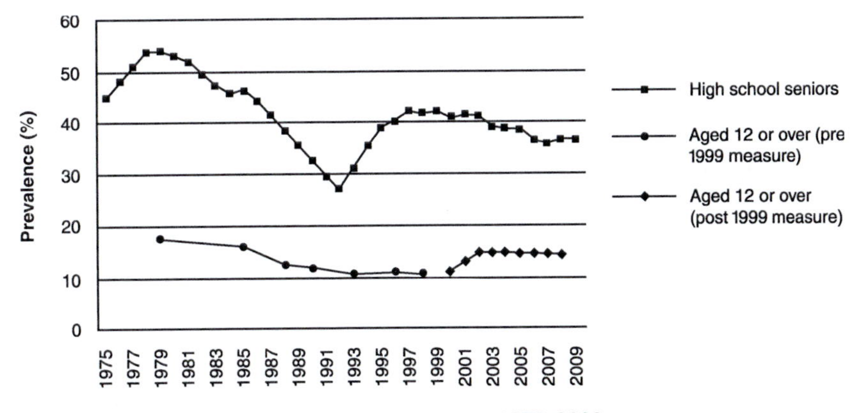

Figure 7.3 Reported past year use of any illicit drug, 1975–2009.

(*Sources:* National Survey on Drug Use and Health and Monitoring the Future. Johnston *et al.* 2009; MTF 2009; SAMHSA 2009b).

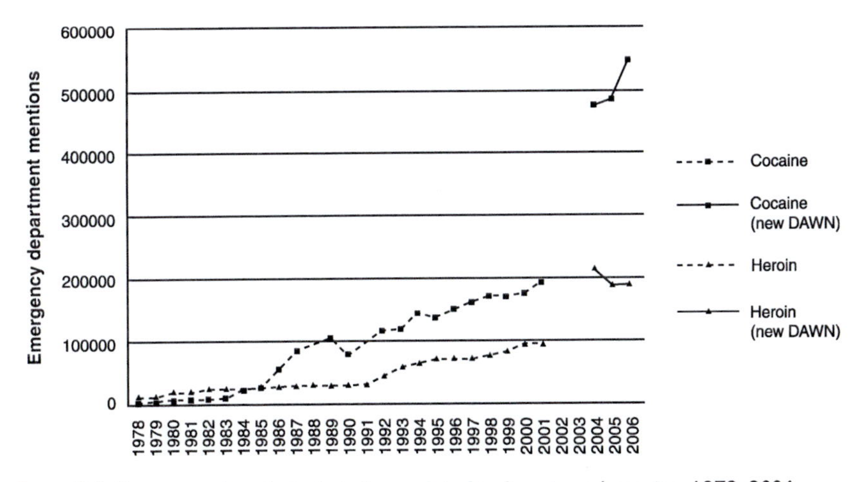

Figure 7.4 Emergency hospital admissions related to heroin and cocaine, 1978–2006.

(*Sources:* NIDA 1987; SAMHSA 2003).

are related to heroin and cocaine after 1979. There was also a steep rise in drug-related deaths (see Figure 7.5). By the early 2000s, drug-induced deaths were more prevalent than deaths induced by alcohol (Paulozzi & Annest 2007). Many of these deaths are related to prescribed opioid painkillers, which have shown dramatic rises in both availability and mortality (Paulozzi 2006; Wisniewski *et al.* 2008). As Drucker (1999) noted, the massive expansion of incarceration has not resulted in a reduction in the most serious drug-related harms, even if drug use overall has fallen.

Explaining incarceration

So if this repressive drug policy has so plainly failed to reduce the burden of drug-related harms, how do we explain its long-standing commitment to the use of law enforcement and penal exclusion as its primary tools? The foremost critic of prohibition in the USA has argued that it is due to a strong cultural attachment to the ideal (if not the practice) of temperance (Nadelmann 2009). Michael Tonry (2009) also highlights the effect of fundamentalist Protestant beliefs which divide the population between worthy citizens and unwelcome freeloaders. With its specifically Protestant origins, the culture[54] of the USA has been more influenced by the call to curtail sensory pleasures in favour of embodying the purity of scripture. This contrasts with European cultures which retain the influence of mediaeval Catholicism in celebrating the sensuous carnality of consumption (Mellor & Shilling 1997). As Max

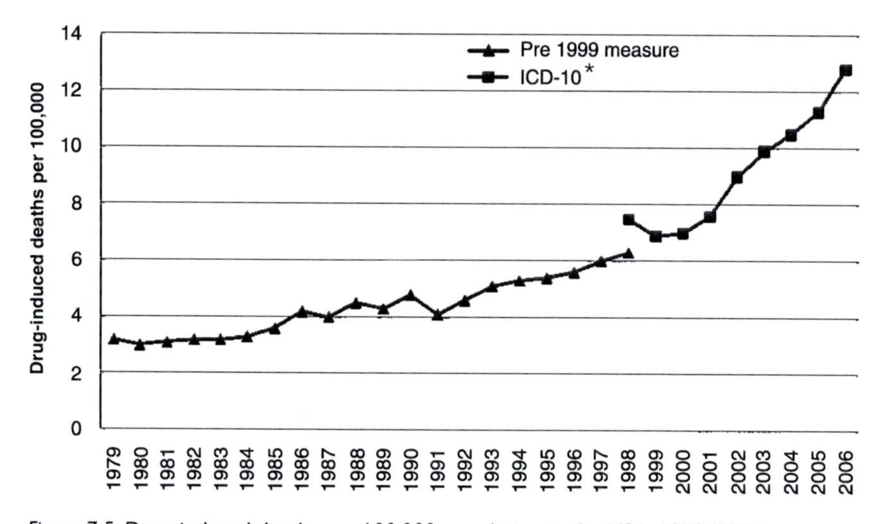

Figure 7.5 Drug-induced deaths per 100,000 population in the USA, 1979–2006.

(*Source:* Annual National Vital Statistics).

* ICD-10 is the International Statistical Classification of Diseases and Related Health Problems. It includes a specific definition of drug related death.

Weber (1920) noted from his American travels, the less-contested influence of Protestantism also led to a purer form of capitalism in the USA. The broader social base of the capitalist 'spirit' in the USA, and the individualism it inspired, has led to less intervention by the state in providing healthcare and welfare support. The predilection for social exclusion of unworthy outsiders can be seen today in at least two areas of American life. The massive use of imprisonment is one. The tendency to exclude people from access to healthcare is another. The idea that people must earn social rights rather than be granted them by virtue of their citizenship or humanity continues to contaminate US public policy, as was seen in the ugly debate of 2009/10 over President Obama's healthcare plans. Continued use of illicit drugs marks people out as being unworthy of inclusion in the main body of US society. Maintaining repressive drug policies is, according to this view, about maintaining the separation between saved believers in the wholesome American dream and the intemperate, undeserving outsiders who threaten it.

This approach is persuasive, but it cannot on its own explain the particular, exceptional form of mass incarceration to which US drug policy has contributed. Drug users could be kept beyond the pale without mass imprisonment, for example, through stigmatizing practices of compulsory treatment and police harassment. Indeed, this was the actual practice in the USA before President Nixon declared war on drugs. A massive apparatus of penal supervision and control has since been created in which to place drug users and sellers for increasing periods of servitude. There are other explanations for this rise of the US carceral state. Jonathan Simon (2007) has, for example, argued that Nixon used drug policy as a political tactic against Democrat opponents who had become associated with the drug-taking culture of the anti-Vietnam war movement. Nixon carried out his own exaggeration of the drug-crime link, claiming that drug-related crime cost the nation about $18 billion per year, even though this was more than 25 times the value of all unrecovered property reported stolen in the USA in 1971 (Epstein 1977). By identifying drugs as 'public enemy number one' to the 'silent majority' of American society, he could implicate his opponents as being similar menaces. He could also use federal funding of the drug war to build a new political network, reaching around Congress and state governments to impose his presidential authority at ground level. Politicians since Nixon have continued to deploy drug policy as a political weapon. Even when caught with their hands firmly stuffed in the illicit drug industry's overflowing till – as the Reagan administration was at the time of Oliver North's campaign against the Nicaraguan government (Sub-Committee On Terrorism, Narcotics and International Operations 1989) – they still continued to lock up increasing numbers of Americans, and especially African Americans, in order to display how firmly they stood against moral corruption. They simultaneously hacked away at the institutions of social security that had been built by the 1930s New Deal and the 1960s War on Poverty. Their legacy is the existence of the prison as the only provider of housing, welfare and healthcare services to large numbers of US citizens (Comfort 2008).

David Garland (2001) and Jock Young (1999) have offered explanations that have focused on the socio-economic and cultural changes associated with the transition to late modernity in American (and British) society. Advanced capitalism has weakened ties between employers and employees. It has restructured both the family and the city. Mass commercial communication exposes us all to myriad choices, but a common consumerist imperative. There has been a rise in both individualism and inequality and a decline in moral absolutes. This means that the state needs new tools to establish its own legitimacy. Imprisonment of young, unemployed minorities provides such a tool, especially when it satisfies the vindictive thirst for punishment that is inspired by a general decrease in feelings of security. Repressive drug laws fit this bill perfectly. Bruce Western (2004) has argued, against Garland, that the rise in imprisonment must be seen as a cause, and not just an effect, of changes in the functioning of American capitalism. He points to the contradiction between the apparent fiscal conservatism of neo-liberal politics and the massive expenditure of taxpayers' money on imprisonment. This, he argues, shows that mass incarceration is a moral enterprise, partly based on racism against African Americans, which has had the economic effect of deepening class and ethnic inequalities. Ruth Gilmore pushes the structural analysis of prison expansion further in arguing that it has enabled the state to mobilize idle surpluses of land, capital and people in responding to the social and economic crises of late capitalism. She presents the building of a string of prisons in rural California as a way of 'putting half the population into prisons so the other half can make money watching them' (Gilmore 2007: 208). The expansion of imprisonment has been one solution to the inability of the US economy to create jobs for its growing population. In the decade from May 1999, it seems that the number of jobs in the private sector actually shrank, if the government-supported sectors of education and healthcare are excluded (Mandel 2009). US state and federal governments have used prisons to substitute for the millions of manufacturing and other jobs that have been moved abroad by US corporations. Many of the people who would in the past have filled these jobs are now either working or languishing in correctional institutions.

Bifurcation in the USA

So religion, politics, culture, and neo-Marxist economics all provide potential explanations for the use of a drug policy tool – mass incarceration – which has so obviously failed to reduce drug-related harms. But we need to be careful. In a country as huge and diverse as the USA, there are bound to be developments which go against the dominant trend. For example, it is surprising to many outsiders that the USA contains one of the longest experiences of cannabis decriminalization. In 1975, the Supreme Court of Alaska ruled that the criminalization of possession of marijuana in one's own home breached the right to privacy that is enshrined in the state's constitution. Some other states – including California, Colorado, Maine, Minnesota, Mississippi, Nebraska, Nevada, New York, North Carolina, Ohio and Oregon – have also decriminalized personal possession of marijuana (Faupel *et al.* 2004). Some use civil fines and retain criminal penalties for repeat offenders and for smoking marijuana in public. The evidence suggests that cannabis use has not been permanently increased by decriminalization in these states (Single *et al.* 2000), although this has been disputed by researchers who argue that it is difficult to test the effects of decriminalization, given the variety of its forms between states, and the fact that most 'non-decriminalized' states have also reduced their penalties for possession of marijuana (Pacula *et al.* 2004). The apparent lack of differences between states may be explained by the fact that citizens of these states are not very well informed about whether cannabis has been decriminalized or not (MacCoun *et al.* 2008).

There are also several states, California being the most prominent, that have enabled marijuana to be purchased legally for medical use. The definition of medical use has become so broad that, in effect, anyone who can both afford the registration fees and convince a doctor that they are in need of pain relief can get a legal supply of marijuana in some areas of these states. However, people living in housing supported by the the United States Department of Housing and Urban Development (HUD) can have their tenancies ended for using this marijuana, under HUD's 'one strike and you're out' policy. Here we see an American example of bifurcation (Cohen 1985). US drug policy has always chosen its targets. Early laws, from the 1875 San Francisco Opium Ordinance to the 1951 Boggs Act, were firmly targeted at drugs and drug users who were perceived as foreign, and not at the domestic users of similar substances (ACLU 2003). Ruth Peterson's (1985) analysis of the 1970 Comprehensive Drug Abuse Prevention and Control Act showed how penalties for marijuana possession were reduced. She argues that this was done with the intent of protecting middle and upper class drug users (referred to in one Congressional hearing as the 'cream of American youth' [Ibid: 256]). Penalties were increased for dealers and traffickers, who were seen as 'enemy deviants' (Ibid: 243). Under contemporary US policy, most dealers and many users (especially if they live in public housing) are liable to be dealt with very firmly, even where marijuana has been decriminalized or legalized for medical use. But some marijuana users and dealers – those who can afford the fees and will submit to medical and state supervision – have legal access to the drug.

Collateral damage

These countervailing examples, then, show that the main thrust of US drug policy still bears down most heavily on the socially and racially marginalized residents of the deindustrialized American city (Wacquant 2006). Large disparities in marijuana arrest rates (e.g. Johnson *et al.* 2008; Levine 2009) and between sentences for crack and powder cocaine (Sabet 2005) mean that the US war on drugs has had its most damaging effects amongst African and Latino Americans. Far from reducing harm, US drug policy has done the opposite. It has damaged the lives of millions of American citizens. It has deprived them of liberty, welfare, education and the right to vote in many states. And it is not just those people who are caught up in the drug war crossfire that suffer these harms (Mauer & Chesney-Lind 2002). The consequences of US drug policy on state budgets and voting patterns mean that it has damaged all Americans who rely on public services for their education, welfare and healthcare. For example, California, which built up its carceral archipelago while credit capital was plentiful, now faces an extreme budget deficit. Governor Schwarzenegger's initial solution to the crisis was to cut $8.6 billion from public education, raise the taxes of low and middle income Californians, but leave the prison budget untouched (Woo & Scheck 2009).[55] The University of California, which has doubled its tuition fees since 1998, was forced to accept a 20 per cent cut in its budget (O'Leary 2009). After several years of squeezes in the education budget, the proportion of Californians over 25 who have graduated high school dropped lower than in 48 other states (Mortenson 2009). As prisons struggle to accommodate the large numbers of poor Californians who are sent to them by the courts for drug offences, the availability and quality of public education – which would otherwise offer them a way out of poverty and crime – is being reduced.[56]

Another example of the damage done beyond the criminal justice system is the effect of drug policy on election results. The Fourteenth Amendment of the US Constitution enables states to stop rebels and other criminals voting. This power was largely targeted at black people in the late nineteenth century (Mauer 2002) as rich, white people found ways to replace slavery as a method of social and labour control in the southern states (Blackmon 2008). It has since expanded so far that over five million Americans have lost the right to vote, about one third of them drug offenders. They are still disproportionately southern, African Americans. The state with the highest number of disenfranchised persons is Florida. Manza and Uggen (2006) calculated that if these 827,000 people had voted at the low level of turnout but with the high rate of Democrat preference estimated from surveys, then Al Gore would easily have won Florida and so denied victory to George W. Bush in the 2000 presidential election. Across the states that have disenfranchised felons and ex-felons there have been tight elections that have turned on the exclusion of these citizens – always in favour of the Republican candidate. Even more insidiously, these people are counted when totting up representation in Congress and in the presidential Electoral College, even though they cannot vote.[57] This further distorts democratic representation. The combined effect is that southern Republicans and their allies have been able more easily to impose policies of penal repression and welfare restriction on the rest of the USA.

Change we can believe in?

The defeat of this political coalition by President Obama has sparked hope that the US drug war might be brought to an end. The repeal of the ban on federal funding of needle exchanges, moves to end the crack/powder cocaine sentencing disparity, the appointment of a relatively liberal team at the head of the Office of National Drug Control Policy (ONDCP)[58] and the spread of medical marijuana legislation all support this optimism, as does the President's personal insight into the reasons why people use drugs (see Chapter 3). He did not campaign on law and order, unlike Bill Clinton (Teague 2009).[59] Instead, Obama chose to highlight the issue of racial disparities in the prison population. His deep awareness of the scars left on the American psyche by racism and slavery (see Obama 2008) equips him to take on the task of reducing their enduring effects.

The huge costs of incarceration may lead to a loss of political popularity for penal policies in times of shrinking public expenditure. A broad and effective alliance of social progressives and fiscal conservatives may be built, as has long been the aim of reformers like the Drug Policy Alliance. But cutting prison budgets is not an inevitable outcome of financial crisis. If the USA's repressive drug policies are, as has been suggested, the result of deep moral attachments to Protestant temperance, political and cultural preferences for punishment (especially of people of colour) and structural adjustments to the systemic underemployment of labour, then President Obama is going to find it difficult to limit the penal complex of drug control. His scope for action in this area is limited, as much of the policy is made at state level. His political capital has already been weakened in the struggle for healthcare reform. It faces further evaporation in the attempt to get carbon emission cuts agreed by the Senate. It will bleed away entirely if the Afghanistan war turns into a Vietnam-style defeat. Will he risk spending any more of this precious capital on a dismantling of repressive drug controls that will leave him open to rhetorical attack for being soft on crime? After all, the factors that led to the US expansion of imprisonment are still in place (Tonry 2009). To a pessimist, it would seem more likely that US drug policy will continue to be intrusive, divisive, expensive and ineffective (Boyum & Reuter 2005).

Sweden: an example of effective, restrictive policies?

If the USA cannot provide an example of effective drug prohibition, maybe other countries can. The United Nations Office on Drugs and Crime has searched the world and settled on Sweden as the poster country for the repressive approach outlined in UN drug conventions. In 2007, UNODC Director Antonio Maria Costa lauded Swedish drug policy. In the foreword to a report on 'Sweden's successful drug policy', he wrote, 'government is responsible for the size of the drug problem in its country. Societies often have the drug problem they deserve' (UNODC 2007: 5).

The official UN story was that Sweden had a liberal approach until Nils Bejerot and his Association for a Drug-Free Sweden called, in 1969, for the criminalization of both drug trafficking and use. Drug laws were gradually tightened. In 1972, the maximum prison sentence for drug offences was raised to ten years. In 1981, legal provisions for compulsory treatment were introduced. In 1988, drug use itself became punishable (not just possession). The Swedish government has refused to distinguish between 'hard' and 'soft' drugs, targeting cannabis as both harmful in itself and as the 'stepping stone' to other drugs. It is the second highest spender on drug policy in Europe (Ibid).[60] In UN negotiations, it has argued for stringent limitations on all classes of drugs, especially stimulants (Sweden's main problematic drugs have historically been amphetamines). On joining the European Union in 1995, Sweden argued strongly for the prohibitionist approach, causing a split in EU drug policy discussions (Chatwin 2003).

The UNODC (2007) attributed several results to Sweden's 'stringent' approach. Rates of drug use are lower amongst adults and young people than in the late 1960s, despite an increase in the 1990s that the UNODC attributed to an economic slowdown and cuts on healthcare spending. Drug-related deaths have fallen since 2001. Rates of reported drug use, problematic use, availability and HIV are lower than the European average, and have also been falling. The UNODC concludes by approving Sweden's aim of creating a drug-free society: 'It is perhaps that ambitious vision that has enabled Sweden to achieve this remarkable result' (Ibid: 52). It neglects to mention the significant expansion of substitution treatment, outpatient care and the provision of housing to problematic drug users that has followed advocacy of greater moves to harm reduction within Sweden (Blomqvist *et al.* 2009).

The UN's view of cause and effect in the Swedish drug situation is highly controversial. A long-time proponent of more liberal European drug policies, Peter Cohen, was quick to give his critique of the UNODC's story. Commenting on an early version of the published analysis, he 'smelled a rat', accusing 'the work of UNODC to be tailor made to arrive at the conclusion that drug control works' (Cohen 2006). He points out that by comparing levels of drug use to the EU average it would be possible to show that Dutch drug policy is a wonderful success, but that French and US policies are catastrophic failures, if only we are naïve enough to believe both that drug use constitutes the drug problem and that it is directly caused by government policy. Cohen cites Ted Goldberg's report that Sweden's rate of drug-related deaths is relatively high, coming close to the level caused by traffic accidents, as well as Goldberg's (2004) article highlighting the continuing tensions between advocates of prohibition and harm reduction within Sweden.

A more detailed rebuttal of the UNODC report was prepared by Börje Olsson (2009) for a conference which took place at the UNODC building in Vienna. He argued that the largest reductions in drug use happened *before* 1969. This is plainly visible in a graph included in the report (UNODC 2007: 25). Olsson accused Nils Bejerot – who takes the UNODC's credit for inspiring Sweden's drug-free policy – of being an unscientific moral entrepreneur who made three erroneous claims. They were: that permissive drug policies lead to increased drug use; that police targeting of users and dealers reduces drug use; and that any drug use by young people is a stepping stone to problematic use. Olsson cites Swedish studies that refute the first two claims. He challenges the 'stepping stone' theory by pointing out that problematic drug use continued to rise, even while drug use among young people was falling. If the theory were correct, then problematic use should have fallen in line with other drug use.

Both Olsson and Cohen accuse the UNODC of hand-picking data in order to support the hypothesis that restrictive policies cause reductions in levels of drug use. There is no evidence to suggest that such policies caused the fall in drug use before 1969, as they were not used in Sweden at the time. The rise in drug use in the 1990s, which the UNODC explains away as being a product of economic changes, actually happened at what Olsson identifies as the high point of police forces' action against drug use. In 1993, they started using drug tests and so discovering and prosecuting more users. Olsson further argues that more recent data suggests that problematic drug use has risen since 2004 and that deaths began to rise in 2007. The UNODC report only includes data up to 2003.

We can add a comparison with the USA to this critique. If restrictive drug policies cause lower rates of drug use, then should not stricter restrictions lead to the lowest levels of use? What the US example shows us, in contrast to this hypothesis, is that rates of marijuana use increased in the 1990s at a time of substantial expansion in the rate of arrests of marijuana users (King & Mauer 2006). The maximum sentence in Sweden for any first-time drug offence, including large-scale trafficking, is ten years. This also happens to be the *minimum* sentence for selling *any* amount of drugs in Alabama, as long as the sale takes place within three miles of both a school[61] and a housing project (Greene *et al.* 2006). The massive difference in sentencing between the USA and Sweden has not reduced drug use in the USA to anywhere near Sweden's low levels. Olsson concludes his demolition of the UNODC report by stating that 'there is no scientific basis to state that the restrictive Swedish drug policy is superior to other policies'. He could have added that there is very little evidence to support the effectiveness of restrictive policies in any country (Babor *et al.* 2010).

The Netherlands: the example of depenalization

The Netherlands was the firmest European opponent of US prohibitionist pressure in the 1920s. It criminalized possession of opium and cocaine in 1928 in order to comply with the Geneva conference resolutions, but rarely enforced these laws (Davenport-Hines 2001). The possession, manufacture and sale of cannabis were eventually prohibited in law in 1953, but various ways have since been tried to avoid criminalization in practice. Crucial to the understanding of these forms of tolerance is the untranslatably Dutch concept of *gedogen* (Uitermark 2004). This refers to activities that are not legal, but are not treated as illegal unless they cause other harms. In the 1960s, use of cannabis and psychedelics in the underground scene was quietly ignored. Youth centres such as Amsterdam's *El Paradiso* emerged from this subculture as a place where drugs were for sale with discreet official connivance (Downes 1988).

As drug use grew, two commissions were set up to examine the issue. The first was led by the prominent abolitionist[62] criminologist, Louk Hulsman, the second by a Chief Inspector of Mental Health, Pieter Baan. They were informed by the work of the social researcher Herman Cohen, who served on both commissions. He argued that drug use is not always deviant or harmful, but that some harms of drug use (e.g. long-term use, dependence and use while at work or driving) are to be avoided. Dutch society was already used to the idea that criminalizing young people did more harm than good. So there was a receptive audience to the similar recommendations of both these commissions – that cannabis users should not be punished. The Hulsman report was more radical, envisioning a longer-term decriminalization of all drugs, but it did not recommend this in the short-term (Cohen 1994). These reports of 1971 and 1972 did not lead to immediate action. The government may have been goaded to take a closer look at their recommendations by the rise in heroin use between 1972 and 1974, which followed the blocking of opium supply and the appearance in Amsterdam of heroin-dependent American GIs from West German military bases (Downes 1988). The eventual revision of the Opium Act in 1976 separated drugs which posed 'unacceptable' risks (cocaine and heroin) from those that posed 'less severe' risks (cannabis and barbiturates). The law retained minimal criminal penalties for possession even of these 'less severe' drugs. The vital development in Dutch drug policy was not this law but the implementation of written guidelines which stated that prosecutors would consider the prosecution of both sale and possession of small amounts of cannabis as their lowest priority. Cannabis was not decriminalized, let alone legalized. It remains a criminal offence to sell and possess cannabis. But Dutch prosecutors have depenalized the drug by deciding not to prosecute these offences under certain conditions.[63]

In the first few years after 1976, there was a gradual development in the number of cannabis sales points. The cannabis market became more commercial in the early 1980s, as more visible coffee shops openly promoted their wares. It is to this commercialization, rather than to the depenalization of cannabis, that MacCoun and Reuter (2001a; 2001b) attribute some of the rise in cannabis use that was seen in the 18–20 age group between 1984 and 1996 (lifetime prevalence rose from 15 per cent in 1984 to 44 per cent in 1996). In their detailed analyzes, these authors acknowledge that other countries also experienced rises in cannabis use in the 1990s. And they point out that rates of drug use were still lower in the Netherlands than in some more restrictive countries (see, for example, Figures 7.1 and 7.2 above). Rates of cannabis use have been fairly stable since the mid 1990s. Admissions to treatment for cannabis have increased, as they have elsewhere in Europe (van Laar & Ooyen-Houben 2009). Increasing restrictions placed on coffee shops in some towns (such as enforcing the rules that prevent them from selling alcohol and closing some that operated near schools or national borders) have reduced their numbers, although they remain more commercialized than had been envisaged by the 1976 reformers (Ibid). In 2007, there were still 702 coffee shops operating in the Netherlands, with at least one of them in 106 of its 443 municipalities (Bieleman *et al.* 2008). In 2009, there were moves by conservative local politicians to close all the coffee shops in the towns of Roosendaal, Bergen op Zoom and in the province of Limburg, as well as to reduce their numbers in both Rotterdam and Amsterdam.

Meanwhile, the heroin market has been dealt with through other means. In the late 1970s, it was hoped that the separation of the heroin market from young cannabis users, combined with the provision of methadone treatment and subsidies to drug user organizations would be enough to limit the problem. This has been characterized as an era of 'limitless tolerance' (Downes 1988: 139). But corruption in the drug user organizations and police frustrations with continued drug dealing led to cynicism that this approach could work. It was superseded from about 1980 by a policy of 'controlled tolerance' (Ibid: 140). City authorities would no longer subsidize community organizations without financial oversight and representation on the board. Methadone programmes continued, and indeed were ramped up, but open street dealing of heroin would no longer be permitted. After the success of the trials of heroin assisted therapy in Switzerland (Uchtenhagen *et al.* 1997) it was imported to the Netherlands and found to be effective in improving the health and reducing the offending of its carefully selected participants (Blanken *et al.* 2010; van den Brink *et al.* 2003). Large numbers of heroin users have been brought into a wide range of treatments. Systems of quasi-compulsory treatment – and even compulsory placement in special penitentiary institutions for treatment – have been developed, although this has not been as successful as hoped (van 't Land *et al.* 2005; van Ooyen-Houben 2008). The Dutch approach in the most recent years has been characterized by a mixture of pressure to get problematic drug users off the streets and into treatment, combined with services to aid their social integration. This has apparently succeeded in reducing the highly visible dealing and other related problems that were apparent to journalists visiting the country in the early 1990s (Barendregt & van de Mheen 2009; Self 2006).

There is some evidence of increasing toughness in the Netherlands policy. As well as increasing restrictions on coffee shops and the use of quasi-compulsory treatment, there has also been an increase in the number of drug offenders in prison. However, in contrast to England and Wales, this increase was in line with the general increase in imprisonment that was seen in the 1990s and early 2000s. Since 2004, imprisonment for drug and other offences have both fallen (see Figure 7.6). New prisons were built as a response to overcrowding in the 1990s. A legal change in 2001 has led to more use of community sentences instead of imprisonment. Some cells are now lying empty and prisons are being closed. The restorative ethos in Dutch penal policy seems to have come back into vogue, despite pessimistic predictions of the extension of intolerant, neo-liberal penal expansion (Downes 2007).

A recent evaluation of the Dutch drug policy (van Laar & Ooyen-Houben 2009) shows encouraging trends in the most serious drug problems. Deaths from heroin and methadone are low by international standards. New HIV and Hepatitis C infections have reduced (van Laar *et al.* 2009). A decline in the number of syringes given out by needle exchanges also suggests that injecting drug use is down. The estimated prevalence of injecting drug use is remarkably low by international standards (Mathers *et al.* 2008). Property crime is falling, although the contribution of drug policy measures to this is unclear. The provision of 'user rooms' where drug users can inject in hygienic, medic-

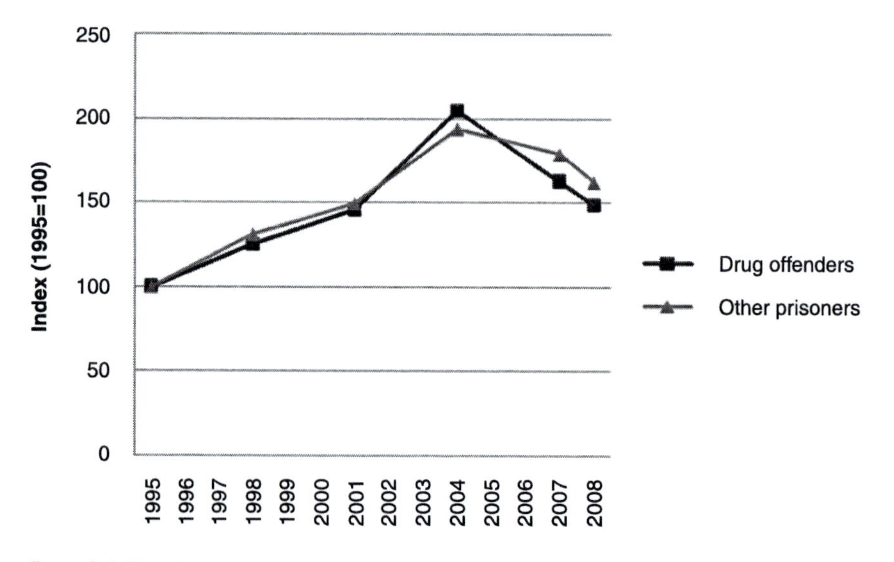

Figure 7.6 Trends in the numbers of people in prison for drug and other offences, 1995–2008.

(*Source:* data supplied by Netherlands Ministry of Justice and ICPS 2009)

ally supervised sites has reduced the level of public nuisance associated with public injecting (see also Hunt & Lloyd 2008; Wright & Tompkins 2004). The average age of the most problematic drug users has increased significantly since the early 1980s (van Laar & Ooyen-Houben 2009). This suggests that market separation has contributed to a reduction in the number of young people who become problematic users. The major failing identified by the evaluation was the continued involvement of major criminal consortia in the large-scale production and trafficking of drugs like cannabis and ecstasy. The pragmatic, depenalizing policy of market separation, controlled tolerance and treatment expansion has succeeded in reducing the most serious drug-related harms, without imposing collateral damage on the rest of society. The continued operation of criminal gangs in the illicit drug trade cannot be solved by depenalization. For the Dutch, the question is whether to retreat to more restrictive forms of control, or to expand tolerance to enable legal regulation of the wholesale cannabis market. For other countries, the question is whether depenalization, which seems to have achieved many of its aims in the Netherlands, would be acceptable and effective in places which do not share the principle of *gedogen*.

Keeping drug problems low: enforcement or equality?

The apparent success of both the Dutch and Swedish approaches in keeping rates of drug use relatively low has led to some bizarre attempts to reinterpret their lessons for other countries. US drug warriors used to criticize the Netherlands for its liberal approach. In advance of a visit there in 1998, ONDCP chief General Barry McCaffrey called the Dutch policy 'an unmitigated disaster' and claimed, incorrectly, that both murder rates and drug use were higher in the Netherlands than the USA (Komarow 1998). Now British drug warriors have moved to praising the Dutch, not for the pragmatic reality of their policy, but for having an imaginary 'tough' approach (Gyngell 2009).

Kathy Gyngell compares rates of British drug use to the lower rates of Sweden and the Netherlands and then claims that these are the result, in both countries, of an unambiguous focus on 'the enforcement of the drug laws; the prevention of all illicit drug use; [and] the provision of addiction care' (Ibid: 62). As my colleague Axel Klein (2009) has noted, it requires a peculiar selection from the available facts to claim that the Netherlands has a tougher approach to drug law enforcement than the UK. Gyngell's claim of an 'unambiguous' focus on enforcement of drug laws obviously conflicts with the existence of the written, AHOJ-G guidelines that openly state that some Dutch drug laws will *not* be enforced. Her statement that the UK has 'one of the most liberal drug policies in Europe' (Gyngell 2009: i) ignores the existence of forms of decriminalization in Portugal, Belgium, Germany, Italy,

Spain and the Czech Republic, as well as the Netherlands' depenalized approach. It also ignores the fact that the maximum sentences for cannabis and heroin trafficking in England and Wales are 14 years and life imprisonment respectively. This compares to four years and 16 years in the Netherlands, and ten years in Sweden for all drugs.[64] Babor *et al.* (2010) classify the UK as a country that has internationally high levels of drug law enforcement.

Gyngell criticizes the finding that drug seizures have little impact on drug markets (Reuter & Stevens 2007) and claims that higher seizures in the Netherlands create a more effective approach. In support of this claim she cites a literature review carried out for the English Home Office (Dorn *et al.* 2005). Nowhere in this report is it suggested that drug seizures have a significant impact on drug availability and use. Indeed, the review makes extensive use of Reuter's findings that seizures have very little effect (Reuter 1984, 1989; Reuter & Haaga 1989; Reuter & Kleiman 1986). Here, Gyngell goes beyond selective use to actual misrepresentation of the available evidence.

The role of inequality and social support

What many commentators – including Gyngell – have missed out is the impact of wider socio-economic factors on patterns of drug use. In his critique of the UNODC's report on Sweden, Cohen (2006) gives a useful list of other factors, outside the scope of drug policy, which might influence rates of drug use. They include demography, urbanization and working hours. Countries, such as Greece, with high proportions of elderly people, low proportions of city-dwellers and less available leisure time for workers tend to have lower rates of drug use than countries which have younger people, larger cities and more free time, such as the Netherlands.

Perhaps an even more relevant factor, which Cohen does not mention, is social inequality. Graphs included in *The Spirit Level* (Wilkinson & Pickett 2008) show that not only is reported drug use higher in more unequal countries, so are a host of other health and social problems. The correlation is stronger between inequality and their index of health and social problems ($r=0.87$, $p<0.01$) than it is between inequality and their index of drug use ($r=0.63$, $p=0.01$).[65] This again suggests that it is the social problems that surround drug use that are more highly associated with inequality than drug use itself. And this correlation is much higher than any that could be observed between the type of drug policy and rates of drug use or related problems. The two most restrictive countries that we have discussed – USA and Sweden – are at opposite ends of the scale to each other, both for drug use and social problems. US and UK policies aiming to eliminate drug use have not saved them from high rates of drug use or other problems, just as the decriminalized or depenalized countries do not inevitably have such high rates.

The suggestion that national drug problems are more directly affected by inequality than they are by drug policy is echoed in other studies that have been done on the link between inequality, welfare spending and imprisonment. Wilkinson and Pickett also find a strong correlation between nations' levels of income inequality and their rates of imprisonment ($r=0.75$, $p<0.01$). But, as Tapio Lappi-Seppälä (2008) has noted, there are many intervening factors between measures of inequality and imprisonment. A crucial one may be the level of welfare spending. Countries choose the level of pain they inflict through the penal system. They also choose how supportive to be of people who cannot support themselves through employment. There seems to be a direct trade-off between these choices. Downes and Hansen (2006) have found that countries that spend a higher proportion of their national wealth on welfare tend to imprison fewer people. This relationship has got stronger over the last two decades and it has also been observed for the states of the USA (Beckett & Western 2001). Lappi-Seppälä (2008) has strengthened our confidence that this relationship is real, rather than an artifact of measures of social spending. He tested it with an index of decommodification as well as against total social expenditure. He found that both these measures of social support were negatively correlated with imprisonment. As social support goes up, imprisonment goes down. Some countries prefer to control the people who do not succeed in the labour market, rather than support them. As Richard Garside (2009: 78) has written, '[w]elfare-state regimes and penal regimes are ultimately different mechanisms for addressing (to a greater or lesser degree of success) underlying social antagonisms, inequalities and the problems that they give rise to'.

Even countries with relatively high inequality and low welfare support can mediate some of their effects by taking policy steps that minimize the harms of drug use. This is shown, for example, by the relative success of the UK in limiting the impact of HIV on injecting drug users, compared to the Iberian countries which implemented harm reduction measures much later in the epidemic (Brugal *et al.* 2005; Hunt & Stevens 2004). But it seems, in general, that it is those countries with high levels of inequality and low levels of social support that also have the highest rates of drug problems. This proposition is hard to test quantitatively, due to the lack of data. But some comparable data has been provided on national rates of injecting drug use (Mathers *et al.* 2008). And we can use levels of income inequality and social support. These are measured by the Gini coefficient, the level of total social expenditure (both available from the website of the Organization for Economic Cooperation and Development) and an index of decommodification (Scruggs & Allan 2006). These indicators allow us to test whether there is a relationship, not just between inequality and drug use, but between various social indicators and the riskiest forms of drug use. The countries chosen for this analysis are the richest Western democracies where late modern capitalism is most highly expressed.[66] The relationships between the prevalence of injecting drug use and both income inequality and total social expenditure are in the expected direction, but fall short of being statistically significant. The relationship between decommodification and injecting drug use is significant ($r = -0.62$, $p<0.05$). Countries with higher levels of inequality and lower levels of social support and decommodification do tend to have higher levels of injecting drug use. Figure 7.7 gives a visual illustration of the relationship between estimated levels of injecting drug use and decommodification. There are many differences between these countries in drug policy, demography, geography, legal contexts, religious and cultural attitudes to drug use, urbanization and working hours. Some of these differences would be expected to dilute the correlation, but it is strong enough to shine through them. This indicates that the provision of social support is more important in affecting the levels of problematic drug use than is the stringency of drug policy.

The countries discussed in this book have made very different choices in how to regulate drug problems. The USA and, to a lesser extent, the UK have chosen high rates of imprisonment of drug offenders and a minimal or limited welfare state. These policies have not prevented relatively serious drug problems, despite the shared rhetoric on the necessity of prohibition. Sweden has also sought the eradication of illicit drugs, but has refused to pursue it through heavy use of imprisonment. Along with the Netherlands, it has instead prioritized treatment and integration of drug users in a social context of high levels of employment and welfare support and low inequality. The

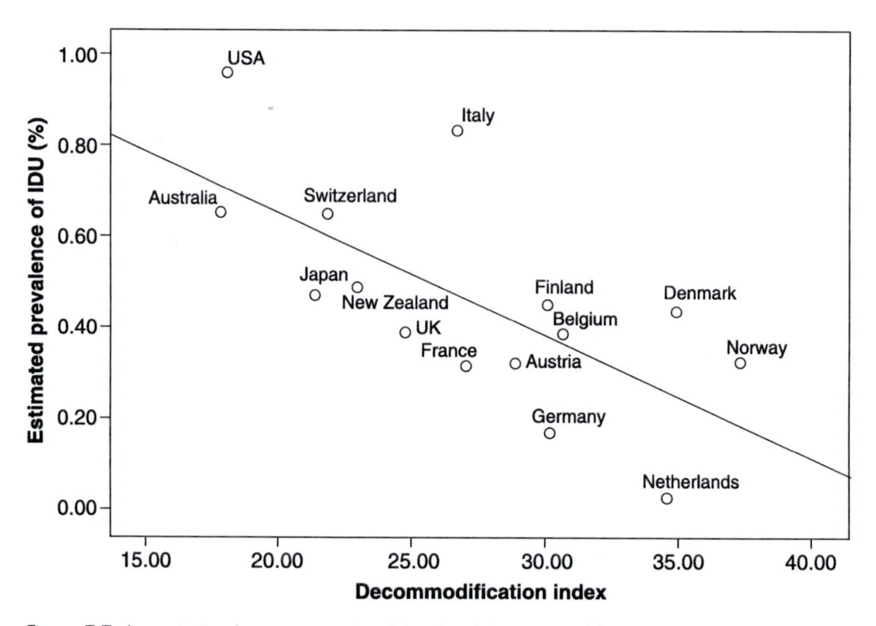

Figure 7.7 Association between national levels of decommodification and estimated levels of injecting drug use.

Netherlands has not insisted, as Sweden has, that abstinence be a condition of social inclusion. In line with its cultural norms of (limited) tolerance, it has offered support and services to people who have problems with drugs, while avoiding the criminalization of its citizens who enjoy cannabis. Simple comparison shows that the levels of drug use and drug problems do not depend on the level of prohibition (see also Reinarman *et al.* 2004). They are more closely associated with the level of social equality and support.

International lessons

This chapter has done a little justice to the complexity of drug policy issues in the USA, Sweden and the Netherlands in the relatively short space that I have given to each. Readers in search of more detailed accounts are encouraged to supplement this chapter by reading other publications (Boekhout van Solinge 2004; Boyum & Reuter 2005; Hallam 2010; Mares 2006). And there are places where they can find information on relevant national experiences that have not been dealt with here, such as those of Portugal (Hughes & Stevens forthcoming), Australia (Degenhardt *et al.* 2006; Hall 2008b; Lenton 2008), Germany (Bollinger 2004), Denmark (Asmussen Frank *et al.* 2008; Houberg forthcoming) and Italy (MacCoun & Reuter 2001b; Solivetti 2001).

Before this review of the implications of various countries' drug policies concludes, it is important to emphasize how unlikely it is that we could succeed in reducing drug problems just by transferring these policies across national borders. I have tried to show how dependent policies and their outcomes are on the various paths that these countries have taken, not just in their drug policy, but in their historical, political and cultural development. It is necessary to take into account the triplet history of fundamentalist Protestantism, populist political structures and racism to understand the US policy of mass incarceration (Tonry 2009). In Sweden the political culture has developed very differently. An insistence on social inclusion and equality, tinged with high levels of social duty and trust, has contributed to the development of a Swedish welfare state that is very generous by the standards of most countries, but demands (and receives) a high level of conformity to established social norms. Even within this society, some people seek out the pleasures and pains of dependent heroin use, as we saw in Chapter 3 (Lalander 2003). The development of controlled tolerance and dynamic harm reduction in the Netherlands also owes something to the role of the Christian church. Uitermark (2004) argues that it was the shift in attitudes in both Catholic and Protestant politicians that enabled the Dutch reforms of the 1970s to occur. These politicians had been very influential in the development of a comprehensive welfare system after the Second World War. In the 1960s and 1970s, they faced a major decline in their vote and feared that enforcement of cannabis laws would alienate young people from them. So they supported depenalization. The role of Christian Democrat politicians in the current movement against the coffee shops and in attempts to reduce welfare show how fragile the gains that have been made in the successful attempt to limit drug problems may be.

If we aspire to the drug policy outcomes of Sweden and the Netherlands (and which US or UK politician would not want to reduce their levels of drug use and related problems to those of these European partners?), then we will need to raise our argument above the level of whether stricter norms or less harsh enforcement will meet our needs. We will have to follow the drug problem upstream to its source in social arrangements that create inequality and reduce the availability of social support. We will not solve the drug problem by legislating, legalizing, educating, arresting, imprisoning or treating our way out of it. Drug policy does have a powerful effect in creating and mediating drug-related harms. Mass imprisonment causes unjustified harm. Treatment and harm reduction measures prevent unnecessary deaths. But long-term solutions to drug problems require change to be effected outside the realm of drug policy. If governments do have the drug problems they deserve it is not because they have neglected to enforce their drug laws, but because they have failed to protect their citizens from the malign effects of inequality.

Chapter 8

Towards progressive decriminalization

All the evidence on drugs, crime and public health that this book will give has already been presented. It has shown that man-made inequality is indispensable to the understanding of contemporary patterns of drug use, drug control and related harms. Chapter two showed that illicit drug use is not an activity that is confined to poor and marginalized groups. Indeed, it seems that rates of illicit drug use are actually higher among the relatively privileged. But the health and criminal harms of problematic drug use are most likely to be experienced by people who are economically, socially and racially excluded, through a process that I described in Chapter 3 as subterranean structuration. In Chapter 4, I showed that, when making policy on illicit substances, members of powerful groups mine the mountains of evidence that have been produced. They do so selectively, in order to find nuggets of evidence to use in stories that mark their tellers out as worthy of recognition, promotion or election. Political tactics contribute to this distorted use of knowledge, but a deeper influence is the use of drug policy as a symbolic discourse which ideologically sustains inequalities in the distribution of power, resources and respect. As many authors have concluded, prohibitionist policy is not a rational response to the existing pains and pleasures of drug use. Neither, as O'Malley and Mugford (1991) argued, is it a result of a conspiracy by a unified, omniscient state in the interests of a homogeneous ruling class. Prohibition, in its many varieties, results from shifting patterns of argument and discourse involving various groups within and around the state.

I ethnographically observed this process in practice in the UK government. I then showed, through an analysis of policy discourse in Chapter 5, that this process has led to policies that are not based on a rational assessment of the full range of available evidence. Rather, the cases of the DTTO, the Drugs Act 2005 and the yo-yoing classification of cannabis suggest that English drug policy operates to create imaginary distinctions between users of various drugs. Some 'domestic' drugs (like alcohol and tobacco) are accepted as tolerable within the law, despite the important harms to which they contribute. 'Foreign' drugs, like cannabis, ecstasy, cocaine and heroin, are kept outside the law. By presenting these illicit substances as inevitably dangerous and as used mainly by dangerous people, we can reassure ourselves that our increasing feelings of late modern insecurity are being attended to. In this way, we distract ourselves from the contribution of increasing inequality, both at home and globally, to the creation of these insecurities. The distortion of the available knowledge does not prevent some advances in the use of evidence to inform policy, especially when this knowledge does not threaten the basic ideological assumption that illicit drugs are all bad and that their users are therefore always in need of either treatment or punishment. The evidence that the largest part of drug use does not lead to health or criminal harms has been repeatedly ignored. The evidence that some people become dependent on drugs and are thereafter more likely to commit a higher volume of crimes has instead been used to justify a large increase in investment in both treatment and penal coercion. Both have been combined in services that use the criminal justice system to encourage people to enter therapy. Chapter 6 suggested that this investment has helped many people to reduce their drug use and their offending. It has been more cost-effective than imprisoning these people would have been. However, the investment in treatment is still smaller than the spending on the police and penal control of drugs. Imprisonment for drug offences has risen substantially, with the heaviest burden of consequent pains being borne by members of visible minorities. Meanwhile, for drug users who are seen as less threatening, the government has reduced the level of punishment while increasing the capacity of state surveillance.

In Chapter 7, I compared different approaches in the USA, Sweden and the Netherlands. The US model is exceptional in the scale of the damage it does to illicit drug users and other people. Here also, people of African heritage bear the brunt of these expensive and ineffective policies. The contrasting examples of Sweden and the Netherlands, and a brief analysis of other international data, support the idea that it is not so much drug policies as social policies that influence the level of drug-related harms. We are left with the impression that, as Young (1971: 225) concluded nearly four decades ago,

> The only method of curing a social problem is socially. That is, we must either remove it from the category of social problems because its psychic or physical effects do not warrant its inclusion, or change the structural position of the individuals concerned so that the problem can be solved in ways which do not involve recourse to mentally destructive, physically incapacitating drugs.

There will, no doubt, be objections that this account is overly simplistic. There are some interesting academic debates to be had. For example, the idea that evidence cannot be disentangled from the values which are embedded in its production and interpretation (e.g. Valentine 2009) would challenge my assumption that evidence is a necessary and useful guide to the development of more effective, less harmful drug policies. Others would even challenge the idea that the production of knowledge about people's behaviours can be anything other than an exercise of disciplinary power/knowledge (Foucault 1979). And yet others would argue that to focus on the political economy of drug policy is to underestimate cultural adaptations to the conditions of late modernity (Seddon *et al.* 2008). The promoters of such ideas will need to explain how they escape the entanglement of knowledge and power. They will have to explain what other tools we have – aside from knowledge – to resist the illegitimate control of our minds and bodies (Oakley 2000). And they will need to show how we can identify human agency in these uses of power so as to resist them. These debates can be had at other times and other places. For now, I assume that many readers will be more interested in the attempt to create alternative ways of dealing with drugs and drug users.

We do not start from scratch here. The last ten years have seen several attempts to come up with better policies. This final chapter will use these existing recommendations in attempting to identify new policies which offer the chance to reduce the problems that this book has identified.

Proposing policies

Table 8.1 provides a summary of independent reports which have recommended changes in English drug policy over the last decade.[67] They share some features. They tend to see cannabis as the drug that is most likely to face imminent legal changes. They see heroin as the most dangerous and problematic drug. They tend to avoid recommending any change to regulations on benzodiazepines, which are among the most widely used illicit drugs and are associated with many drug-related deaths. They make little mention of the problems associated with emerging drugs, like GHB, GBL, BZP, mephedrone, methylone, modafinil and the newer 'smart' drugs. Some, like the report from the Royal Colleges of Psychiatrists and of Physicians, are relatively conservative (Working Party of the Royal College of Psychiatrists and the Royal College of Physicians 2000). Given the history of the medical profession in advocating for medical control of psychoactive substances (Berridge 1999), it is not surprising that this report did not call for major changes, either to the law or to the practice of prescribing methadone to large numbers of dependent heroin users. It predicted that heroin prescription will become more widespread, either through the authorities turning a blind eye to wider prescribing or by formal expansion of this type of treatment. In effect, this is an argument for a return towards the old 'British system' of doctors being allowed to prescribe according to their own professional judgement, with relatively little interference from the Home Office and the Department of Health.

The Police Foundation report is also fairly conservative (Independent Inquiry into the Misuse of Drugs Act 1971 2000). The major change that it

Table 8.1 Recommendations made by non-governmental organizations on British drug policy, 2000–2009

	Police Foundation	*Royal Colleges*	*RSA Commission*	*Centre for Social Justice*	*Transform*
Year	2000	2000	2007	2007	2009
Misuse of Drugs Act	Retain it, and strengthen asset seizure against traffickers.	Retain it, but experiment with minor alterations.	Replace with Misuse of Substances Act (to include tobacco and alcohol).	Retain it, but review classification system.	Advocates significant revision of national legislation.
Cannabis	Move to class C and make possession (and home growing) non-arrestable. Enable medical supply.	Encourage policy experiments. Enable medical prescription, if clinical trials support it.	*De jure* or *de facto* legalization of possession. Consider licensing of legal supply.	Move back from class C to B.	Enable licensed sales, adapting the Dutch model. Move towards legal supply.
Hallucinogens	Move LSD from class A to B. Mushrooms not considered.	As is.	Depending on their place in an index of harm (to be created).	Not covered.	Enable licensed supply to members of psychedelics clubs.
Amphetamine-type stimulants	As is.	Provide realistic information on ecstasy.	Depending on their place in an index of harm.	No recommendation.	Enable licensed users to buy high strength products. Over-the-counter sales for low-strength preparations.
Benzodiazepines	Combine with flumazenil in pills to discourage injecting.	As is.	Not covered.	Not covered.	Not covered.
Coca derivatives	As is.	As is.	Depending on their place in an index of harm.	Develop programmes in prisons for people who use crack.	Enable licensed users to buy cocaine powder from pharmacists. License sales of low-strength coca drinks.

Opiates/opioids	Buprenorphine from class C to B.	Predicts *de facto* legalization of heroin, as police turn blind eye to local prescribing.	Retain criminal penalties for supply. Consider replacing criminal with administrative penalties for possession of heroin.	Expand abstinence-based treatment in and outside prisons.	High-strength opiates (e.g. heroin, fentanyl) to be licitly available only on prescription. Less restriction for less refined opium products (e.g. poppy tea).
Emerging drugs	Invest in early warning systems.	Not covered.	To be regulated according to their place in the harms index.	Not covered.	Default prohibition of new psychoactive substances. Research to be carried out on them non-commercially.
Drug treatment	Reallocate resources from punishment to treatment.	Invest in the most cost effective treatment (i.e. methadone) and improve quality.	Expand, improve and integrate treatment services with primary care, employment and housing.	Expand abstinent and residential treatment. Replace focus on coercion with focus on recovery.	Combine provision of treatment/recovery services with 'holistic social support'.
Trafficking and supply offences	Introduce a defence for 'social supply'. Reduce prison sentence lengths.	Consider reallocating resources spent on interdiction to treatment.	Focus attention on organized crime, not small-scale supply.	Increase spending on enforcement. Do not differentiate between drugs in punishing supply offences. Focus on reduction of supply.	Expand existing systems for licit production, but with fair trade. Maintain enforcement of the new drug regulations.
Drug-related crime	More research needed.	No recommendation.	Abandon drug testing on arrest and shrink DIP. Expand drug courts.	More drug courts and abstinence-based treatment in prison.	Crime will fall as users abandon the expensive illicit market.

(Continued Overleaf)

Table 8.1 Continued

	Police Foundation	*Royal Colleges*	*RSA Commission*	*Centre for Social Justice*	*Transform*
Harm reduction	Repeal section 9A of the MDA to enable provision of safer paraphernalia.*	No recommendation.	Enable the opening of drug consumption rooms.	Conduct clinical review of harm reduction services which are accused of 'contributing to more complex problems for future treatment'.	Advocates expansion of harm reduction principles, including supervised injecting facilities.
Education	Focus education on harms of heroin and cocaine.	Cut spending on ineffective programmes.	Start drug education at primary schools. Educate for harm reduction at secondary schools.	Introduce drug testing in schools. Expand and trial drug education.	Provide realistic education and 'meaningful alternatives to drug use'.
International	As is.	As is.	Not covered.	Intercept drugs and smugglers in the countries of origin.	Reform the UN conventions. Poverty reduction in drug-producing countries.
Research priorities	Investment in monitoring statistics and evaluation of drug law enforcement.	Raise spending on research to 1% of the annual drugs budget.	Creation of a drug harms index.	Treatments that may be effective in creating abstinence, including neuro-electric therapy.	Effects of alternative policy models.

* This section was amended in 2003, but provision of foil to encourage heroin users to switch from injecting to smoking may still be illegal.

recommended – which was subsequently partly implemented[68] and then reversed – was that cannabis should be moved to class C. This had been recommended by the ACMD as far back as 1979 (ACMD 1979), as the report makes clear. The commission that created the report was established by the Police Foundation, but only two of the group's thirteen members were police officers. Nevertheless, it followed the advice of the Association of Chief Police Officers in the recommendations it made for reclassification. As shown by the discussion of Warburton *et al.*'s (2005b) study in Chapter 6, many police officers believe that arresting cannabis users is a waste of time. They see the benefits of reducing the amount of time they spend on very common but relatively minor offences. They also benefit from the retention of the power to criminalize drug users and suppliers. This maintains the power of the police to intervene in the lives of the people whom they characterize as creating the highest levels of harm (Collison 1995).

The RSA report provided thorough evidence of the failures of current drug policy, but in the end it pulled its punches (RSA Commission on Illegal Drugs Communities and Public Policy 2007). It did recommend replacing the Misuse of Drugs Act with a Misuse of Substances Act, which would include alcohol and tobacco. But it provided little information on how this Act would actually operate. It suggested that legalization of possession might apply to both cannabis and heroin, but postponed more detailed discussion to await the creation of a more accurate index of drugs according to their harmfulness. This suggests that it is possible to create a definitive list of drug harmfulness, without taking into account the environments and the expectations with which these drugs interact. This assumption is challenged by the idea (presented in Chapter 3) that the process of subterranean structuration creates drug harms, not just the inherent properties of any particular drug. The recommendation to merge the regulation of alcohol, tobacco and currently illicit drugs under a Misuse of Substances Act frames all use of these psychoactive substances as misuse. So it presents teetotal abstinence as the only worthwhile state of consciousness, in apparent ignorance of the ubiquitous human pursuit of intoxication (Bancroft 2009; O'Malley & Mugford 1991).

The two most recent sets of recommendations came from opposite ends of the drug policy spectrum. The first was the Centre for Social Justice's (CSJ) report on addictions (Gyngell 2007). This included some of the arguments on the supposedly tougher Dutch policies that I criticized in Chapter 7.[69] There is direct conflict between the recommendations of the CSJ report and that of the Royal Colleges. The CSJ argued that substitution treatment is less effective than abstinence-based treatments in curing addiction. The collected wisdom of the physicians and psychiatrists was that residential abstinence treatment is not much more effective than methadone, but it is much more expensive. The available experimental evidence shows weak or contradictory evidence for the effectiveness of the type of abstinence-based treatments that CSJ recommends for use in structured day care (Ferri *et al.* 2006; Kaskutas

2009).[70] The CSJ estimates the cost of residential treatment at £26,000 per person per annum. It compares this to the higher cost of imprisonment in order to argue that treatment would be more cost-effective. It is probably true that residential treatment would be more cost-effective than prison, as other reports have found (Matrix Knowledge Group 2007; National Center on Addiction and Substance Abuse 2003). But this is not the correct comparator here. The CSJ does not argue for replacing prison with treatment. Indeed, it argues for more use of imprisonment to back tougher enforcement of drug laws. According to the CSJ, residential treatments would replace methadone prescriptions. It uses an estimate of the annual cost of substitution treatment of £2,020 per person. It does not explain how we are to bridge the large gap (£23,980) that separates this from the cost of residential treatment. It may be true that the majority of dependent users want to stop drug use altogether when they enter treatment (McKeganey *et al.* 2004). But it is also true that most of them will fail to do so, even if they enter abstinence-based treatment (McKeganey *et al.* 2006). Are we to deny effective treatments to people who cannot stop using opiates in order to pay for the treatment of a smaller number that can? This would be an argument for more death and more infectious disease. The CSJ also recommends investment in drug prevention education and drug testing in schools. This is despite the failures of even the best-designed drug education programmes to reduce drug use (Blueprint Evaluation Team 2009), and of the evidence on school drug testing to show that it does anything other than provide an incentive for pupils to move to less easily detected and more harmful patterns of drug use (McKeganey 2005; Yamaguchi *et al.* 2003).

The final report considered here is the least likely to be implemented any time soon. The Transform Drug Policy Foundation report provides a global plan for how drug regulation would operate if we were to stop using the criminal law as its main instrument (Transform 2009a). Transform had already provided detailed arguments against prohibition (Rolles 2007). It had also argued against incremental change within the prohibitionist regime which is laid out by the UN conventions. It stated that this would leave in place the harms caused by illegal drug production and supply. It argued instead that prohibition should be replaced by a legally regulated system for drug manufacture and distribution (Transform 2006). The evidence from both these reports is synthesized in its ambitious 2009 *Blueprint for Regulation*. This presents five different modes of legal regulation, all of which are already in place for some licit psychoactive substances. They are: prescription; pharmacy sales; licensed sales; licensed premises; and unlicensed sales. It recommends a phased introduction of the use of these models for drugs that are currently illegal, with strict restrictions on advertising. Cocaine could eventually be sold by licensed pharmacists, with cannabis being more widely available through a legally regulated supply. Heroin would remain as a prescription-only drug. The book notes that both heroin and cocaine are currently manufactured legally for analgesic and anaesthetic use. It advocates the expansion of existing systems for such licit production. It suggests that principles of fair trade should be applied in order that sustainable development is supported in the producer countries.

The principle objection to these proposals – other than moralistic pandering to the idea that some drug use is inherently wrong – is that they represent significant steps into the unknown (Edwards 2004). Speculation is rife. Prices would probably fall if they reflected the costs of production and distribution, rather than the profiteering of an illegal market. It is convincingly posited that consumption would then increase, just as alcohol consumption has risen as it has become more affordable (The Academy of Medical Sciences 2004). Prices could be controlled at higher levels, but this would increase the size of the black market which would persist alongside existing markets for smuggled alcohol and tobacco. It is also argued that higher rates of drug use would lead to higher rates of drug-related health problems, in line with the positive correlation between trends in population levels of alcohol consumption and the related harms (Ibid; Elder *et al.* 2010). All these objections and more are dealt with in Transform's various publications. As the current UN conventions have outlawed experimentation with alternative forms of regulation, few of Transform's rebuttals can have the force of evidence behind them.

Also, Transform's arguments focus on the legal status of drugs and not the social circumstances that surround them. Although inequality in the harms for drug use and control are referred to, Transform's proposals are still open to the charge that they would lead to even greater levels of drug-related harms in the vulnerable, deprived communities which already suffer the most (Inciardi 2008; Singer 2008). As I mentioned in the last chapter, there is an emerging two-tier market for cannabis in California. People who need it to reduce pain and stress can get it legally if they pay the medical fees. Other people – many of whom cannot afford the upfront fees or convince a doctor that they are the sort of person who deserves a prescription – still rely on the illegal market, with all its dangers. In a fundamentally unequal society, some of Transform's proposals could well lead to similar and even more damaging splits between legal and illegal markets. It is very likely that drugs would be diverted from the legal market, however carefully the issues of licensing and registration were attended to. The US experience of rapid growth in deaths related to OxyContin shows that legally prescribed opioids can be very harmful indeed (Van Zee 2009). The effects of some different forms of drug regulation on social and individual norms and decisions, and therefore the resultant harms, are almost completely unpredictable in advance.

Drug policy proposals and ideology

The reason that Transform's proposals are not likely to be adopted in the immediate future is not because they are speculative. The postulated benefits of prohibition are equally hypothetical, even though its harms are well documented. The UNODC (2009) claims that rates of drug use and related harms would be higher if it were not for prohibition. This may be true, but we have no way of testing this proposition. The reason that the evidence which Transform presents is unlikely to be translated into action is that it does not fit the ideological process of evidence selection. Prohibition is ideological in the narrow sense. It depends on viewing the world in a certain, pre-defined way. It is not amenable to change by evidence that comes from outside this world view. It is also ideological in a wider sense. Drug prohibition originates in the ability of certain powerful groups in society to impose controls on the behaviours of other people. Through symbolic and material exclusion of some drug users, it then reproduces these inequalities of power and resources.

If both kinds of ideology influence the use of evidence, then some of the proposals made by these reports are more likely than others to have impact on policy. The partial implementation of the Police Foundation's report showed that the police reclassification recommendations had some purchase on policy. The more recent re-reclassification of cannabis shows that it has been possible for politicians to accommodate police wishes to spend less time on cannabis possession offences while also using cannabis policy for fragmentary and bifurcatory purposes (see Chapter 6). The Police Foundation's other recommendations are not supportive of the ideological separation of illicit drug users from the wholesome body of society, and so are less likely to find powerful supporters for implementation. The Royal Colleges' wish that prescribing of opiate substitutes and of heroin itself be expanded have been fulfilled. Methadone maintenance prescriptions have vastly increased, and a trial of heroin assisted treatment has been implemented (Lintzeris *et al.* 2006; Strang *et al.* 2005). The recommendations to invest heavily in research and drug policy experiments have so far been ignored, as ministers have seen evidence on drug policy as surplus to their requirements. This was shown in the sacking of Professor Nutt (see Chapter 5) and also in a letter sent to Transform by Prime Minister Gordon Brown. He wrote:

> [w]e do not intend to undertake an impact assessment comparing the costs and benefits of different legislative options for domestic drug policy. We see no merit in embarking upon such an undertaking in view of our longstanding position that we do not accept that legalisation and regulation are now, or will be in the future, an acceptable response to the presence of drugs.
>
> (Brown 2010)

The Centre for Social Justice relies heavily on the narrow ideology of prohibition as a source for its proposals. Its recommendation that cannabis be moved back to class B has been implemented. Its recommendations on abstinence-based services have put the Director of the National Treatment Agency on the offensive (Hayes 2008) and informed the thinking of the prospective Conservative government (Green 2009b). Despite the wider evidence base for opiate substitution than for abstinence-based services, few would argue that treatment should not aim to help the many drug users who want to become abstinent. But two questions arise. One, outlined above, is about where the money to pay for increased residential treatment is to come from. The other is about the role of social inequality in the creation and cure of problematic drug use. The CSJ report pays minimal attention to the role of addiction in 'cementing' deprivation. It pays none at all to the role of inequality in creating drug dependencies. It does not address the psycho-social stress of relative poverty (Wilkinson 2005), which creates mental ill-health and self-medicating drug use. It completely ignores the social processes which leave illicit drug markets as the only arena in which many people can find respect, cash and comfort. These social processes take place in the highly unequal social conditions that are structured by both the narrow and broad conceptions of drug policy ideology. Should we not seek to prevent the development of problematic drug use before we argue over how to promote recovery from it?

Progressive decriminalization: an agenda for social reform

The Centre for Social Justice is not alone in ignoring the lack of actual social justice in making its drug policy recommendations. Few people who make drug policy proposals link them explicitly to the need to reduce inequalities. I will attempt here to create an agenda for policies that are more effective in reducing the harms that are related to drugs. It is not a list of things that are definitively settled as having to be done. It is rather a list for discussion. It takes suggestions from the previous policy proposals that have been discussed and from the broader field of social policy reform. It contains three main elements. The first is the reduction of inequalities. The second is the reform of international law. The third is a gradual, evidence-dependent shift towards the decriminalization and regulation of currently illicit drugs.

The possibility of some of these changes being put into practice may seem remote. The capitalist motor of late modernity drives us down a road of increasing inequality, harsh punishment and a 'lawless masculinity' that is equally apparent in peripheral housing estates and the financial heart of the City of London, even if it expresses itself in different forms of social harm (Lea 2002: 130). The ideological operation of drug policy plays its part in the intensification of these tendencies. Its symbolic legitimation of inequality reduces the possibility that they will face popular opposition. If we are to reduce the harms related to drugs according to this analysis, we are left with three choices: inactive despair; socialist or other forms of utopianism; or an active engagement with the existing structures of power. The worst excesses of capitalism have been tamed before. Large reductions in inequality happened in the first half of the twentieth century in the UK and the USA. Their beneficial effects are still visible in the European countries that have embraced social democracy. Social changes that were once unthinkable have been repeatedly achieved in the past. They were not created by people sitting it out, waiting to see how bad things could get. They did not rely on the total overthrow of all existing social arrangements. They were created by people joining together, organizing and voting for change. This is an effort of the imagination as much as it is of the will. If we are to create less harmful ways of dealing with drugs, then we will need to 'shift the mental and institutional boundaries of the present' (Loader 1998: 208). This agenda aims to contribute to that effort.

Reducing inequalities

Illicit drug markets are expanded by inequality, both domestically and internationally. Global inequality of wealth drives the cultivation and export of drugs in producer countries. Affluence in the developed countries gives people the time and money to spend on drugs. Inequality in these countries concentrates the most harmful markets in deprived communities. Drug harms are not the most widespread and deathly damages that are associated with these inequalities. Internationally, they drive starvation, preventable disease and war. Domestically, they drive serious reductions in life expectancy and mental health among the more deprived. Reducing inequality would reduce these harms as well as reducing the damages related to psychoactive substances. According to the analysis presented in this book, there are three types of inequality that need addressing. The most obvious is income inequality. Closely related to this are inequalities in power. A third category is inequality in recognition. As Lister (2008) has argued, the experience of inequality is not just about having less money than other people. It is about being made to feel inferior in every social situation: being looked down on in schools, shops and cinemas; being made to believe that nobody cares what you think or feel. This kind of poverty encourages people to seek respect in harmful drug markets.

As I wrote in Chapter 2, the policies that the British government introduced from 1997 onwards have failed to prevent an increase in income inequality. The reason is that underlying inequalities in income and wealth have grown so fast that Labour's redistributive policies have only limited the increase in relative poverty. Wilkinson and Pickett (2008) note that there are at least two paths towards greater income equality. Sweden achieves it through fiscal redistribution of earnings. Japan has low levels of underlying wage inequality, so has less need for progressive taxation. It seems that the UK government will need to take both paths if it hopes to reverse, rather than entrench, the deep inequality that has arisen in the last 30 years. This will mean increasing the minimum wage, closing tax loopholes and increasing taxes on very high pay. It will also mean countering the increase in underlying wage inequality. A start could be made on this by adopting the multiparty proposal for a high pay commission to create policies to limit very high salaries.[71] Wilkinson and Pickett themselves argue for the spread of employee ownership in businesses throughout the economy. They note that profitable, productive cooperatives, such as the Mondragón Corporation in Spain, tend to have much lower pay differentials than other corporations. Whatever steps are taken to reduce inequality, we will also have to reduce the pains of poverty that lead so many people to seek refuge in dependent drug use. This will mean defending and developing welfare, education, housing and health programmes that can reduce the impact of inequality.

One significant barrier to the achievement of greater equality has been inequality in power. The wealthy have a virtual stranglehold on the most senior positions in powerful elites (Sampson 2005). The British constitution is notoriously unwieldy. It creates such a high degree of centralization that it is very difficult for people to mobilize around alternative policies. The Labour government devolved some powers to national governments in Scotland, Wales and Northern Ireland. This provides an opportunity for new policies to be tested in practice, such as the Scottish government's current proposal to introduce a minimum alcohol price. In England, however, the grip of the central executive has been tightened through its top-down management of local initiatives, by sidelining the role of Parliament in checking its authority and by refusing to enable electoral reform (which was promised back in 1997). If we are to see real, sustainable movements for greater equality, we will need a revitalization of local democracy, an enhanced role for elected representatives in deciding policy, and the implementation of some form of proportional representation.[72] This would allow new people and ideas to enter the policy stream from outside the current wellsprings of power. Some of these ideas, such as those pushed by far-right and other extremist parties, would be unpalatable and wrong. But it is not the role of the constitution to protect us from hearing odious arguments. It is to protect us, through guarantees of our human rights, from their implementation.

The opening up of democracy would enable the voices of many people who are currently silent or silenced to be heard. Many people are so alienated from the political process, so excluded from the cultural capital which enables political engagement, that reform of political arrangements would not be enough to bring them into the attempt to create higher levels of social equality, recognition and respect. For this reason, it would be necessary to invest in skilled, sustained community development with the groups that are most vulnerable. This would recognize the cultural particularities of diverse communities: people who have recently arrived from other countries as well as people whose families have lived here for generations; women whose femininity is performed in the face of violence and dependency as well as men whose masculinity is threatened by lifelong redundancy; people who are divided by all the specificities of sexuality, bodily ability, spiritual belief, ethnicity, gender and class, but who share the same human rights and duties. It would involve genuine consultation with communities affected by policy change. It would also enable them to take an active role in setting the direction of change and deciding how it is to be carried out (Stevens *et al.* 1999; Wright 2000). There have been previous waves of community development, but they have tended to founder on the rarely anticipated but hardly surprising consequence of giving more power to people who have little. Their interests clash with those of the people who already have power and who have used it to corner the market in material and cultural resources. So participation leads to conflict (Godbout 1983; Stevens *et al.* 2003). Community development must therefore go hand-in-hand with democratic renewal in order to allow these conflicts to be expressed and resolved through deliberative, public discussion, as advocated by both Gewirth (1996) and Habermas (1996). Community organization from below, now apparent in forms such as the Transition Towns movement, will help to build the social trust that is necessary in order to create support for the policies that will reduce inequality (Rothstein & Uslaner 2005). A key role should be reserved for people who have had problems with drugs, whether they are still using or they have become abstinent. Their insights into how drug problems arise, and how they can be overcome, will be important in reducing levels of drug-related harm, whatever legal or social policy regime is in place.

International law reform

The USA and its allies in the international war on drugs have used the UN conventions and the International Narcotics Control Board to limit the freedoms of other countries who wish to experiment with new forms of regulation (Bewley-Taylor 2005; Jelsma 2003). Even the UNODC has recognized that the pursuit of prohibition has caused the development of a damaging criminal market and has displaced policy efforts away from the promotion of public health (Costa 2008). Negotiations at the Commission on Narcotic Drugs have repeatedly foundered on the inability to put together – and then hold together – a coalition of countries to push for even relatively minor changes. In 2009, for example, a coalition of European and other governments and worldwide non-governmental organizations was making progress towards the inclusion of the term 'harm reduction' in official UN drug policy (it is already included in official UN policy on AIDS [UN General Assembly 2006]). Then the Pope made a statement that harm reduction was 'anti-life' and Italy dropped out of the coalition (Campbell 2009b). Harm reduction was excluded from the eventual political declaration (United Nations Economic and Social Council 2009).

In the meanwhile, several countries have kept to the letter – if not the spirit – of the UN conventions while effectively decriminalizing drug possession. The preamble to the 1988 convention states that the aim of drug control is to eradicate illicit drug markets. The 1971 convention obliges signatory states to establish sanctions or punishments for 'any action contrary to a law or regulation' that follows the convention. But neither document states that drug use or possession must be criminalized (Dorn & Jamieson 2000). Countries like Portugal, Italy, Spain, Germany, the Netherlands, Mexico, Bolivia, Uruguay, Paraguay and Colombia have realized that drug use cannot be eradicated. So they have introduced policies to reduce the harms of prohibition, while taking care to stay within the conventions by retaining sanctions against drug markets. This shows that we do not need to wait for reform of the conventions before we start research on other forms of regulation. However, as they stand, the UN conventions operate as generators of prohibition-related harms (Buxton 2006). They also put a brake on the development of knowledge on how we might better address drug-related problems around the world. The 1988 convention requires countries to criminalize the 'production, manufacturing, extraction, preparation, offering, offering for sale, distribution, delivery on any terms whatsoever, brokerage, dispatch, dispatch in transit, transport, importation or exportation' of the substances targeted by the conventions. So countries cannot experiment with ways of enabling drug users to access a safe, legal supply. The Netherlands would have great difficulty, for example, in resolving the 'back door' problem of cannabis production and distribution without breaking the 1988 convention. We need a new international settlement that enables the development of better evidence on all the steps in the chain of drug supply and use. It should recognize national sovereignty and the right of each nation to regulate its own social problems, while providing a framework for international cooperation on drug-related problems which cross national frontiers.

The steps to such a settlement have been examined by several authors (e.g. Bewley-Taylor 2002; Room *et al.* 2010). The first, necessary step is to generate the political will to make change happen. This will require more of the international mobilization and campaigning by governmental and non-governmental organizations which emerged in the run-up to the 2009 UN negotiations. It will be a long and awkward process. The history of international meetings on drug policy, ever since the Shanghai convention of 1909, is one of discord and delay. The main obstacle to creating a more flexible system has always been the USA. As this prime proponent of prohibition scales down the drug war rhetoric at home, is it too much to ask for that it might engage more helpfully in the effort to create a less harmful international regime of drug regulation?

Creating the evidence for more effective policy

The evidence of the harms imposed by drug prohibition, and the moral argument for limited rights to use drugs that was presented in the first chapter, imply that we should move towards drug policies that are less damaging to human rights and well-being. These policies would impose the lightest controls that are consistent with the prevention of harm to people's basic, non-subtractive and additive rights (in that order of priority). Currently, we have little reliable evidence on where this eventual balance might lie. So we need to move away from speculative arguments and start generating the evidence around which people can mobilize for change. We should follow the advice of the Royal Colleges and invest in research. This evidence will not be able to resolve policy arguments purely on its own methodological merits. It will provoke debate and face attempts to silence it, especially when findings conflict with the interests and beliefs of powerful groups. However, it will strengthen the hand of any group that enters into discursive struggle with the evidence behind them. Powerful groups currently exercise their power in making convenient choices from the existing, limited evidence base. As this evidence base grows, and as more convincing positions emerge from it, advocates will be able to use it to erode the legitimacy and authority of any policy stance that conflicts with the evidence. They will use it to win more support, within and outside the state. It may help them exert pressure for policy change. Or it may strengthen support for the status quo, if this should happen to emerge from the new evidence as the least harmful option. It will not – and should not – be the only factor in drug policy decisions. Legitimate discussion over the value of various harms that are related to drugs and their control will continue. But research will at least enable us to discuss these harms with more confidence that we know what they actually are.

There are at least three kinds of research that deserve more attention: psychopharmacology; treatment; and policy research. Research on the psychopharmacology of illicit substances is rapidly developing. We still know too little about the long-term harms and therapeutic benefits of drugs like ecstasy and cannabis. Several studies have been commissioned in these areas, and the next few years will no doubt see some important findings emerge. There is a bigger hole in our knowledge about the harms posed by novel psychoactive compounds. Mephedrone is the latest to attract attention from the media and people who are in the market for drug-induced pleasure (Measham *et al.* 2010). Very little is yet known about how harmful it might be. Even if effective measures are found to control this drug or its precursors, other new drugs have already been invented that will challenge legal boundaries. These include pharmaceutical products that have failed to find a medical use, as well as substances produced by underground chemists (e.g. Shulgin & Shulgin 1991). We need to develop the existing systems for the analysis of substances which are not yet widely used. Unregulated experimenters, such as the Shulgins, and government scientists, like Les King,[73] have demonstrated the potential for research on new substances. Their work needs to be built on by envisioning the substances that are most likely to enter the market and testing their potential effects and harms. The first time that drug policy makers encounter a particular substance should not be when it has been extracted from the corpse of a 17 year-old partygoer.

Treatment research has produced a massive outpouring of findings in the last 40 years. Many of them have been positive. They have suggested that some currently used methods for treating drug dependency and minimizing drug-related harm are significantly better than doing nothing. None have provided a miracle cure for drug use. The search for vaccines that will somehow inoculate us against our desires for intoxication will no doubt continue. In the meanwhile, there is plenty of existing research that awaits the widespread implementation it deserves. The results of rigorous trials of heroin assisted treatment (Uchtenhagen 2008) suggest that it should be more widely available to people who cannot control their use of heroin through methadone substitution. Similarly, findings from studies of supervised injection sites (aka drug consumption rooms, Hunt & Lloyd [2008]) suggest that more people and cities that currently experience the harms related to public injecting would benefit from their introduction. Emerging findings on the effectiveness of take-home naloxone in preventing overdose deaths also point the way towards lifesaving implementation of research (Gaston *et al.* 2009). These examples demonstrate the potential benefits of shifting the priority in drug policy from criminal law enforcement towards the enhancement of public health. The implementation of these approaches should be studied in order to learn how best to effect this change.

The existing research has not yet given us enough information on how we can help people who face drug dependency to move towards the independent lives that they want to lead. Too many people have had the terrible experience of watching friends and relatives go through the cycle of drug use, attempts at abstinence, relapse and repeat until death. We know that people are more likely to escape this cycle if they find a way out through stable accommodation and employment. We should not wait for political change to make these supportive factors more widely available to the people who are most likely to become dependent on drugs. We need to create services that can help young people to avoid slipping into such damaging patterns of drug use. And we need to find out how best to support people in their search for security and stability as they mature. The findings of the *Early Exit* project suggested that people are most likely to engage in drug treatment if they are offered services which they do not experience as stigmatizing, that are provided to them at convenient times and locations, and that attends to their full range of needs (including housing and income) (Stevens *et al.* 2008). It struck us, as it has others (e.g. McGrail 2007), that such services may be provided better in the context of mainstream health services than in specialist drug treatment settings. This speculation needs to be tested, as do other, relatively under-researched treatment modalities, such as the abstinence-based structured day care programmes that the CSJ recommends.

The third area of priority for research presents the greatest methodological challenges. Testing the effects of drug policy changes is not impossible. But it is very difficult to use the standard methods to achieve valid and reliable results. It would be very difficult, for example, to carry out a randomized controlled trial of cannabis decriminalization. Even quasi-experimental studies will be rare, given the absence of comparison groups of states or countries that are similar in every aspect except their drug policy. Nevertheless, we can use observational studies and natural experiments to test some of the speculations about drug policy outcomes. The experiences of various states and countries have been used to show, for example, that increased drug use is not an inevitable result of decriminalization (Hughes & Stevens forthcoming; MacCoun & Reuter 2001b; Reuter & Stevens 2007; Room *et al.* 2010). One potential way to test drug policy speculations is to compare real-life observations to sophisticated models. These studies could use advances in modelling techniques (Grass *et al.* 2008) to generate hypotheses from the data and assumptions that already exist. Each potential new regime for drug regulation should be modelled on the basis of assumptions about the behaviour of potential users, suppliers, advertisers and regulators. Drug policy changes that were found to offer a good likelihood of better outcomes in such models could then be tested by the phased introduction of these regimes. Data would be collected to compare against the modelled, hypothetical outcomes. These should include impacts on public health, crime, the environment and inequality – not just changes in rates of drug use or public spending. As time went on and more such studies were carried out, cumulative evidence would be generated about the reliability of each of the speculations that currently inform drug policy debates. There is no need to limit such research to policy on drugs that are currently illicit. Work at the University of Sheffield (Meier *et al.* 2009) shows that it is already being applied to the potential effects of the proposed Scottish method for reducing the harms of alcohol use.

The reduction of penalties for possession and small-scale production of cannabis seems to be a policy change that is closest to being possible on both sides of the Atlantic. The introduction of warnings in place of arrests for cannabis possession in England and Wales in 2004 appears to have been accompanied by a fall in cannabis use. As restrictions on cannabis users are reduced in other places, research should be done to observe subsequent trends for comparison against scenarios generated by modelling of such policy changes. Proposals to shorten prison sentences of crack offenders in the USA, and of drug importers in the UK, are also already in the political process. These should also be implemented for comparative, observational study. If studies continue to suggest that reducing the punishments of drug users has little negative effect on drug-related harms, then we should continue to mobilize public opinion in favour of further advances. We should test alternative regimes for the supply of illicit substances, including those suggested in Transform's *Blueprint*. This will require reform of the international control system, especially the 1988 convention. The logical consequence of emerging evidence on the regulation of alcohol, tobacco and illicit drugs may be to bring them together in a new Act for the Regulation of Psychoactive Substances. This would replace the Misuse of Drugs Act, as suggested by the RSA Commission, although it would have a different name to their suggested replacement and would not necessarily be based on an index of harms that are measured on a single metric. It would rather be designed to enable flexible regulation of each drug, or category of drugs, according to evidence and public opinion about the most appropriate regimes.

We need to retain some caution about the use of modelling techniques in advancing drug policy. Even sophisticated models cannot account for the wonderful complexity of human life. Models are not reality. We only need to look at the models that were predicting a smooth economic future prior to the bank crashes of 2008 for confirmation of this basic point. These crashes show the dangers of believing the models, rather than preparing for the risk that they might not be true. Sociological research will be necessary, both to develop the assumptions that are entered into the models and to make observations of reality to test their predictions. A combination of sociological, economic, psychological, anthropological, political and legal research will help us to advance our understanding of drug policy dilemmas. This research will not provide answers that can be implemented without public discussion and assent. It will provide 'experiments in government' (O'Malley 2008: 457) that help us to reduce social harms while increasing individual freedoms and the scope for democratic debate.

Endpoint

It seems unlikely that the 'psychic or physical' harms of drug use will be significantly reduced without changes to the structural position of the most-harmed drug users. So we must work towards social solutions if we want to reduce these harms. Social inequality is associated with a wide range of problems. Some of them cause much more harm than drug use does. The harms that are increased by the combination of psychoactive drugs and inequality include crime, illness and early death. The methods we currently use to control drugs contribute to the continuation and deepening of this inequality. Current drug policies tell stories which dissimulate the harms of inequality, fragment society between worth and unworthy drug users and so legitimate the unequal distribution of power and resources. I have argued that we need to move beyond the stalemated, speculative debate between prohibition and legalization. We need an understanding of drug use and related problems that takes into account the social – as well as the legal – constraints which shape people's choices about how they are going to use drugs. The argument for progressive decriminalization rests on a foundational idea of justice. It is that our prospects for freedom to act towards our own purposes mean that we all have rights and duties which we owe to each other. In order to respect these rights, and to expand the scope of our freedom, we need to reduce inequalities of income, power and recognition. This would also reduce the pressures under which people become dependent on damaging substances.

In order to reduce these pressures, we need to develop more reliable evidence on which to build drug policy. Justified scepticism about political uses of evidence should not prevent us from creating and using knowledge that can help us to perform our duties and protect our rights. We need to link the campaign against the unjustified infliction of pain on people who use drugs to the call for greater equality. We should take care to ensure that any suggested improvements to drug policy do not have the effect of deepening inequalities, as so many drug policy innovations of the past have done. Action to improve drug policy should complement initiatives to create wider social justice. This will include building coalitions between drug users, researchers, campaign groups, unions and politicians in ways which build support for greater equality and reduce the perceived electoral dangers of less punitive drug policies. Then we will have a chance to increase freedom while reducing harm.

Endnotes

1 Current controversies over the use of cannabis as a medicine show how hard it is to draw the boundary between medical and non-medical use of drugs. For this discussion, illicit drugs will be treated as if they had no medical value, as this provides the strongest test of whether there is a right to use them.
2 This stipulation may mean that illicit drug sellers are not respecting the rights of their customers to full information on the contents and potential harms of their wares. It could also lead to a discussion of whether the consequences of criminalizing the sale of these substances makes it more likely that consumers are denied their rights to full information. In the absence of this information, it is still within the scope of the user's freedom of action as to whether to take the risk of consuming these substances.
3 For example to *Living with Drugs* (Gossop 2007), to *Drugs, Society and Human Behavior* (Ksir *et al.* 2006), or to the website of Drugscope (http://www.drugscope.org.uk/)
4 The UN conventions that relate to illicit drugs are: *The Single Convention on Narcotic Drugs*, 1961; *The Convention on Psychotropic Substances*, 1971; and *The United Nations Convention Against Illicit Traffic in Narcotic Drugs and Psychotropic Substances*, 1988.
5 Some of these drugs have different names within and between countries. So, for example, I have referred to products of the *cannabis sativa* plant as cannabis in the British context, and marijuana in the US context. I use the term 'opiates' to describe alkaloids of the opium poppy (such as morphine) and derivatives of such alkaloids (such as heroin). For convenience, I will follow other authors in also using the term to cover methadone, even though this is, strictly speaking, a synthetic opioid.
6 When this book uses the term dependence, it will usually be referring to a behavioural pattern characterized by a compulsion to use drugs. When it uses the term addiction, it will usually be in the context of approaches to this behavioural pattern which assume it is caused by an identifiable disease.
7 This refers to the tendency of Foucauldian scholars to reject moral judgements about the normative values of social tendencies, such as the expansion of penal control, while decrying the existence of these phenomena. Without a normative judgement, there can be no basis for decrying anything.
8 Among the self-serving myths put about by advocates of this branch of pseudo-economics are:

- That reducing income tax rates would increase the overall tax take. It would not (Page 2005).

- That countries with higher income differentials would incentivize wealth creation and so improve economic growth. They have not (de Dominicis *et al.* 2008).
- That hypothetical increases in the tax take and economic growth justify the harms caused by inequality. They do not.

9 Sometimes proponents of genetic explanations of inequality go to absurd lengths. Take, for example, an example in a magazine which seduces its well-heeled readers with the title *Intelligent Life*. In between adverts for Patek Phillipe watches and Chanel jewellery, there is an article on cleverness. The author (Joyce 2007) interprets the work of a prominent writer on IQ as explaining away environmental effects with the statement that 'superior genes cause superior performance by co-opting superior environments'. The example is given of tall identical twins whose initial advantage in height is multiplied by recruitment into basketball training programmes. A slight initial advantage is turned into massive sporting superiority by the genes 'co-opting' a beneficial environment. This illogical but relatively benign tale of the basketball court turns nasty when it is applied to race, and the apparent differences in IQ between white and black Americans. Here it is argued that 'blackness itself in a still-biased society means their genes can only co-opt inferior environments'. What kind of nonsense is this? The idea is that miniscule helices of DNA can go behind our backs, co-opting environments for us. The complex social histories that created a ball game which is both highly socially valued and best played by people of gigantic height are ignored. Instead, we are led to believe that genes act in some mysterious way to choose the beneficial environment of the high school gym. And as for the implication that we should ignore the history of slavery by blaming African genes for not 'co-opting' a less racist society in which to live? Let's hope that readers of *Intelligent Life* can look past the adverts for $20,000 watches and see that their own intelligence is being insulted.

10 The argument that low intelligence is the common cause of both poor health and poor socio-economic status has been disconfirmed by analysis of two longitudinal datasets that tracked over 30,000 American participants' intelligence, socio-economic status and health. It found that, if you control for the effects of income and education, intelligence has no significant effect on people's health (Link *et al.* 2008). The authors report that their data supports the idea that health is more dependent on the effects of socio-economic status on 'knowledge, money, power, prestige, and beneficial social connections' p. 72.

11 Sex surveys suggest that, on average, men have had several more partners than women. This is a mathematical impossibility unless there are some women who have very high numbers of sexual partners who are not being counted. Women like this (such as those who are selling sex) may well exist (Brewer *et al.* 2000). But this explanation does not save the validity of sex surveys, which have apparently failed either to reach these women or to persuade them to report their prolific activities.

12 Sitting here listening to the radio (currently playing *Ulysses* by Franz Ferdinand, with its repeated, ignored instruction 'let's get high'), I think of David Davis' appearance on *Desert Island Discs*. Davis, who is a prominent British, Conservative, prohibitionist politician, chose Pink's *Get the party started* as one of the songs he would take to his desert island. He has repeatedly talked up the dangers of ecstasy and campaigned against reducing the punishment of its users. I guess he does not know that the opening lines of Pink's song ('I'm comin' up, so you better get this party started') make a very clear reference to the euphoric onset of MDMA.

13 The questions on dependence were:

- During the past 12 months, have you used (name of drug) every day for two weeks or more?
- In the past 12 months have you used (name of drug) to the extent that you felt like you needed it or were dependent on it?
- In the past 12 months have you tried to cut down on (name of drug) but found you could not do it?
- In the past 12 months did you find that you needed larger amounts of (name of drug) to get an effect, or that you could no longer get high on the amount you used to use?
- In the past 12 months have you had withdrawal symptoms such as feeling sick because you stopped or cut down on (name of drug)?

14 The strongest correlation between indicators of deprivation, with Kendall's tau b at 0.438, was between low income and unemployment.
15 The usual assumption is that drug use and dependence are features of poor people. Results from the SPM suggest otherwise. A US study of the health behaviours of over 12,000 Americans also found a positive relationship between excessive drinking, illicit drug use and higher income (Stockdale *et al.* 2007).
16 The central nervous system includes sensors of high levels of carbon dioxide and low levels of oxygen in the blood. In opiate-induced respiratory depression, the brain fails to stimulate the lungs to breathe in response to these sensors.
17 In the Web of Knowledge, a bibliographic database of journal citations, it was recorded as being cited 209 times by March 2009, more than any other article which focused on the drugs-crime link.
18 See Chapter 2, p. 29.
19 It is highly possible that the apparent link between drug use and psychopharmacological violence was influenced by other variables that are not included in Weiner *et al*'s model, such as early childhood experiences, environmental stress, low educational achievement, unemployment or mental health. These factors have been found in other studies to predict both drug use and violence, which can occur simultaneously without one causing the other.
20 Fourteen per cent were classed as psychopharmacological (of which 68 per cent were linked to alcohol and 16 per cent to crack), only four per cent were classed as economic-compulsive, and fully 74 per cent were classed as systemic (61 per cent crack, 27 per cent powder cocaine and four per cent marijuana).
21 The priority given to proving (not testing) the framework is evident in the passage, '[e]mpirically, it was not always possible to ascertain the full motivation for robbery/homicides involving dealers. Conceptually, it was felt that such homicides most rightly belonged within the system of drug distribution' (Ibid: 673).
22 A sophisticated student of social theory might object to my joining together, here, the work of Bourdieu and Giddens. There are important differences between them in the emphases they place on the roles of structure and agency in influencing social action. The use made in this book of their concepts focuses on their shared interest in how structure and agency interact to reproduce the constraints within which people act.
23 Hall *et al.* (2008) have diagnosed an even more extreme expression of a similar, criminally consumerist tendency in drug markets in the deprived estates of Northeast England.
24 It could be argued that this term, like 'underclass', looks at the poor from the top down. It is true that 'subterranean structuration' is unlikely to be picked up in

conversations in the streets, prisons and treatment centres populated by the people whose activities it describes. But it avoids fixing their identities for them. It is an 'analytical concept' of the type used by Loïc Wacquant (2007) to argue against rhetorical categories which obscure both the actions of the powerful in relegating large numbers of people to the margins of society and the actions of these relegated people in creating responses which provide partial solutions to this marginalization, while also contributing to the reproduction of the social limits that they face.

25 Home Office estimates of the number of problematic drug users suggest that 22 per cent of all recent users of heroin and crack are female (Hay *et al.* 2007). Women make up about six per cent of the total prison population (Ministry of Justice 2009b). A psychiatric survey of the prison population found that 41 per cent of female remand prisoners and 23 per cent of female sentenced prisoners reported symptoms of drug dependence in the year before imprisonment. This compared to 26 per cent and 18 per cent of male prisoners (Singleton *et al.* 1997).

26 This downward spiral is not only experienced by women. Pryor reports that his heroin use also became self-perpetuating once it had got under way. He writes '[t]o become an addict, the experience of the drug must answer some urgent need, must soften some searing pain, must provide a way out from some inner disaster . . . As the habit establishes itself, the pain of addiction, the withdrawal symptoms, overcome and subsume the pain the drug is answering. It becomes a self-fulfilling prediction' (Pryor 2003: 64).

27 Henri Bergeron's (2009) useful summary shows that these connections have also been discovered by French writers.

28 Scepticism about the possibility of value-neutral, technocratic, evidence-based policy is nothing new, as demonstrated by this 'doggerel' composed by a previous sociological interloper into Whitehall from the University of Kent: 'But facts ('tis said) speak for themselves, (And some people believe in fairies and elves), But facts – let's face it – we *select*, And values guide what we detect' (Pahl 1977: 148).

29 Of course, countless first-hand accounts of the policy making process have been published in the form of political memoirs and diaries. But these accounts usually attempt to justify rather than explain the decisions that were made. Their contribution to the sociological analysis of policy making is therefore limited, although they would make fascinating source material for discourse analysis in this field.

30 This approach was so widespread that a meeting on workforce development concluded that there was a need for colleagues to be trained in 'research methods' other than Google.

31 When I asked Peter, he said it was because senior people think that specialists might have divided loyalties; that developing such knowledge also meant developing too much fellow feeling with people who provide services in that area. This criticism was backed up by occasions where I heard various departments, or sections within departments, described as 'producer-captured'. But there may be other reasons.

32 Her gender is probably significant. Despite explicit efforts to achieve greater gender equality (the current government target is to increase the proportion of women in top civil service management posts to 34 per cent), the most senior ranks of the civil service are dominated by men. And so were the informal networking events that I observed. During evenings in the pub and football games in the park, personal connections of mutual affection and trust were developed. There were informal and formal events designed for women only. I obviously could not observe these, but it strikes me that they would be less likely

to lead to useful connections with current or future superiors, given the relative absence of women at the top echelons of the civil service.

33 A policy making civil servant who had been involved since the beginning of this process attributed these problems with NOMS to the strong opposition of public sector managers and the failure of a succession of short-lived ministers to overcome it.

34 The persistence of the appeal of intuition to civil servants can be seen by comparing this quote to one recorded by Garrett (1972) from one civil servant about his colleagues. He said they have 'an almost unanimous reliance on intuition and a distrust of systematic argument' (quoted by Garrett 1972: 38).

35 Alan Johnson's demand for the resignation of the Chair of the Advisory Council of the Misuse of Drugs shows a similar approach to narrative in drug policy (see Chapter 5 for more on this controversy). The Home Secretary said that Professor Nutt had to go because he was causing confusion between the evidence and government policy. It was not because he got the evidence wrong, but because he could not keep the story straight. The minister had obviously had enough of having his mind blown.

36 There may also be a third face of academic reason, restricting the performance of rationality to narratives that are somehow fashionable, original or otherwise confirmatory of senior academics' self-image and consequent desire to promote their performers. But this would require another, rather navel-gazing study to be done.

37 This language may sound simplistic. Less direct euphemisms were usually used. But the underlying assumption of dualism between a law-abiding majority and a reckless, feckless minority was expressed at one conference in the phrase 'the job of policing is to protect the goodies and to stop the baddies'.

38 This salience was demonstrated in graphs in some of the PowerPoint packs I worked on. These charts tracked MORI opinion poll data, showing that crime and anti-social behaviour were consistently high up the list of public concerns, at least until the credit crunch of 2008/9 displaced these fears.

39 This concept is based on Habermas' theory of the 'ideal speech situation', which lays out the presuppositions of communicative action. When the reaching of consensus through dialogue is bypassed by the use of money or power, then communication loses its ideal, emancipatory character. This distorts the principles which give the possibility of meaning to communication.

40 http://www.cabinetoffice.gov.uk/strategy/about.aspx [accessed 12 January 2010].

41 Johnson said in a television interview, '[w]hat you cannot have is a chief adviser at the same time stepping into the political field and campaigning against government decisions. You can do one or the other. You can't do both.' (BBC 2009)

42 Literally 'without seed' – the unpollinated buds of the female plant provide the strongest concentration of the active ingredient THC (delta-9-tetrahy drocannabinol).

43 Although caution should again be applied in interpreting this study, which used non-random sampling and rejected many seized samples for being too small for analysis.

44 E.g. 'we remain rigid in our opposition to those who sell the drugs, abuse our young people and derive profit from it. We are not ashamed to say that we will not move one jot in terms of the 14 years that should follow such people' (Baroness Scotland of Asthal 2003).

45 The *Daily Mail* has been accused of mendacity in its exaggeration of drug harms since the early days of British drug control. Davenport-Hines (2001) found a cutting from the paper in the Home Office archives. In the margins of a 1923

article with the headline 'HASHISH PERIL', a civil servant had scrawled the word 'Liar!'

46 This was developed after legal challenge from nearly 200 ex-prisoners, who had been denied appropriate treatment (Hayes 2010). It still refuses to implement evidence-based needle exchange programmes in prisons (see Stevens *et al.* 2010; Stöver & Nelles 2003)

47 Regression to the mean is the statistical phenomenon which means that people or groups who have extreme scores at one point in time are likely to have less extreme scores at a later point in time. Donald Campbell sardonically recommended that 'trapped administrators' use it to ensure that their programmes come out of evaluation in a positive light (Campbell 1969: 426). Home Office civil servants seem, in this case at least, to have taken Campbell's advice to heart. Hope (2008) goes further, arguing that the separation between science and politics has collapsed and that civil servants have gone on the offensive against academic sources of counter-expertise. I have experienced such an attack myself, while trapped in a lift with a civil servant who was in charge of DIP. I had just made this point about regression to the mean in a conference session. He made it clear that he was not happy with this critique of his methodology.

48 The inverted commas around 'voluntarily' are there because many drug users who enter drug treatment without formal pressure from the legal system still feel some forms of pressure to be in treatment (Stevens *et al.* 2006).

49 It may seem naïve to trust people's own reports about their offending. However, studies comparing self-reports to other indicators have shown that such self-report can be a valid and reliable indicator of offending behaviour (Gossop *et al.* 2006; Nurco 1985).

50 The EuropASI score uses answers to questions on the frequency of use of various drugs in the previous 30 days to create a composite score for the severity of addiction (Koeter & Hartgers 1997).

51 The data from the 2004 *Offending, Crime and Justice Survey* were retrieved from the UK Data Archive at the University of Essex. They were created by the Home Office Research, Development and Statistics Directorate, National Centre for Social Research and BMRB. The data are Crown Copyright.

52 Such debate, according to at least one commentator, is immaterial to the development of more intensive methods for surveillance and control. According to Haggerty (2009), we need to challenge the reasoning behind the development of such expansive systems of state supervision. If we focus narrowly on their effectiveness, we risk ceding the argument to advocates of expansion who see nothing wrong with the state monitoring ever-increasing elements of our lives.

53 Decommodification is a term associated with the work of Esping-Anderson (1990) on welfare regimes. It means the level of access to goods and services that the people of a country have when they do not have access to the labour market. It is measured by an index based on three types of welfare support: unemployment benefits, sickness pay and pensions.

54 Culture is used here to refer to a system within which people hold each other accountable for their adherence to expected standards of behaviour (Douglas 1992).

55 The Governor was subsequently forced to accept cuts of $1.2 billion to the 2009/10 prison budget, but as of November 2009 this budget was forecast to be overspent by $1.4 billion – giving a net *increase* of $200 million at a time of financial crisis (Drug Policy Alliance 2009). He now seems to have reconsidered this imbalance and has proposed to amend California's constitution to ensure that

no more is spent on prisons than on higher education (Office of the Governor 2010).

56 This tactic of disinvesting in human potential in favour of the politics of vengeful exclusion is unfortunately being replicated in England and Wales. In December 2009, the government announced a package of severe cuts to university budgets, but plans are still active to build more prisons.

57 This provides another echo of slavery. Until it was amended in 1868, the Constitution of the United States included a clause that stated that slaves would be counted (at three fifths of their actual number) in deciding the level of representation of each state in the federal government.

58 The Director of the ONDCP is now Gil Kerlikowske, a former Seattle Police Chief. His Deputy is Thomas McLellan, who is an internationally renowned researcher, with a track record of calling for expansion of evidence-based treatment for drug addicts. Kerlikowske has stated that US drug control policy will no longer be presented as a 'war on drugs'. In a recent speech, he called for more priority to be given to public health approaches and highlighted the problem of prisoner re-entry. However, his suggested solutions did not include reducing the prison population and expanding harm reduction services. Rather, he advocated expanded surveillance of drug prescribers and users and drug testing of ex-prisoners as 'technological fixes' (Kerlikowske 2009b).

59 Obama's Democrat predecessor presided over the largest increase in imprisonment of any US leader and was also an enthusiastic extender of 'invisible' punishments, including the exclusion of first-time drug offenders from public housing (Rubinstein & Mukamal 2002).

60 That this ranking is irrelevant to drug policy outcomes is suggested by the unremarked-upon fact that the Netherlands is first on the list and the UK is third. The Netherlands has higher rates of drug use than Sweden, but low rates of drug problems. The UK has much higher rates of both use and related problems.

61 The assumption that enhanced penalties for dealing drugs near schools would somehow protect young people has been challenged by research in Massachusetts (Brownsberger *et al.* 2004). It showed that the school zone statute 'fails to push drug dealing away from schools'. It also showed how this type of statute falls disproportionately on poor, urban dwellers, as they are the most likely to live and work within these densely populated zones.

62 Hulsman was an abolitionist in that he wanted to do away with the use of criminal laws to resolve social conflicts (van Swaaningen 2010).

63 The prosecution guidelines are known by the acronym AHOJ-G: no advertising (*Affichering*); no selling hard drugs (*Harddrugs*); no nuisance (*Overlast*); no selling to minors (*Jeugdigen*); and no selling of large quantities (*Grote hoeveelheden*). The initial amount of 30 grams of cannabis under which buyers and sellers would not be prosecuted was reduced to five grams in 1995. Coffee shops are not punished if they hold less than 500g of cannabis in stock. They still engage in crime when they purchase this stock. This semi-tolerated legal anomaly has come to be known as the 'backdoor problem'.

64 The maximum sentences are rarely applied in any of these countries. They do give an indication of the relative severity with which drug offenders are treated, as do the comparable scenarios given in the country reports to the European Legal Database on Drugs (see http://eldd.emcdda.europa.eu/html.cfm/index5174EN.html#).

65 For readers unfamiliar with correlation coefficients, it is generally thought that a value of 'r' of between 0.4 and 0.7 indicates a moderate correlation. Figures between 0.7 and 0.9 indicate a strong correlation. The value of 'p' indicates how

likely it is that this correlation is a result of random variation. Values below 0.01 suggest that the probability of this is less than one per cent.

66 Data was not available for injecting drug use in Sweden, Ireland or Israel. The figure for Canada was excluded as an outlier in the analysis. Its estimated prevalence of injecting drug use was 1.3 per cent. Its decommodification index value was 25.

67 I have excluded the report that I wrote with Peter Reuter for the UK Drug Policy Commission (Reuter & Stevens 2007) as we deliberately refrained from making specific policy recommendations.

68 The fact that the power of arrest was retained for cannabis possession when it was reclassified to class C in 2004 undermined the intent of the Police Foundation recommendation.

69 The CSJ report also engages in a rewrite of drug policy history by arguing that the Labour government's commitment to harm reduction services represents a 'fundamental shift' from previous policies. In fact, as I showed in Chapter 6, there was a great deal of continuity from the Thatcher and Major Conservative governments to the policies pursued under Labour. The commitment to harm reduction began during the prime ministerial tenure of Margaret Thatcher. The multi-agency structure for drug treatment was created under Major. The focus on methadone as the frontline treatment for heroin users goes back even further. The rise of methadone took off in the 1970s, after restrictions were imposed on the old British system of heroin prescription (Marks 1993). Labour's innovations were to pour money into these structures and to insist on a greater degree of collaboration between health and criminal justice agencies. There was no fundamental shift.

70 My own experience of researching outcomes from an abstinence-based structured day care programme, as part of the *QCT Europe* study, was that many clients dropped out in the first few days and weeks of the programme. They were unable to comply with the abstinence requirement. The smaller number who stayed with the programme were able to use it to help them reduce their drug use.

71 The campaign for this commission notes that British workers would have to do a 40 hour week on minimum wage for 226 years to earn the average annual pay of a FTSE 100 company's chief executive.

72 Some measures to strengthen the independent role of Parliament have recently been proposed (House of Commons Reform Committee 2009), but seem unlikely to be fully implemented.

73 Les King worked for nearly 30 years at the British Forensic Science Service. He has advised the European Monitoring Centre on Drugs and Drug Addiction that the existing European Early Warning System should anticipate drugs that may emerge, as well as studying existing substances (King 2009). He resigned from the Advisory Council on the Misuse of Drugs in autumn 2009 in protest at the sacking of Professor Nutt.

Bibliography

ACLU (2003) *Race and the War on Drugs*, New Haven, CT: American Civil Liberties Union Drug Policy Litigation Project.

ACMD (1979) *Report on a Review of the Classification of Controlled Drugs and of Penalties under Schedules 2 and 4 of the Misuse of Drugs Act 1971*, London: Home Office.

ACMD (1988) *AIDS and Drug Misuse: Part One*, London: Department of Health and Social Security.

ACMD (1998) *Drug Misuse and the Environment*, London: The Stationery Office.

ACMD (2002) *The Classification of Cannabis under the Misuse of Drugs Act, 1971*, London: Home Office.

ACMD (2008a) *MDMA ('ecstasy'): a review of its harms and classification under the Misuse of Drugs Act 1971*, London: Home Office.

ACMD (2008b) *Cannabis: Classification and Public Health*, London: Home Office.

ACPO (2009) *ACPO Guidance on Cannabis Possession for Personal Use*, London: Association of Chief Police Officers.

Allen, C. (2007) *Crime, Drugs and Social Theory: A Phenomenological Approach*, Aldershot: Ashgate.

Amon, J.J., Garfein, R.S., Ahdieh-Grant, L., Armstrong, G.L., Ouellet, L.J., Latka, M.H., Vlahov, D., Strathdee, S.A., Hudson, S.M., Kerndt, P., Des Jarlais, D. and Williams, I.T. (2008) 'Prevalence of Hepatitis C virus infection among injection drug users in the United States, 1994–2004', *Clinical Infectious Diseases*, 46(12): 1852–58.

Aneshensel, C.S. and Sucoff, C.A. (1996) 'The neighborhood context of adolescent mental health', *Journal of Health and Social Behavior*, 37(4): 293–310.

Anglin, M.D. and Speckart, G. (1988) 'Narcotics use and crime: a multisample, multiperiod analysis', *Criminology*, 26: 197–233.

Arseneault, L., Cannon, M., Witton, J. and Murray, R.M. (2004) 'Causal association between cannabis and psychosis: Examination of the evidence', *British Journal of Psychiatry*, 184(2): 110–17.

Asmussen Frank, V., Bjerge, B. and Houberg, E. (eds) (2008) *Drug Policy: History, Theory and Consequences*, Aarhus: Aarhus University Press.

Asthana, S., Gibson, A., Moon, G., Brigham, P. and Dicker, J. (2004) 'The demographic and social class basis of inequality in self reported morbidity: an exploration using the Health Survey for England', *Journal of Epidemiology and Community Health*, 58(4): 303–07.

Atkinson, A.B. (2008) *The Changing Distribution of Earnings in OECD Countries*, Oxford: Oxford University Press.

Aust, R. and Smith, N. (2003) *Ethnicity and drug use: key findings from the 2001/2002 British Crime Survey. Findings 209*, London: Home Office.

Babor, T., Caulkins, J., Edwards, G., Fischer, B., Foxcroft, D., Humphreys, K., Obot, I., Rehm, J., Reuter, P., Room, R., Rossow, I. and Strang, J. (2010) *Drug Policy and the Public Good*, Oxford: Oxford University Press.

Bailey, R., Fuller, E. and Ormston, R. (2010) 'Smoking, drinking and drugs: reactions to reforms', in A. Park, J. Curtice, K. Thomson, M. Phillips, E. Clery and S. Butt (eds), *British Social Attitudes. The 26th Report*, London: Sage.

Ball, J.C., Rosen, L., Flueck, J.A. and Nurco, D.N. (1981) 'The criminality of heroin addicts: When addicted and when off opiates', in J.A. Inciardi (ed.), *The Drugs-Crime Connection*, Beverley Hills: Sage.

Bancroft, A. (2009) *Drugs, Intoxication and Society*, Cambridge: Polity Press.

Barendregt, C. and van de Mheen, D. (2009) 'Then there was silence on the streets. Developments in the street scene of Rotterdam in the last decade', *Drugs: Education, Prevention and Policy*, 16(6): 497–511.

Baroness Scotland of Asthal (2003) *Lords Hansard: 12th November 2003. Column 1501*, London: Stationery Office.

Barton, A. (2003) *Illicit Drugs: Use and Control*, London: Routledge.

Bauman, Z. (2007) *Consuming Life*, Cambridge: Polity Press.

BBC (2009) *Drugs adviser was wrong – Johnson*, 1st November 2009. Available <http://news.bbc.co.uk/1/hi/8336509.stm> (accessed 25 January 2010).

Beatty, P., Petterutti, A. and Ziedenberg, J. (2007) *The Vortex: The Concentrated Racial Impact of Drug Imprisonment and the Characteristics of Punitive Countries*, Washington, DC: Justice Policy Institute.

Becker, H. (1963) *Outsiders: Studies in the Sociology of Deviance*, New York: The Free Press.

Beckett, K. and Western, B. (2001) 'Governing social marginality: Welfare, incarceration, and the transformation of state policy', *Punishment and Society*, 3(1): 43–59.

Bennett, T. (1998) *Drugs and crime: the results of research on drug testing and interviewing arrestees*, London: Home Office Research and Statistics Directorate.

Bennett, T. and Holloway, K. (2005) *Understanding Drugs, Alcohol and Crime*, Maidenhead: Open University Press.

Bennett, T. and Holloway, K. (2007) *Drug-Crime Connections*, Cambridge: Cambridge University Press.

Bennett, T., Holloway, K. and Farrington, D. (2008) 'The statistical association between drug misuse and crime: A meta-analysis', *Aggression and Violent Behaviour*, 13: 107–18.

Benoit, E. (2003) 'Not just a matter of criminal justice: States, institutions, and North American drug policy', *Sociological Forum*, 18(2): 269–95.

Bergeron, H. (2009) *Sociologie de la Drogue*, Paris: Éditions la Découverte.

Berridge, V. (1999) *Opium and the People*. revised edition, London: Free Association Books.

Berridge, V. and Strong, P. (1991) 'AIDS in the UK: Contemporary history and the study of policy', *Twentieth Century British History*, 2(2): 150–74.

Berridge, V. and Thom, B. (1996) 'Research and policy: What determines the relationship', *Policy Studies*, 17(1): 23–34.

Bewley-Taylor, D. (2002) 'Habits of a Hegemon: The United States and the Future of the Global Drug Prohibition Regime', in A. Armenta, M. Jelsma, T. Blickman, V. Montañés and R. Vargas (eds), *Polarisation and Paralysis in UN Drug Control. Breaking the Impasse*, Amsterdam: Transnational Institute.

Bewley-Taylor, D.R. (2005) 'Emerging policy contradictions between the United Nations drug control system and the core values of the United Nations', *International Journal of Drug Policy*, 16(6): 423–31.

Bhaskar, R. (1978) *A Realist Theory of Science*, Sussex: Harvester Press.

Bieleman, B., Beelen, A., Nijkamp, R. and de Bie, E. (2008) *Coffeeshops in Nederland 2007: Summary*, Groningen: Intraval.

Bishop of Oxford (1997) *Lords Hansard. 27th October 1997: Column 957*, London: Stationery Office.

Black, N. (2001) 'Evidence based policy: proceed with care', *British Medical Journal* 323: 275–79.

Blackman, S. (2004) *Chilling Out: The Cultural Politics of Substance Consumption, Youth and Drug Policy*, Maidenhead: Open University Press.

Blackmon, D.A. (2008) *Slavery by Another Name: The Re-Enslavement of Black People in America from the Civil War to World War II*, New York: Doubleday.

Blanken, P., Hendriks, V.M., van Ree, J.M. and van den Brink, W. (2010) 'Outcome of long-term heroin-assisted treatment offered to chronic, treatment-resistant heroin addicts in the Netherlands', *Addiction*, 105: 300–08.

Blomqvist, J., Palm, J. and Storbjörk, J. (2009) ' "More cure and less control" or "more care and lower costs"? Recent changes in services for problem drug users in Stockholm and Sweden', *Drugs: Education, Prevention and Policy*, 16(6): 479–96.

Bloor, M., Gannon, M., Hay, G., Jackson, G., Leyland, A.H. and McKeganey, N. (2008) 'Contribution of problem drug users' deaths to excess mortality in Scotland: secondary analysis of cohort study', *British Medical Journal*, 337(7666): a478.

Blueprint Evaluation Team (2009) *Blueprint Drugs Education: The Response of Pupils and Parents to the Programme*, Stirling: Institute for Social Marketing.

Blumstein, A. and Wallman, J. (eds) (2000) *The Crime Drop in America*, New York: Cambridge University Press.

Boekhout van Solinge, T. (2004) *Dealing with Drugs in Europe: An Investigation of European Drug Control Experiences: France, the Netherlands and Sweden*, The Hague: BJu Legal Publishers.

Bollinger, L. (2004) 'Drug law and policy in Germany and the European Community: Recent developments', *Journal of Drug Issues* (Summer): 491–510.

Bonnie, R.J. and Whitebread, C.H. (1974) *The Marijuana Conviction: A History of Marijuana Prohibition in the United States*, Charlottesville: University of Virginia Press.

Bouchard, M. Culture hydroponique et capacité organisationelle du marché domestique de marijuana, paper presented to the Societies of Criminology 1st Key Issues Conference, Paris, May 2004.

Bourdieu, P. (1984) *Distinction: A Social Critique of the Judgment of Taste*, Boston, MA: Harvard University Press.

Bourdieu, P. (1990) *The Logic of Practice*, Cambridge: Polity Press.

Bourdieu, P. (1998) *Practical Reason: On the Theory of Action*, Cambridge: Polity Press.

Bourdieu, P. (2000) *Pascalian Meditations*, Cambridge: Polity Press.

Bourgois, P. (1996) *In Search of Respect: Selling Crack in El Barrio*, Cambridge: Cambridge University Press.

Bourgois, P. (1997) 'Résistance et autodestruction dans l'apartheid américain', *Actes De La Recherche En Sciences Sociales*, (120): 60–68.

Bourgois, P. (2000) 'Disciplining addictions: The bio-politics of methadone and heroin in the United States', *Culture Medicine and Psychiatry*, 24(2): 165–95.

Bowling, B. (1999) 'The rise and fall of New York murder: Zero tolerance or crack's decline?' *British Journal of Criminology*, 39(4): 531–54.

Bowling, B. and Phillips, C. (2002) *Racism, Crime and Justice*, Harlow: Longman.

Bowling, B. and Phillips, C. (2007) 'Disproportionate and discriminatory: Reviewing the evidence on police stop and search', *Modern Law Review*, 70(6): 936–61.

Boyd, S. (1999) *Mothers and Illicit Drugs: Transcending the Myths*, Toronto: University of Toronto Press.

Boyum, D. and Reuter, P. (2005) *An Analytic Assessment of U.S. Drug Policy*, Washington, DC: The AEI Press.

Brewer, D.D., Potterat, J.J., Garrett, S.B., Muth, S.Q., Roberts, J.M., Kasprzyk, D., Montano, D.E. and Darrow, W.W. (2000) 'Prostitution and the sex discrepancy in reported number of sexual partners', *Proceedings of the National Academy of Sciences of the United States of America*, 97(22): 12385–88.

Brewer, M., Muriel, A. and Wren-Lewis, L. (2009a) '*Accounting for changes in inequality since 1968: decomposition analyses for Great Britain*', London: Government Equalities Office. Online. Available <http://www.equalities.gov.uk/pdf/Accounting%20for%20changes%20in%20inequality.pdf> (accessed 25 January 2010).

Brewer, M., Muriel, A., Phillips, D. and Sibieta, L. (2009b) *Poverty and Inequality in the UK: 2009*, London: Institute for Fiscal Studies.

Brochu, S., da Agra, C. and Cousineau, M.-M. (eds) (2002) *Drugs and Crime Deviant Pathways*, Aldershot: Ashgate.

Brown, G. (2010) '*Letter to Danny Kushlick*', London: Transform Drug Policy Foundation. Online. Available <http://transform-drugs.blogspot.com/2010/01/gordon-brown-responds-to-transforms.html> (accessed 21 January 2010).

Brownsberger, W.N., Aromaa, S.E., Brownsberger, C.N. and Brownsberger, S.C. (2004) 'An empirical study of the school zone anti-drug law in three cities in Massachusetts', *Journal of Drug Issues*, 34(4): 933–49.

Brugal, M.T., Domingo-Salvany, A., Puig, R., Barrio, G., Garcia de Olalla, P. and de la Fuente, L. (2005) 'Evaluating the impact of methadone maintenance programmes on mortality due to overdose and AIDS in a cohort of heroin users in Spain', *Addiction*, 100(7): 981–89.

Buchanan, J. and Young, L. (2000) 'The war on drugs – a war on drug users?' *Drugs: Education, Prevention and Policy*, 7(4): 409–22.

Bui, H.S. (2009a) 'Prisons and Race Equality', in H.S. Bui (ed.), *Race and Criminal Justice*, London: Sage.

Bui, H.S. (2009b) 'Foreign National Prisoners: Issues and Debates', in H.S. Bui (ed.), *Race and Criminal Justice*, London: Sage.

Burr, A. (1987) 'Chasing the dragon: Heroin misuse, dependency and crime in the context of South London culture', *The British Journal of Criminology*, 27(4): 333–57.

Buxton, J. (2006) *The Political Economy of Narcotics: Production, Consumption and Global Markets*, London: Zed Books.

Camber, R. (2008) 'Tetra Pak billionaire pair told to take monthly drug test', *Daily Mail*, 7 August 2008.

Campbell, A. (2008) *'Letter to Professor David Nutt'*, London: Home Office. Online. Available <http://press.homeoffice.gov.uk/documents/2009-02-10-Campbell-Nutt-Ec1.pdf> (accessed 22 November 2009).

Campbell, D. (2009a) 'Cocaine drug of choice for under-25s, NHS figures suggest', *The Observer*, 4 October 2009.

Campbell, D. (2009b) 'Vatican's stance on UN drugs policy "risks lives" ', *The Guardian*, 27 February 2009.

Campbell, D.T. (1969) 'Reforms as experiments', *American Psychologist*, 24(4): 409–29.

Care Quality Commission (2010) *Count me in census 2009*, London: Care Quality Commission.

Carlen, P. (2008) 'Imaginary Penalities and Risk-crazed Governance', in P. Carlen (ed.), *Imaginary Penalities*, Cullompton: Willan.

Carlen, P. and Worrall, A. (2004) *Analysing Women's Imprisonment*, Cullompton: Willan.

Carmichael, A. (2005) *Commons Hansard: Standing Committee F. Thursday 27 January 2005. Column 15*, London: The Stationery Office.

Carnwath, T. and Smith, I. (2002) *Heroin Century*, London: Routledge.

Carter, P. (2003) *Managing Offenders, Reducing Crime: A New Approach*, London: Prime Minister's Strategy Unit.

Caulkins, J.P., Knoll, C., Tragler, G. and Zuba, D. (2004) 'Modelling dynamic trajectories of initiation and demand: The case of the US cocaine epidemic', *Healthcare Management Science*, 7: 319–29.

Chambliss, W.J. (1976) 'The State and Criminal Law', in W.J. Chambliss and M. Mankoff (eds.), *Whose Law, What Order? A Conflict Approach to Criminology*, New York: John Wiley & Sons.

Chatwin, C. (2003) 'Drug policy developments within the European Union', *British Journal of Criminology*, 43: 567–82.

Chein, I., Gerard, D.L., Lee, R.S. and Rosenfeld, E. (1964) *The Road to H: Narcotics, Delinquency and Social Policy*, New York: Basic Books.

Chen, C.-Y., Storr, C.L. and Anthony, J.C. (2009) 'Early-onset drug use and risk for drug dependence problems', *Addictive Behaviors*, 34(3): 319–22.

Chesney-Lind, M. (2002) 'Imprisoning Women: The Unintended Victims of Mass Imprisonment', in M. Mauer and M. Chesney-Lind (eds), *Invisible Punishment: The Collateral Consequences of Mass Imprisonment*, New York: The New Press.

Chomsky, N. (1973) 'Psychology and ideology', in N. Chomsky (ed.), *For Reasons of State*, New York: Vintage.

Chowdry, H., Crawford, C. and Goodman, A. (2009) *Drivers and Barriers to Educational Success: Evidence from the Longitudinal Study of Young People in England*, London: The Institute for Fiscal Studies.

Christie, N. (1986) 'Suitable Enemies', in H. Bianchi and R. v. Swaaningen (eds), *Abolitionism: Towards a Non-repressive Approach to Crime*, Amsterdam: Free University Press.

Christie, N. (2000) *Crime Control as Industry: Towards Gulags Western Style*. 3rd edn, London: Routledge.

Clark, D.B. (2004) 'The natural history of adolescent alcohol use disorders', *Addiction*, 99(Supplement 2): 5–22.

Clarke, C. (2005) *Commons Hansard debates. 18 January 2005: Column 696*, London: www.parliament.uk.

Cloward, R.A. and Ohlin, L.E. (1960) *Delinquency and Opportunity: A Theory of Delinquent Gangs*, New York: The Free Press.

Cohen, P. The case of the two Dutch drug policy commissions. An exercise in harm reduction 1968–1976, paper presented to the 5th International Conference on the Reduction of Drug related Harm, Toronto, 1994.

Cohen, P. (2006) *Looking at the UN, smelling a rat. A comment on 'Sweden's successful drug policy: a review of the evidence' UNODC September 2006*, Online. Available <http://www.cedro-uva.org/lib/cohen.looking.html> (accessed 23 December 2009).

Cohen, P. and Sas, A. (1994) 'Cocaine use in Amsterdam in nondeviant subcultures', *Addiction Research*, 2(1): 71–94.

Cohen, S. (1985) *Visions of Social Control*, Cambridge: Polity Press.

Cohen, S. and Taylor, L. (1992) *Escape Attempts: The Theory and Practice of Resistance to Everyday Life. Second edition*, London: Routledge.

Collison, M. (1993) 'Punishing drugs: criminal justice and drug use', *British Journal of Criminology*, 33(3): 382–99.

Collison, M. (1995) *Police, Drugs and Community*, New York: Free Association Books.

Collison, M. (1996) 'In search of the high life: Drugs, crime, masculinities and consumption', *British Journal of Criminology*, 36(3): 428–44.

Colman, A.M. and Gorman, L.P. (1982) 'Conservatism, dogmatism, and authoritarianism in British police officers', *Sociology* 16(1): 1–11.

Comfort, M. (2008) ' "The best seven years I could'a done": the reconstruction of imprisonment as rehabilitation', in P. Carlen (ed.), *Imaginary Penalities*, Cullompton: Willan.

Commons Hansard Debates (1997a) *Drugs and Crime: 22 December 1997*, London: Stationery Office.

Commons Hansard Debates (1997b) *Illegal Drugs: 27 October 1997*, London: Stationery Office.

Cook, D. (2006) *Criminal and Social Justice*, London: Sage.

Coomber, R. and Maher, L. (2006) 'Street-level drug market activity in Sydney's primary heroin markets: Organization, adulteration practices, pricing, marketing and violence', *Journal of Drug Issues*, 36(3): 719–53.

Costa, A.M. (2008) *Making drug control 'fit for purpose': Building on the UNGASS decade. Report by the Executive Director of the United Nations Office on Drugs and Crime as a contribution to the review of the twentieth special session of the General Assembly*, Vienna: United Nations Office on Drugs and Crime.

Coulthard, M., Farrell, M., Singleton, N. and Meltzer, H. (2002) *Tobacco, alcohol and drug use and mental health*. London: Office for National Statistics.

Courtwright, D.T. (2001) *Dark Paradise. A History of Opiate Addiction in America*, Cambridge, MA: Harvard University Press.

CSDH (2008) *Closing the gap in a generation: health equity through action on the social determinants of health. Final Report of the Commission on Social Determinants of Health*, Geneva: World Health Organization.

Currie, E. (1993) *Reckoning: Drugs, the Cities, and the American Future*, New York: Hill and Wang.

Curtis, R. and Wendel, T. (2007) ' "You're always training the dog": Strategic interventions to reconfigure drug markets', *Journal of Drug Issues*, 37: 867–92.

D'Souza, D.C. (2007) 'Cannabinoids and psychosis', in A. Abi-Dargham and O. Guillin (eds), *Integrating the Neurobiology of Schizophrenia. International Review of Neurobiology, Volume 78*, Amsterdam: Elsevier.

Davenport-Hines, R. (2001) *The Pursuit of Oblivion: A History of Narcotics, 1500–2000*, London: Weidenfeld and Nicolson.

Davies, C., English, L., Lodwick, A., McVeigh, J. and Bellis, M.A. (eds) (2009) *United Kingdom drug situation: annual report to the European Monitoring Centre for Drugs and Drug Addiction (EMCDDA) 2009*, London: Department of Health.

DDN (2009) 'Watershed for the ACMD', *Drink and Drug News*, 16 November 2009.

de Dominicis, L., Florax, R.J.G.M. and de Groot, H.L.F. (2008) 'A meta-analysis on the relationship between income inequality and economic growth', *Scottish Journal of Political Economy*, 55(5): 654–82.

Dean, K. (1997) 'Book review: The Imperative of Health: Public Health and the Regulated Body, by Deborah Lupton', *Social Science & Medicine*, 44(7): 1077–79.

Degenhardt, L., Hall, W.D. and Lynskey, M.T. (2003) 'Testing hypotheses about the relationship between cannabis use and psychosis', *Drug and Alcohol Dependence*, 71: 37–48.

Degenhardt, L., Day, C., Gilmour, S. and Hall, W. (2006) 'The "lessons" of the Australian "heroin shortage" ', *Substance Abuse Treatment, Prevention, and Policy*, 1(11).

Deitch, D., Koutsenok, I. and Ruiz, A. (2000) 'The relationship between crime and drugs: What we have learned in recent decades', *Journal of Psychoactive Drugs*, 32(4): 391–97.

DeNavas-Walt, C., Proctor, B.D., Smith, J.C. and U.S. Census Bureau (2009) *Income, Poverty, and Health Insurance Coverage in the United States: 2008*, Washington, DC: US General Printing Office.

Donoghue, K. (2002) 'Casualties of war: Criminal drug law enforcement and its special costs for the poor', *New York University Law Review*, 77(6): 1776–804.

Dorling, D. 'Crime, Poverty and Place'. 17th Eve Saville Memorial Lecture, London, June 2006.

Dorling, D., Rigby, J., Wheeler, B., Ballas, D., Thomas, B., Fahmy, E., Gordon, D. and Lupton, R. (2007) *Poverty, Wealth and Place in Britain, 1968 to 2005*, York: Joseph Rowntree Foundation.

Dorn, N. and Jamieson, A. (2000) *Room for Manoeuvre. Overview of comparative legal research into national drug laws of France, Germany, Italy, Spain, the Netherlands and Sweden and their relation to three international drugs conventions*, London: Drugscope.

Dorn, N., Murji, K. and South, N. (1992) *Traffickers: Drug Markets and Law Enforcement*, London: Routledge.

Dorn, N., Levi, M. and King, L. (2005) *Literature review on upper level drug trafficking. Online report 22/05*, London: Home Office.

Dostoyevsky, F. (1989 [1864]) *Notes from Underground*, New York: Norton.

Douglas, M. (1987) *How Institutions Think*, London: Routledge & Kegan Paul.

Douglas, M. (1992) *Risk and Blame*, London: Routledge.

Doward, J., Hinsliff, G. and McKie, R. (2009) 'Ministers face rebellion over drug tsar's sacking', *The Observer*, 1 November 2009.

Downes, D. (1988) *Contrasts in Tolerance: Post-War Penal Policy in the Netherlands and England and Wales*, Oxford: Clarendon Press.

Downes, D. (2007) 'Visions of penal control in the Netherlands', *Crime and Justice*, 36(1): 93–126.

Downes, D. and Hansen, K. (2006) *Welfare and punishment. The relationship between welfare spending and imprisonment*, London: Crime and Society Foundation.

Drucker, E. (1999) 'Drug prohibition and public health: 25 years of evidence', *Public Health Reports*, 114(1): 14–29.

Drug Policy Alliance (2009) 'Press release: California Budget Deficit Balloons, While Prisons on Schedule to Overspend by $1.4 Billion'. Online. Available <http://www.drugpolicy.org/news/pressroom/pressrelease/pr111809a.cfm> (accessed 22 December 2009).

Duke, K. (2003) *Drugs, Prisons and Policy-Making*, Basingstoke: Palgrave.

Duke, K. (2006) 'Out of crime and into treatment?: The criminalization of contemporary drug policy since "Tackling Drugs Together" ', *Drugs: Education, Prevention and Policy*, 13(5), 409–15.

Dunn, W.N. (1993) 'Policy reforms as arguments', in F. Fischer and J. Forester (eds), *The Argumentative Turn in Policy Analysis and Planning*, Durham, NC: Duke University Press.

Duster, T. (1970) *The Legislation of Morality: Drugs, Law and Moral Judgement*, New York: The Free Press.

Eagle, M. (2009) *Hansard Written Answers. 26 October 2009: Column 88W*, London: www.parliament.uk.

Easton, M. (2008) *Drug Treatment – Success or Failure?* Online. Available <http://www.bbc.co.uk/blogs/thereporters/markeaston/2008/10/drug_treatment_officials_were.html> (accessed 17 December 2009).

Edwards, G. (2004) *Matters of Substance: Drugs – and why everyone's a user*, London: Picador.

Egg, R. (1993) *Drogenabhängige Straftäter. Therapiemotivation durch justiziellen Zwang? Sonderdruck des Verfassers*, Erlangen-Nürnberg: Universität Erlangen-Nürnberg.

Eisenbach-Stangl, I., Moskalewicz, J. and Thom, B. (eds) (2009) *Two Worlds of Drug Consumption in Late Modern Societies*, Farnham: Ashgate.

Elder, R.W., Lawrence, B., Ferguson, A., Naimi, T.S., Brewer, R.D., Chattopadhyay, S.K., Toomey, T.L. and Fielding, J.E. (2010) 'The effectiveness of tax policy interventions for reducing excessive alcohol consumption and related harms', *American Journal of Preventive Medicine*, 38(2): 217–29.

EMCDDA (2009a) *Annual report 2009: The state of the drugs problem in Europe*, Luxembourg: Office for Official Publications of the European Communities.

EMCDDA (2009b) *Selected Issue. Drug Offences: Sentences and Other Outcomes. Online annex*, Lisbon: European Monitoring Centre on Drugs and Drug Addiction.

Epstein, E.J. (1977) *Agency of Fear: Opiates and Political Power in America*, New York: G. P. Putnam and Sons.

Esping-Anderson, G. (1990) *The Three Worlds of Welfare Capitalism*, Princeton, NJ: Princeton University Press.

Ettore, E. (1992) *Women and Substance Use*, Basingstoke: The Macmillan Press.

Faupel, C.E., Horowitz, A.M. and Weaver, G. (2004) *The Sociology of American Drug Use*, New York: McGraw-Hill.

Fergusson, D.M. and Horwood, L.J. (1998) 'Early conduct problems and later life opportunities', *Journal of Child Psychology and Psychiatry*, 39(8): 1097–108.

Fergusson, D.M. and Boden, J.M. (2008) 'Cannabis use and later life outcomes', *Addiction*, 103(6): 969–76.

Fergusson, D.M., Horwood, L.J. and Lynskey, M.T. (1997) 'The effects of unemployment on psychiatric illness during young adulthood', *Psychological Medicine*, 27(2): 371–81.

Fergusson, D.M., Horwood, L.J. and Woodward, L.J. (2001) 'Unemployment and psychosocial adjustment in young adults: causation or selection?', *Social Science & Medicine*, 53(3): 305–20.

Ferrell, J., Hayward, K. and Young, J. (2008) *Cultural Criminology: An Invitation*, London: Sage.

Ferri, M., Amato, L. and Davoli, M. (2006) 'Alcoholics Anonymous and other 12-step programmes for alcohol dependence', *Cochrane Database of Systematic Reviews*: DOI: 10.1002/14651858.CD005032.pub2.

Finestone, H. (1957) 'Cats, kicks and colour', *Social Problems*, 5(1): 3–13.

Fischer, C.S., Hout, M., Sanchez, M., Lucas, S.R., Swidler, A. and Voss, K. (1996) *Inequality by Design: Cracking the Bell Curve*, Princeton, NJ: Princeton University Press.

Flood-Page, C. and Mackie, A. (1998) *Sentencing Practice: an examination of decisions in magistrates' courts and the Crown Court in the mid-1990's. Home Office Research Study 180*, London: Home Office.

Flood-Page, C., Campbell, S., Harrington, V. and Miller, J. (2000) *Youth Crime: Findings from the 1998/99 Youth Lifestyles Survey. Home Office Research Study 209*, London: Home Office.

Foucault, M. (1979) *Discipline and Punish: The Birth of the Prison*, London: Penguin.

Foucault, M. (1998) *The History of Sexuality Vol.1: The Will to Knowledge*, London: Penguin.

Friedli, L. (2009) *Mental health, resilience and inequalities*, Copenhagen: World Health Organization.

Friedman, M. (1992) 'The Drug War as a Socialist Enterprise', in A.S. Trebach and K.B. Zeese (eds), *Friedman & Szasz on Liberty and Drugs*, Washington, DC: The Drug Policy Foundation.

Friedman, S.R. (1998) 'The political economy of drug-user scapegoating – and the philosophy and politics of resistance', *Drugs: Education Prevention and Policy*, 5(1): 15–32.

Frisher, M., Martino, O., Crome, I. and Croft, P. (2009a) 'Trends in drug misuse recorded in primary care in the UK from 1998 to 2005', *Journal of Public Health*, 31(1): 69–73.

Frisher, M., Crome, I., Martino, O. and Croft, P. (2009b) 'Assessing the impact of cannabis use on trends in diagnosed schizophrenia in the United Kingdom from 1996 to 2005', *Schizophrenia Research*, 113 (2): 123–28.

Frost, N. and Griffiths, P. (2008) *Assessing illicit drugs in wastewater: Potential and limitations of a new monitoring approach. Insights No. 9*, Lisbon: EMCDDA.

Gans, H.J. (1971) 'Social Science for Social Policy', in I.L. Horowitz (ed.), *The Use and Abuse of Social Science*, New Brunswick, NJ: Transaction Books.

GAO (2005) *Adult Drug Courts: Evidence Indicates Recidivism Reductions and Mixed Results for Other Outcomes. GAO-05-219*. Washington, DC: General Accountability Office.

Garland, D. (2001) *The Culture of Control: Crime and Social Order in Contemporary Society*, Oxford: Oxford University Press.
Garrett, J. (1972) *The Management of Government*, Harmondsworth: Penguin.
Garside, R. (2009) 'Why does Britain have such a high prison population?' in J. Collins and S. Siddiqui (eds.), *Transforming Justice: New approaches to the criminal justice system*, London: Criminal Justice Alliance.
Gaston, R., Best, D., Manning, V. and Day, E. (2009) 'Can we prevent drug related deaths by training opioid users to recognize and manage overdoses?', *Harm Reduction Journal*, 6(1): 26.
Gelsthorpe, L. and Burney, E. (2007) 'Parenting as crime control: a critique of government policy', paper presented to the 7th Annual Conference of the European Society of Criminology, Bologna.
Gendreau, P., Goggin, C., Cullen, F.T. and Paparozzi, M. (2002) 'The Common Sense Revolution and Correctional Policy', in J. McGuire (ed.), *Offender Rehabilitation and Treatment: Effective Programmes and Policies to Reduce Re-offending*, John Wiley & Sons: Chichester.
Gershon, P. (2004) *Releasing resources to the front line: independent review of public sector efficiency*, London: HM Treasury.
Gewirth, A. (1978) *Reason and Morality*, Chicago: University of Chicago Press.
Gewirth, A. (1982) *Human Rights: Essays on Justification and Applications*, Chicago: University of Chicago Press.
Gewirth, A. (1996) *The Community of Rights*, Chicago: University of Chicago Press.
Giddens, A. (1979) *Central Problems in Social Theory: Action, structure and contradiction in social analysis*, London: The Macmillan Press.
Gilmore, R.W. (2007) *Golden Gulag. Prisons, Surplus, Crisis, and Opposition in Globalizing California*, Berkeley: University of California Press.
Glaser, B.G. and Strauss, A.L. (1967) *The Discovery of Grounded Theory: Strategies for Qualitative Research*, New York: Aldine.
Glees, A. (2005) 'Evidence-based policy or policy-based evidence? Hutton and the government's use of secret intelligence', *Parliamentary Affairs*, 58(1): 138–55.
Godbout, J. (1983) *La participation contre la démocratie*, Montréal: Editions coopératives Albert Saint-Martin.
Godfrey, C., Eaton, G., McDougall, C. and Culyer, A. (2002) *The economic and social costs of Class A drug use in England and Wales, 2000. Home Office Research Study 249*. London: Home Office.
Goggins, P. (2005) *Hansard, House of Commons Written Answers for 5 February 2005, column 1429W*, London: The Stationery Office.
Goldberg, T. (2004) 'The evolution of Swedish drug policy', *Journal of Drug Issues*, 34(3): 551–76.
Goldkamp, J. (1994) 'Miami's treatment drug court for felony defendants: Some implications of assessment findings', *The Prison Journal*, 73(2): 110–66.
Goldkamp, J., White, M. and Robinson, J. (2001) 'Do drug courts work? Getting inside the drug court black box', *Journal of Drug Issues*, 31: 27–72.
Goldstein, P. (1985) 'The drugs-violence nexus: A tripartite framework', *Journal of Drug Issues*, 15: 493–506.
Goldstein, P., Brownstein, H., Ryan, P. and Bellucci, P. (1989) 'Crack and homicide in New York: A conceptually based event analysis', *Contemporary Drug Problems*, 16(4): 651–87.

Gossop, M. (2007) *Living With Drugs*, 6th edn, Aldershot: Ashgate.

Gossop, M., Marsden, J. and Stewart, D. (2000) 'Drug selling among drug misusers before intake to treatment and at 1-year follow-up: results from the National Treatment Outcome Research Study (NTORS)', *Drug and Alcohol Review*, 19(2): 143–51.

Gossop, M., Stewart, D., Treacy, S. and Marsden, J. (2002) 'A prospective study of mortality among drug misusers during a 4-year period after seeking treatment', *Addiction*, 97(1): 39–47.

Gossop, M., Marsden, J., Stewart, D. and Kidd, T. (2003) 'The National Treatment Outcome Research Study (NTORS): 4–5 year follow-up results', *Addiction*, 98: 291–303.

Gossop, M., Trakada, K., Stewart, D. and Witton, J. (2006) *Levels of conviction following drug treatment: Linking data from the National Treatment Outcome Research Study and the Offenders Index. Findings 275*, London: Home Office.

Gossop, M., Marsden, J., Stewart, D., Lehmann, P., Edwards, C., Wilson, A. and Segar, G. (1998) 'Substance use, health and social problems of service users at 54 drug treatment agencies', *British Journal of Psychiatry*, 173: 166–71.

Granfield, R. and Cloud, W. (2001) 'Social context and "natural recovery": the role of social capital in the resolution of drug-associated problems', *Substance Use and Misuse*, 36(11): 1543–70.

Grass, D., Caulkins, J.P., Feichtinger, G., Tragler, G. and Behrens, D.A. (2008) *Optimal Control of Nonlinear Processes With Applications in Drugs, Corruption, and Terror*, Berlin: Springer-Verlag.

Graves, J.L. (2004) *The Race Myth*, New York: Penguin.

Green, D.A. (2009a) 'Feeding wolves: Punitiveness and culture', *European Journal of Criminology*, 6(6): 517–36.

Green, P. (1991) *Drug Couriers*, London: Howard League for Penal Reform.

Green, W. (2009b) 'Tory Government to take hard line on drugs', *The Journal*. Online. Available <http://blogs.journallive.co.uk/journalblogcentral/2009/08/tory-government-to-take-hard-l.html> (accessed 20 January 2010).

Greene, J., Pranis, K. and Ziedenberg, J. (2006) *Disparity by Design: How drug-free zone laws impact racial disparity – and fail to protect youth*, Washington, DC: Justice Policy Institute.

Grover, C. (2008) *Crime and Inequality*, Cullompton: Willan.

Gusfield, J.R. (1987) 'Passage to Play: Rituals of Drinking Time in American Society', in M. Douglas (ed.), *Constructive Drinking: Perspectives on Drink from Anthropology*, Cambridge: Cambridge University Press.

Gyngell, K. (2007) *Breakthrough Britain: Ending the costs of social breakdown. Volume 4: Addictions*. London: Conservative Party.

Gyngell, K. (2009) *The Phoney War on Drugs*, London: Centre for Policy Studies.

Habermas, J. (1984) *Communication and the Evolution of Society*, Cambridge: Polity Press.

Habermas, J. (1987) *The Philosophical Discourse of Modernity*, Cambridge: Polity Press.

Habermas, J. (1996) *Between Facts and Norms: Contributions to a Discourse Theory of Law and Democracy*, Cambridge, MA: MIT Press.

Habermas, J. (2002 [1981]) 'Social Action, Purposive Activity and Communication', in M. Cooke (ed.), *On the Pragmatics of Communication*, Cambridge: Polity Press.

Haggerty, K.D. (2009) 'Methodology as a knife fight: The process, politics and paradox of evaluating surveillance', *Critical Criminology*, 17: 277–91.

Hajer, M.A. (1993) 'Discourse Coalitions and the Institutionalisation of Practice: The Case of Acid Rain in Britain', in F. Fischer and J. Forester (eds), *The Argumentative Turn in Policy Analysis and Planning*, Durham, NC: Duke University Press.

Hajer, M.A. (1995) *The Politics of Environmental Discourse: Environmental Modernization and the Policy Process*, Oxford: Oxford University Press.

Hales, J., Nevill, C., Pudney, S. and Tipping, S. (2009) *Longitudinal Analysis of the Offending, Crime and Justice Survey 2003–06. Research report 19*, London: Home Office.

Hall, S., Winlow, S. and Ancrum, C. (2008) *Criminal Identities and Consumer Culture. Crime, Exclusion and the New Culture of Narcissism*, Cullompton: Willan.

Hall, W. (2008a) 'The Adverse Health Effects of Cannabis and their Policy Implications.' Paper presented to the Second Annual Conference of the International Society for the Study of Drug Policy, Lisbon.

Hall, W. (2008b) 'The contribution of research to the development of a national cannabis policy in Australia,' *Addiction*, 103(7): 712–20.

Hallam, C. (2010) *What Can We Learn from Sweden's Drug Policy Experience*, Oxford: Beckley Foundation.

Hammer, T. (1992) 'Unemployment and use of drugs and alcohol among young people – a longitudinal study in the general population', *British Journal of Addiction*, 87(11): 1571–81.

Hammer, T. (1997) 'History dependence in youth unemployment', *European Sociological Review*, 13(1): 17–33.

Hanlon, T.E., Nurco, D.N., Kinlock, T.W. and Duszynski, K.R. (1990) 'Trends in criminal activity and drug use over an addiction career', *Journal of Drug Issues*, 16: 223–38.

Hannon, L. and Cuddy, M.M. (2006) 'Neighborhood ecology and drug dependence mortality: An analysis of New York City census tracts', *American Journal of Drug and Alcohol Abuse*, 32(3): 453–63.

Harcourt, B.E. (2002) *Illusion of Order: The False Promise of Broken Windows Policing*, Cambridge, MA: Harvard University Press.

Harden, K.P., Turkheimer, E. and Loehlin, J.C. (2007) 'Genotype by environment interaction in adolescents' cognitive aptitude', *Behavior Genetics*, 37(2): 273–83.

Hardwick, S. and King, L. (2008) *Home Office Cannabis Potency Study*, London: Home Office.

Harris, P. (2005) *Drug Induced: Addiction and Treatment in Perspective*, Lyme Regis: Russell House.

Hashibe, M., Morgenstern, H., Cui, Y., Tashkin, D.P., Zhang, Z.-F., Cozen, W., Mack, T.M. and Greenland, S. (2006) 'Marijuana use and the risk of lung and upper aerodigestive tract cancers: Results of a population-based case-control study', *Cancer Epidemiology Biomarkers & Prevention*, 15(10): 1829–34.

Haugaard, L., Sánchez-Garzoli, G., Isacson, A., Walsh, J. and Guitteau, R. (2008) *Compass for Colombia*, Washington, DC: Latin American Working Group Education Fund, Washington Office on Latin America, Center for International Policy, and U.S. Office on Colombia.

Hay, G., Gannon, M., MacDougall, J., Millar, T., Eastwood, C. and McKeganey, N. (2007) *National and regional estimates of the prevalence of opiate use and/or crack cocaine use 2005/06: a summary of key findings. Home Office Online Report 21/07*, London: Home Office.

Hayes, P. (2005) *Debate: This house believes that we need more coercive testing and treatment services, National Drug Treatment Conference*. London: Exchange Supplies.

Hayes, P. (2006) *Less crime, not more treatment, ACPO Drugs Conference*. Manchester, 21st November 2006: Association of Chief Police Officers.

Hayes, P. (2008) 'Evidence over ideology', *Druglink* (March/April): 22.

Hayes, P. (2010) 'We do offer drug addicts treatment in prison', (3rd February 2010). Online. Available <http://www.guardian.co.uk/commentisfree/2010/feb/03/drug-users-heard-by-system> (accessed 5 February 2010).

Hearnden, I. (2000) 'Problem drug use and probation in London: an evaluation', *Drugs-Education Prevention and Policy*, 7(4): 367–80.

Heaven, O. and Hudson, B. (2005) ' "Race", Ethnicity and Crime', in C. Hale, K. Hayward, A. Wahidin and E. Wincup (eds), *Criminology*, Oxford: Oxford University Press.

Helmer, J. (1975) *Drugs and Minority Oppression*, New York: The Seabury Press.

Herrnstein, R.J. and Murray, C. (1994) *The Bell Curve: Intelligence and Class Structure in American Life*, New York: Free Press.

Hills, J., Brewer, M., Jenkins, S., Lister, R., Lupton, R., Machin, S., Mills, C., Modood, T., Rees, T. and Riddell, S. (2010) *An anatomy of economic inequality in the UK: Report of the National Equality Panel*, London: Government Equalities Office.

Hillyard, P., Pantazis, C., Tombs, S., Gordon, D. and Dorling, D. (2005) *Criminal Obsessions. Why harm matters more than crime*, London: Crime and Society Foundation.

Hoare, J. (2009) *Drug Misuse Declared: Findings from the 2008/09 British Crime Survey. England and Wales. Home Office Statistical Bulletin 12/09*, London: Home Office.

Home Affairs Select Committee (2002) *The Government's Drug Policy: Is It Working? Third Report Session 2001–2002 HC 318*. London: The Stationery Office.

Home Office (2007) *Drugs Value for Money Review July 2007 Report*, London: Home Office.

Home Office (2008a) *'Evidence of the impact of the Drug Interventions Programme – Summaries and sources'*, London: Home Office. Online. Available <http://drugs.homeoffice.gov.uk/publication-search/dip/DIP-impact-evidence-round-up-v22835.pdf?view=Binary> (accessed 21st January 2010).

Home Office (2008b) *Drugs: protecting families and communities. The 2008–2018 drug strategy*, London: Home Office.

Home Office (2008c) *Press release: Government crackdown on cannabis*, London: Home Office.

Home Office (2009) *Stakeholder Key Messages for the Drug Interventions Programme – October 2009*, London: Home Office.

Hood, R. (1992) *Race and Sentencing*, Oxford: Clarendon Press.

Hope, T. (2001) 'Crime Victimisation and Inequality in Risk Society', in R. Matthews and J. Pitts (eds), *Crime, Disorder and Community Safety: A new agenda?*, London: Routledge.

Hope, T. (2008) 'The First Casualty: Evidence and Governance in a War Against Crime', in P. Carlen (ed.), *Imaginary Penalities*, Cullompton: Willan.

Horsley, S. (2007) *Dandy in the Underworld*, London: Sceptre.

Houberg, E. (forthcoming) 'Drug policy, control and welfare', *Drugs: Education, Prevention and Policy*.

Hough, M. and Turnbull, P. (2006) 'Over-regulation or legitimate control?', *International Journal of Drug Policy*, 17(3): 242–43.

Hough, M., Clancy, A., McSweeney, T. and Turnbull, P.J. (2003) *The impact of Drug Treatment and Testing Orders on offending: two-year reconviction results. Findings 184*, London: Home Office Research, Development and Statistics Directorate.

House of Commons Reform Committee (2009) *Rebuilding the House. First Report of Session 2008–09*, London: The Stationery Office.

House of Commons Science and Technology Committee (2006) *Drug classification: Making a hash of it?* London: The Stationery Office.

HPA (2008) *Shooting Up: Infections among injecting drug users in the United Kingdom 2007. An update*, London: Health Protection Agency.

Hughes, C. and Stevens, A. (forthcoming) 'What can we learn from the Portuguese decriminalisation of illicit drugs?', *British Journal of Criminology*.

Hughes, P., Crawford, G., Barker, N., Schumann, S. and Jaffe, J. (1971) 'The Social Structure of a Heroin-Copping Community', *American Journal of Psychiatry*, 128(5): 551–58.

Human Rights Watch (2009) *'Please, do not make us suffer any more . . .'. Access to Pain Treatment as a Human Right*, New York: Human Rights Watch.

Humar, A., Crotteau, S., Gruessne, A., Kandaswamy, R., Gruessner, R., Payne, W. and Lake, J. (2007) 'Steroid minimization in liver transplant recipients: impact on hepatitis C recurrence and post-transplant diabetes', *Clinical Transplantation*, 21(4): 526–31.

Hunt, N. and Stevens, A. (2004) 'Whose harm? Harm and the shift from health to coercion in UK drug policy', *Social Policy & Society*, 3(4): 333–42.

Hunt, N. and Lloyd, C. (2008) 'Drug Consumption Rooms: Between Evidence and Opinion', in A. Stevens (ed.), *Crossing Frontiers: International Developments in the Treatment of Drug Dependence*, Brighton: Pavilion Publishing.

Husak, D.N. (1992) *Drugs and Rights*, Cambridge: Cambridge University Press.

ICPS (2009) *'Prison Brief for Netherlands'*, London: International Centre for Prison Studies. Online. Available <http://www.kcl.ac.uk/depsta/law/research/icps/worldbrief/wpb_country.php?country=157> (accessed 13 January 2010).

IFS (2009) *'Spreadsheet: figures derived from Family Resources Survey'*, London: Institute for Fiscal Studies. Online. Available <http://www.ifs.org.uk/projects/127> (accessed 25 January 2010).

Inciardi, J.A. (1990) 'The Crack-Violence Connection Within a Population of Hard Core Adolescent Offenders', in M. De La Rosa, E.Y. Lambert and B. Gropper (eds), *Drugs and Violence: Causes, Correlates, and Consequences. NIDA Research Monograph 103*, Rockville, MD: National Institute on Drug Abuse.

Inciardi, J.A. (1999) 'Legalizing Drugs: Would it Really Reduce Violent Crime?', in J.A. Inciardi (ed.), *The Drug Legalization Debate, Second Edition*, Thousand Oaks, CA: Sage.

Inciardi, J.A. (2008) *The War on Drugs IV: The Continuing Saga of the Mysteries and Miseries of Intoxication, Addiction, Crime and Public Policy*, Boston, MA: Pearson.

Independent Inquiry into the Misuse of Drugs Act 1971 (2000) *Drugs and the Law*, London: Police Foundation.

Inglis, B. (1976) *The Opium War*, London: Hodder & Stoughton.

IRS (2006) *Table 5.–Returns with Positive Adjusted Gross Income (AGI)*, Washington, DC: Internal Revenue Service.

Jacques, S. and Wright, R. (2008) 'The relevance of peace to studies of drug market violence', *Criminology*, 46(1): 221–54.

James, S.E., Johnson, J. and Raghaven, C. (2004) ' "I couldn't go anywhere". Contextualising violence and drug abuse: A social network study', *Violence Against Women*, 10(9): 991–1014.

Jelsma, M. (2003) *The Erratic Crusade of the INCB. TNI Drug Policy Briefing No. 4*, Amsterdam: Transnational Institute.

Jelsma, M. and Kramer, T. (2009) *Redefining Targets: Towards a Realistic Afghan Drug Control Strategy*, Amsterdam: Transnational Institute.

John, P. (1998) *Analysing Public Policy*, London: Pinter.

Johnson, A. (2009) 'Memorandum: Advisory Council on the Misuse of Drugs'. Online. Available <http://www.parliament.uk/documents/upload/091118_b)_Letter_from_Alan_Johnson.pdf> (accessed 22 November 2009).

Johnson, B.D., Golub, A. and Dunlap, E. (2008) 'An analysis of alternatives to New York City's current marijuana arrest and detention policy', *Policing: An International Journal of Police Strategies & Management*, 31(2): 226–50.

Johnson, B.D., Goldstein, P.J., Preble, E., Schmeidler, J., Lipton, D.S., Spunt, B. and Miller, T. (1985) *Taking Care of Business: The Economics of Crime by Heroin Abusers*, Lexington, MA: Lexington Books.

Johnson, M. (2007) *Wasted: Violence, Addiction – and Hope*, London: Sphere.

Johnston, L.D., O'Malley, P.M., Bachman, J.G. and Schulenberg, J.E. (2009) *Monitoring the Future National Survey Results on Drug Use, 1975–2008. Volume I: Secondary School Students*, Bethesda, MD: National Institute on Drug Abuse.

Jones, A., Weston, S., Moody, A., Millar, T., Dollin, L., Anderson, T. and Donmall, M. (2007) *The Drug Treatment Outcomes Research Study (DTORS): Baseline Report*, London: Home Office.

Jones, A., Donmall, M., Millar, T., Moody, A., Weston, S., Anderson, T., Gittins, M., Abeywardana, V. and D'Souza, J. (2009) *The Drug Treatment Outcomes Research Study (DTORS): Final outcomes report*, London: Home Office.

Jowell, T. (1997) *Hansard: 19 November 1997. Column 431*, London: Stationery Office.

Joyce, H. (2007) 'How clever are we?', *Intelligent Life*, 1(2): 87–93.

Kant, I. (1981 [1785]) *Grounding for the Metaphysics of Morals*, Indianapolis, IN: Hackett Publishing Company.

Kaskutas, L.A. (2009) 'Alcoholics Anonymous effectiveness: Faith meets science', *Journal of Addictive Diseases*, 28(2): 145–57.

Katz, J. (1988) *Seductions of Crime. Moral and Sensual Attractions in Doing Evil*, New York: Basic Books

Keene, J. (2005) 'A case-linkage study of the relationship between drug misuse, crime, and psychosocial problems in a total criminal justice population', *Addiction Research and Theory*, 13(5): 489–502.

Kerlikowske, R.G. (2009a) 'A better-targeted drug fight'. Online. Available <http://pushingback.com/blogs/pushing_back/archive/2009/12/03/49335.aspx> (accessed 18 December 2009).

Kerlikowske, R.G. (2009b) Statement to the Public Services Summit. Stockholm. Online. Available <http://www.whitehousedrugpolicy.gov/news/speech09/121009_Stockholm.pdf> (accessed 17 December 2009).

King, L. (2009) New drugs coming our way: what are they and how do we detect them. Presentation to EMCDDA Conference on Identifying Europe's Information Needs for Effective Drug Policy, Lisbon: EMCDDA.

King, R. (2008) *Disparity By Geography: The War on Drugs in America's Cities*, Washington, DC: The Sentencing Project.

King, R. and Mauer, M. (2006) 'The war on marijuana: The transformation of the war on drugs in the 1990s', *Harm Reduction Journal*, 3(1): 6.

Kingdon, J. (1984) *Agendas, Alternatives, and Public Policies*, Boston, MA: Little, Brown.

Kleiman, M. (1989) *Marijuana: Costs of Abuse, Costs of Control*, New York: Greenwood Press.

Klein, A. (2008) *Drugs and the World*, London: Reaktion Books.

Klein, A. (2009) 'The Phoney Argument for a New Drug War', *Transform Media Blog*. Online. Available <http://transform-drugs.blogspot.com/2009/05/phoney-argument-for-new-drug-war.html> (accessed 4 January 2010).

Koeter, M. and Hartgers, C. (1997) *European Addiction Severity Index: Preliminary procedure for the computation of the EuropASI composite scores*, Amsterdam: Amsterdam Institute for Addiction Research.

Kokkevi, A. and Hartgers, C. (1995) 'Europe ASI: European adaptation of a multidimensional assessment instrument for drug and alcohol dependence', *European Addiction Research*, 1(4): 208–10.

Komarow, S. (1998) 'Dutch take offense to drug czar's allegation', *USA Today*.13 July 1998.

Kramer, T. (2009) *From Golden Triangle to Rubber Belt? The Future of Opium Bans in the Kokang and Wa Regions*, Amsterdam: Transnational Institute.

Kroll, B. and Taylor, A. (2008) *Interventions for children and families where there is parental drug misuse. Executive summary*, London: London School of Hygiene and Tropical Medicine.

Ksir, C., Hart, C. and Ray, O. (2006) *Drugs, Society and Human Behavior*, New York: McGraw-Hill.

Kübler, D. (2001) 'Understanding policy change with the Advocacy Coalition Framework: An application to Swiss drug policy', *Journal of European Public Policy*, 8(4): 623–41.

Labour Party (1997) *New Labour: Because Britain Deserves Better*, London: Labour Party.

Labour Party (2008) *Press release: Labour crackdown on cannabis*, London: Home Office.

Laidler, K.J. and Hunt, G. (2001) 'Accomplishing femininity among the girls in the gang', *British Journal of Criminology*, 41(4): 656–78.

Lalander, P. (2003) *Hooked on Heroin: Drugs and Drifters in a Globalized World*, Oxford: Berg.

Landis, D., Gaylord-Harden, N.K., Malinowski, S.L., Grant, K.E., Carleton, R.A. and Ford, R.E. (2007) 'Urban adolescent stress and hopelessness', *Journal of Adolescence*, 30(6): 1051–70.

Lane, S.D., Lurie, P., Bowser, B., Kahn, J. and Chen, D. (1999) 'The Coming of Age of Needle Exchange: A History Through 1993', in J.A. Inciardi and L.D. Harrison (eds), *Harm Reduction: National and International Perspectives*, Thousand Oaks, CA: Sage.

Lappi-Seppälä, T. (2008) 'Trust, welfare, and political culture: Explaining differences in national penal policies', *Crime and Justice*, 37(1): 313–88.

Latin American Commission on Drugs and Democracy (2009) '*Drugs and Democracy: Towards a Paradigm Shift*': Latin American Commission on Drugs and Democracy.

Online. Available <http://www.drogasedemocracia.org/Arquivos/declaracao_ ingles_ site.pdf> (accessed 24 January 2010).

Layder, D. (1998) *Sociological Practice: Linking Theory and Social Research*, London: Sage.

Le Grand, J. (1991) 'Equity as an Economic Objective', in B. Almond and D. Hill (eds), *Applied Philosophy: Morals and Metaphysics in Contemporary Debate*, London: Routledge.

Lea, J. (2002) *Crime and Modernity: Continuities in Left Realist Criminology*, London: Sage.

Lee, J.A. (1981) 'Some Structural Aspects of Police Deviance in Relations with Minority Groups', in C. Shearing (ed.), *Organizational Police Deviance*, Toronto: Butterworth.

Lee, W. [Burroughs, W.] (1953) *Junkie: Confessions of an Unredeemed Drug Addict. An Ace Original*, New York: Ace Books.

Lenton, S. (2008) 'Working with Windows: Translating Drug Research into Drug Policy', in D. Moore and P. Dietze (eds.), *Theory, Evidence and Context: Contemporary Innovations in Alcohol and Other Drug Practice in Australia*, Melbourne: Oxford University Press.

Lévi-Strauss, C. (1964) *Totemism*, trans. R. Needham, London: Merlin Press.

Levine, H.G. (2009) '*New York City's Marijuana Arrest Crusade. . . Continues*', New York: City University of New York. Online. Available <http://dragon.soc. qc. cuny.edu/ Staff/levine/NYC-MARIJUANA-ARREST-CRUSADE-CONTINUES-SEPT-2009.pdf> (accessed 4th January 2010).

Levitt, S.D. and Venkatesh, S.A. (2000) 'An economic analysis of a drug-selling gang's finances', *Quarterly Journal of Economics*, 115(3): 755–89.

Lewis, J. (2008) 'Prince Charles backs Tetra Pak couple Rausings and declares "they deserve a second chance" ', *Daily Mail*, 9 August 2008.

Liang, C., McClean, M.D., Marsit, C., Christensen, B., Peters, E., Nelson, H.H. and Kelsey, K.T. (2009) 'A population-based case-control study of marijuana use and head and neck squamous cell carcinoma', *Cancer Prevention Research*, 2(8): 759–68.

Lindert, P.H., Anthony, B.A. and Bourguignon, F. (2000) 'Three Centuries of Inequality in Britain and America', in B.A. Anthony and F. Bourguignon (eds.), *Handbook of Income Distribution*, Oxford: Elsevier.

Link, B.G., Phelan, J.C., Miech, R. and Westin, E.L. (2008) 'The resources that matter: Fundamental social causes of health disparities and the challenge of intelligence', *Journal of Health and Social Behavior*, 49(1): 72–91.

Lintzeris, N., Strang, J., Metrebian, N., Byford, S., Hallam, C., Lee, S., Zador, D. and RIOTT Group (2006) 'Methodology for the Randomised Injecting Opioid Treatment Trial (RIOTT): evaluating injectable methadone and injectable heroin treatment versus optimised oral methadone treatment in the UK', *Harm Reduction Journal*, 2006(3): 28.

Lister, R. (2008) 'Recognition and Voice: The Challenge for Social Justice', in G. Craig, T. Burchardt and D. Gordon (eds.), *Social Justice and Public Policy: Seeking Fairness in Diverse Societies*, Bristol: The Policy Press.

Lloyd, C. (2008) The cannabis classification debate in the UK: full of sound and fury, signifying nothing, paper presented to the Second Annual Conference of the International Society for the Study of Drug Policy, Lisbon.

Loader, I. (1998) 'Criminology and the Public Sphere: Arguments for Utopian Realism', in P. Walton and J. Young (eds), *The New Criminology Revisited*, Basingstoke: Palgrave Macmillan.

London, E.D. (2009) 'Studying addiction in the age of neuroimaging', *Drug and Alcohol Dependence*, 100(1–2): 182–85.

Lopez, A.D., Mathers, C.D., Ezzati, M., Jamison, D.T. and Murray, C.J.L. (2007) *Global Burden of Disease and Risk Factors*, Geneva: The World Bank and Oxford University Press.

Lord President of the Council and Leader of the House of Commons, Secretary of State for the Home Department, Secretary of State for Health and Secretary of State for Education and the Paymaster General (1995) *Tackling drugs together: a strategy for England 1995–98*, London: HMSO.

Lukes, S. (1974) *Power, a Radical View*, London: Macmillan.

Lupton, D. (1995) *The Imperative of Health: Public Health and the Regulated Body*, London: Sage.

Lurigio, A.J. and Schwartz, J.A. (1999) 'The nexus between drugs and crime: theory, research and practice', *Federal Probation*, 63: 67–72.

McAra, L. and McVie, S. (2005) 'The usual suspects? Street-life, young people and the police', *Criminal Justice*, 5(1): 5–36.

MacCoun, R. and Reuter, P. (2001a) 'Evaluating alternative cannabis regimes', *British Journal of Psychiatry*, 178: 123–28.

MacCoun, R. and Reuter, P. (2001b) *Drug War Heresies: Learning from Other Vices, Times, & Places*, Cambridge: Cambridge University Press.

MacCoun, R., Kilmer, B. and Reuter, P. (2003) 'Research on Drugs-Crime Linkages: The Next Generation', in National Institute of Justice (ed.), *Towards a Drugs and Crime Agenda for the 21st Century*, Washington, DC: NIJ.

MacCoun, R., Pacula, R.L., Chriqui, J.F., Harris, K.M. and Reuter, P.H. (2008) '*Do Citizens Know Whether Their State Has Decriminalized Marijuana? A Test of the Perceptual Assumption in Deterrence Theory*': JSP/Center for the Study of Law and Society. Online. Available <http://papers.ssrn.com/sol3/papers.cfm?abstract_id=1120930> (accessed 5 February 2010).

MacDonald, Z. and Pudney, S. (2000) 'Illicit drug use, unemployment, and occupational attainment', *Journal of Health Economics*, 19(6): 1089–115.

McGlothlin, W.H., Anglin, M.D. and Wilson, D.B. (1977) *An evaluation of the California Civil Addict Program*, Washington, DC: National Institute on Drug Abuse.

McGrail, S. (2007) 'Frozen out: How not to treat drug users', *Druglink*, 22(1): 20–22.

McGrail, S. and MacKintosh, D. (2009) *Making it local: A report on the London Drug Policy Forum Strategic Drug Partnership Delivery Project for the Home Office*, London: London Drug Policy Forum.

MacGregor, S. (1998) 'Pragmatism or Principle? Continuity and Change in the British Approach to Treatment and Control', in R. Coomber (ed.), *The Control of Drugs and Drug Users*, London: CRC Press.

MacGregor, S. (2009) 'Policy Responses to the Drug Problem', in S. MacGregor (ed.), *Responding to Drug Misuse*, London: Routledge.

McKeganey, N. (2005) *Random drug testing of schoolchildren: A shot in the arm or a shot in the foot for drug prevention?* York: Joseph Rowntree Foundation.

McKeganey, N., Morris, Z., Neale, J. and Robertson, M. (2004) 'What are drug users looking for when they contact drug services: abstinence or harm reduction?', *Drugs: Education, Prevention, and Policy*, 11(5): 423–35.

McKeganey, N., Bloor, M., Robertson, M., Neale, J. and MacDougall, J. (2006) 'Abstinence and drug abuse treatment: Results from the Drug Outcome Research in Scotland study', *Drugs: Education, Prevention, and Policy*, 13(6): 537–50.

McLaren, J.A., Silins, E., Hutchinson, D., Mattick, R.P. and Hall, W. (2010) 'Assessing evidence for a causal link between cannabis and psychosis: A review of cohort studies', *International Journal of Drug Policy*, 21(1): 10–19.

McSweeney, T. (2009) The impact of 'quasi-compulsory' drug treatment in one English region, paper presented to the 10th Meeting of the Expert Forum on Criminal Justice. Strasbourg, September 2009, London: Institute for Criminal Policy Research. Online. Available <http://www.kcl.ac.uk/content/1/c6/01/22/42/DIPandRe-Offending.pdf> (accessed 29 January 2010)

McSweeney, T., Stevens, A., Hunt, N. and Turnbull, P. (2007) 'Twisting arms or a helping hand? Assessing the impact of "coerced" and comparable "voluntary" drug treatment options', *British Journal of Criminology*, 47(3): 470–90.

McSweeney, T., Stevens, A., Hunt, N. and Turnbull, P. (2008) 'Drug testing and court review hearings: uses and limitations', *Probation Journal*, 55(1): 53–67.

Maddison, A. (2001) *The World Economy: A Millennial Perspective*, Paris: Organisation for Economic Cooperation and Development.

Maher, L. (1997) *Sexed Work. Gender, Race and Resistance in a Brooklyn Drug Market*, Oxford: Clarendon Press.

Mandel, M. (2009) 'A lost decade for jobs', *Business Week*. Online. Available <http://www.businessweek.com/the_thread/economicsunbound/archives/2009/06/a_lost_decade_f.html> (accessed 4 January 2010).

Manza, J. and Uggen, C. (2006) *Locked Out: Felon Disenfranchisement and American Democracy*, New York: Oxford University Press.

Mares, D.R. (2006) *Drug Wars and Coffeehouses: The Political Economy of the International Drug Trade*, Washington, DC: CQ Press.

Marks, J. (1993) 'The Paradox of Prohibition', in C. Brewer (ed.), *Treatment Options in Addiction: Medical Management of Alcohol and Opiate Abuse*, London: Gaskell.

Marmot, M. and Wilkinson, R.G. (eds) (1999) *Social Determinants of Health*, Oxford: Oxford University Press.

Marsden, J., Eastwood, B., Bradbury, C., Dale-Perera, A., Farrell, M., Hammond, P., Knight, J., Randhawa, K. and Wright, C. (2009) 'Effectiveness of community treatments for heroin and crack cocaine addiction in England: a prospective, in-treatment cohort study', *The Lancet*, 374(9697): 1262–70.

Mascini, P. and Houtman, D. (2006) 'Rehabilitation and repression: Reassessing their ideological embeddedness', *British Journal of Criminology*, 46(5): 822–36.

Mathers, B.M., Degenhardt, L., Phillips, B., Wiessing, L., Hickman, M., Strathdee, S.A., Wodak, A., Panda, S., Tyndall, M., Toufik, A. and Mattick, R.P. (2008) 'Global epidemiology of injecting drug use and HIV among people who inject drugs: a systematic review', *The Lancet*, 372(9651): 1733–45.

Mathiesen, T. (2004) *Silently Silenced: Essays on the Creation of Acquiescence in Modern Society*, Winchester: Waterside Press.

Matrix Knowledge Group (2007) *The Economic Case For and Against Prison*, London: Matrix Knowledge Group.

Matza, D. (1961) 'Subterranean traditions of youth', *The Annals of the American Academy of Political and Social Science*, 338(1): 102–18.

Matza, D. and Sykes, G.M. (1961) 'Juvenile delinquency and subterranean values', *American Sociological Review*, 26(5): 712–19.

Mauer, M. (2002) 'Mass Imprisonment and the Disappearing Voters', in M. Mauer and M. Chesney-Lind (eds.), *Invisible Punishment: The Collateral Consequences of Mass Imprisonment*, New York: The New Press.

Mauer, M. and Chesney-Lind, M. (eds.) (2002) *Invisible Punishment: The Collateral Consequences of Mass Imprisonment*, New York: The New Press.

May, T., Duffy, M., Warburton, H. and Hough, M. (2007) *Policing cannabis as a Class C drug: An arresting change?* York: Joseph Rowntree Foundation.

Measham, F. and Shiner, M. (2009) 'The legacy of "normalisation": The role of classical and contemporary criminological theory in understanding young people's drug use', *International Journal of Drug Policy*, 20(6): 502–08.

Measham, F., Moore, K., Newcombe, R. and Wel, Z. (2010) 'Tweaking, bombing, dabbing and stockpiling: The emergence of mephedrone and the perversity of prohibition', *Drugs and Alcohol Today*, 10(1): 14–21.

Meier, P., Purshouse, R., Meng, Y., Rafia, R. and Brennan, A. (2009) *Appraisal of alcohol minimum pricing and off-trade discount bans in Scotland*, Sheffield: ScHARR, University of Sheffield.

Mellor, P.A. and Shilling, C. (1997) *Re-Forming the Body: Religion, Community and Modernity*, London: Sage Publications.

Menard, S. and Mihalic, S. (2001) 'The tripartite conceptual framework in adolescence and adulthood: Evidence from a national sample', *Journal of Drug Issues*, 31(4): 905–39.

Merton, R.K. (1938) 'Social structure and anomie', *American Sociological Review*, 3: 672–82.

Messerschmidt, J.W. (1997) *Crime as Structured Action: Gender, Race, Class and Crime in the Making*, London: Sage Publications.

Mill, J.S. (1974 [1859]) *On Liberty*, Harmondsworth: Penguin.

Mills, J.H. (2003) *Cannabis Britannica: Empire, Trade and Prohibition*, Oxford: Oxford University Press.

Mills, K. (2009) 'Racism, Ethnicity and Drug Misuse', in H.S. Bui (ed.), *Race and Criminal Justice*, London: Sage.

Ministry of Justice (2009a) *Sentencing statistics quarterly brief. January to March 2009. England and Wales. Ministry of Justice Statistical Bulletin*, London: Ministry of Justice.

Ministry of Justice (2009b) *Offender Management Caseload Statistics 2008*, London: Ministry of Justice.

Ministry of Justice (2009c) *Story of the prison population 1995–2009. England and Wales. Ministry of Justice Statistics bulletin*, London: Ministry of Justice.

Monaghan, M. (2008) 'Appreciating cannabis: the paradox of evidence in evidence-based policy making', *Evidence & Policy: A Journal of Research, Debate and Practice*, 4: 209–31.

Moore, D. (2004) 'Beyond "subculture" in the ethnography of illicit drug use', *Contemporary Drug Problems*, 31(2): 181–212.

Moore, T.H.M., Zammit, S., Lingford-Hughes, A., Barnes, T.R.E., Jones, P.B., Burke, M. and Lewis, G. (2007) 'Cannabis use and risk of psychotic or affective mental health outcomes: a systematic review', *The Lancet*, 370(9584): 319–28.

Mortenson, T. (2009) *California at the Edge of a Cliff*, Sacramento, CA: California Faculty Association.

MTF (2009) '2009 Data from In-School Surveys of 8th-, 10th-, and 12th-Grade Students'. Online. Available <http://www.monitoringthefuture.org/data/09data.html#2009data-drugs> (accessed 22nd December 2009).

Muennig, P., Fiscella, K., Tancredi, D. and Franks, P. (2009) 'The relative health burden of selected social and behavioral risk factors in the United States: Implications for policy', *American Journal of Public Health*, published online ahead of print December 17, 2009: AJPH.2009.165019.

Musto, D. (1999) *The American Disease: The Origins of Narcotics Control*, New York: Oxford University Press.

Nadelmann, E. (2009) Interview with Jean-Marc Coicaud, *World Opinion Café Forum*. Online. Available <http://www.ony.unu.edu/events-forums/MDForums/2009/after-the-war-on-drugs-1.html> (accessed 21st December 2009).

Najman, J.M., Toloo, G. and Williams, G.M. (2008) 'Increasing socio-economic inequalities in drug-induced deaths in Australia: 1981–2002', *Drug and Alcohol Review*, 27(6): 613–18.

National Audit Office (2009) *The National Offender Management Information System*, London: National Audit Office.

National Center on Addiction and Substance Abuse (2003) *Crossing the Bridge: An Evaluation of the Drug Treatment Alternative-to-Prison (DTAP) Program. A CASA White Paper*. New York: National Center on Addiction and Substance Abuse, Columbia University.

Naughton, M. (2005) 'Evidence-based policy and the government of the criminal justice system – only if the evidence fits!', *Critical Social Policy*, 25(1): 47–69.

Neale, J. (2002) *Drug Users in Society*, Basingstoke: Palgrave Macmillan.

Neisser, U., Boodoo, G., Bouchard, T.J., Boykin, A.W., Brody, N., Ceci, S.J., Halpern, D.F., Loehlin, J.C., Perloff, R., Sternberg, R.J. and Urbina, S. (1996) 'Intelligence: Knowns and unknowns', *American Psychologist*, 51(2): 77–101.

Newburn, T. and Sparks, R. (eds) (2004) *Criminal Justice and Political Cultures: National and International Dimensions of Crime Control*, Cullompton: Willan.

Newcomb, M.D., Schieier, L.M. and Bentler, P.M. (1997) 'Effects of Adolescent Drug Use on Adult Mental Health: A Prospective Study of a Community Sample', in G.A. Marlatt and G.R. Vandenbos (eds), *Addictive Behaviours: Readings on Etiology, Prevention and Treatment*, Washington, D.C.: American Psychological Association.

NICE (2004) *Interferon alfa (pegylated and non-pegylated) and ribavirin for the treatment of chronic hepatitis C. Technology appraisal 75*, London: National Institute for Health and Clinical Excellence.

NICE (2006) *Peginterferon alfa and ribavirin for the treatment of mild chronic hepatitis C. NICE technology appraisal guidance 106*, London: National Institute for Health and Clinical Excellence.

NIDA (1987) *Topical data from the Drug Abuse Warning Network (DAWN), 1976–1985*, Rockville, MD: National Institute on Drug Abuse.

Nolan, J.L. (2001) *Reinventing Justice: The American Drug Court Movement*, Princeton, NJ: Princeton University Press.

NTA (2008) *Press release. Funding for drug treatment moves towards a fairer system*, London: National Treatment Agency for Substance Misuse.

NTA (2009a) *Statistics for drug treatment activity in England 2008/09. National Drug Treatment Monitoring System*, London: National Treatment Agency for Substance Misuse.

NTA (2009b) *Breaking the link: the role of drug treatment in tackling crime*, London: National Treatment Agency for Substance Misuse.

Nurco, D.N. (1985) 'A Discussion of Validity', in B.A. Rouse, N.J. Kozel and L.G. Richards (eds), *Self-Report Methods of Estimating Drug Use: Meeting Current Challenges to Validity. NIDA Research Monograph 57*, Rockville, MD: National Institute on Drug Abuse.

Nutley, S.M. and Davies, H.T.O. (2000) 'Making a reality of evidence-based practice: Some lessons from the diffusion of innovations', *Public Money and Management*, 20(4): 35–42.

Nutley, S.M., Walter, I. and Bland, N. (2002) 'The institutional arrangements for connecting evidence and policy: The case of drug misuse', *Public Policy and Administration*, 17(3): 76–94.

Nutt, D. (2009a) Estimating drug harms: a risky business?, Lecture at the Centre for Crime and Justice Studies, London.

Nutt, D. (2009b) 'Response to the request from the Science and Technology Select Committee for information about the background to the sacking of Prof Nutt from the ACMD on the 30th October 2009'. Online. Available <http://www.parliament.uk/documents/upload/091118_a)_Letter_from_Prof_Nutt.pdf> (accessed 22nd November 2009).

Nutt, D. (2009c) 'Editorial: Equasy – an overlooked addiction with implications for the current debate on drug harms', *Journal of Psychopharmacology*, 23(3): 3–5.

O'Brien, M. (1998) *Crime and Disorder Bill (Lords). House of Commons Standing Committee B. 19 May 1998*, London: Stationery Office.

O'Bryan, L. (1989) 'Young People and Drugs', in S. MacGregor (ed.), *Drugs and British Society: Responses to a Social Problem in the 1980s*, London: Routledge.

O'Leary, K. (2009) 'California's Crisis Hits Its Prized Universities', *Time*, 18 July 2009.

O'Malley, P. (2002) 'Drugs, Risks and Freedoms: Illicit Drug Use and "Misuse" under Neo-liberal Governance', in G. Hughes, E. McLaughlin and J. Muncie (eds), *Crime Prevention and Community Safety: New Directions*, London: Sage.

O'Malley, P. (2008) 'Experiments in risk and criminal justice', *Theoretical Criminology*, 12(4): 451–69.

O'Malley, P. and Mugford, S. (1991) 'The demand for intoxicating commodities: Implications for the "War on Drugs" ', *Social Justice*, 18(4): 49–75.

Oakley, A. (2000) *Experiments in Knowing: Gender and Method in the Social Sciences*, Cambridge: Polity Press.

Obama, B. (2004) *Dreams from My Father: A Story of Race and Inheritance*, New York: Crown Publishers.

Obama, B. (2008) 'A More Perfect Union', in B. Obama (ed.), *Change We Can Believe In*, Edinburgh: Canongate.

OECD (2008) *Are we growing unequal? New evidence on changes in poverty and incomes over the past 20 years*, Paris: Organisation for Economic Cooperation and Development.

Oeuvray, K., Stevens, A., Hunt, N., McSweeney, T. and Heckmann, W. (in preparation) 'Court ordered commitment: enabling (or hindering) conditions of the emergence of commitment to change in quasi compulsory treatment for drug using offenders'.

Office of the Governor (2010) 'Press release: Gov. Schwarzenegger Provides Constitutional Amendment Language to Increase Higher Education Funding, Shift Funding from Prisons'. Online. Available <http://gov.ca.gov/press-release/14129/> (accessed 11th January 2010).

Olsson, B. (2009) 'Dressed for Success? A critical review of 'Sweden's Successful Drug Policy: A Review of the Evidence', paper presented to the 3rd Annual Conference of the International Society for the Study of Drug Policy, Vienna.

ONDCP (2010) '*FY 2011 Drug Control Program Highlights*', Washington, DC: Office of National Drug Control Policy. Online. Available <http://www.whitehouse drugpolicy.gov/publications/policy/11budget/fy11factsheet.pdf> (accessed 5 February 2010).

Ousey, G.C. and Lee, M.R. (2002) 'Examining the conditional nature of the illicit drug market-homicide relationship: A partial test of the theory of contingent causation', *Criminology*, 40(1): 73–102.

Ousey, G.C. and Lee, M.R. (2007) 'Homicide trends and illicit drug markets: Exploring differences across time', *Justice Quarterly*, 24(1): 48–79.

Owen, J. (2007) 'Cannabis: An apology', *The Independent on Sunday*, 18 March 2007.

Pacula, R., Chriqui, J. and King, J. (2004) *Marijuana Decriminalization. What does it Mean in the United States*, Santa Monica, CA: RAND.

Page, B. (2005) *Analyzing the Economic and Budgetary Effects of a 10 Percent Cut in Income Tax Rates*, Washington, DC: Congressional Budget Office.

Pahl, R. (1977) 'Playing the Rationality Game: The Sociologist as a Hired Expert' in C. Bell and H. Newby (eds), *Doing Sociological Research*, London: George Allen & Unwin.

Palmer, G., MacInnes, T. and Kenway, P. (2007) *Monitoring poverty and social exclusion 2007*, York: Joseph Rowntree Foundation.

Parker, H., Aldridge, J. and Measham, F. (1998) *Illegal Leisure. The Normalization of Adolescent Recreational Drug Use*, London: Routledge.

Parkin, F. (1972) *Class Inequality and Political Order*, St Albans: Paladin.

Paulozzi, L.J. (2006) 'Opioid analgesic involvement in drug abuse deaths in American metropolitan areas', *American Journal of Public Health*, 96(10): 1755–57.

Paulozzi, L.J. and Annest, J.L. (2007) 'US data show sharply rising drug-induced death rates', *Injury Prevention*, 13(2): 130–32.

Paulozzi, L.J. and Xi, Y. (2008) 'Recent changes in drug poisoning mortality in the United States by urban-rural status and by drug type', *Pharmacoepidemiology and Drug Safety*, 17(10): 997–1005.

Pearson, G. (1987a) *The New Heroin Users*, Oxford: Basil Blackwell.

Pearson, G. (1987b) 'Social Deprivation, Unemployment and Patterns of Heroin Use', in N. Dorn and N. South (eds.), *A Land Fit for Heroin: Drug Policies, Prevention and Practice*, Basingstoke: Macmillan Education.

Pearson, G. (1991) 'Drug-Control Policies in Britain', in M. Tonry (ed.), *Crime and Justice Review, Vol. 14*, Chicago: Chicago University Press.

Peters, R. and Murrin, M. (2000) 'Effectiveness of treatment based drug courts in reducing criminal recidivism', *Criminal Justice and Behavior*, 27: 72–96.

Peterson, R.D. (1985) 'Discriminatory decision making at the legislative level', *Law and Human Behavior*, 9(3): 243.

PMSU (2003a) *SU Drugs Report. Phase 1 report: Understanding the issues*, London: Prime Minister's Strategy Unit.

PMSU (2003b) *SU Drugs Report. Phase 2 report: Diagnosis and recommendations*, London: Prime Minister's Strategy Unit.

Preble, E. and Casey, J. (1969) 'Taking care of business – The heroin user's life of the street', *The International Journal of the Addictions*, 4(1): 1–24.

Prendergast, M.L., Podus, D., Chang, E. and Urada, D. (2002) 'The effectiveness of drug abuse treatment: a meta-analysis of comparison group studies', *Drug and Alcohol Dependence*, 67(1): 53–72.

President of the Council (1998) *Tackling Drugs to Build a Better Britain: The Government's Ten-Year Strategy for Tackling Drugs Misuse*, London: Her Majesty's Stationery Office.

Prior, L. (2003) *Using Documents in Social Research*, London: Sage.

Projektgruppe Rauschmittelfragen (1991) *Forschungsprojekt 'Amsel'. Abschlussbericht Band 1*, Frankfurt/Main: Jugendberatung und Jugendhilfe e.V.

PRS (2002) *Evaluation of Lambeth's Pilot of Warnings for Possession of Cannabis – Summary of final report*, London: PRS Consultancy Group.

Pryor, W. (2003) *Survival of the Coolest*, Bath: Clear Press.

Pudney, S. (2002) *The road to ruin? Sequences of initiation into drug use and offending by young people in Britain*, London: Home Office.

Radcliffe, P. and Stevens, A. (2008) 'Are drug treatment services only for "thieving junkie scumbags"? Drug users and the management of stigmatized identities', *Social Science & Medicine*, 67(7): 1065–73.

Ram, R. (2005) 'Income inequality, poverty, and population health: Evidence from recent data for the United States', 61(12): 2568–76.

Ramírez Cuellar, F. (2005) *The Profits of Extermination*, Monroe, ME: Common Courage Press.

RDS NOMS (2007) *Sentencing Statistics 2006. Statistical Bulletin*, London: Ministry of Justice.

Reinarman, C., Cohen, P.D.A. and Kaal, H.L. (2004) 'The limited relevance of drug policy: Cannabis in Amsterdam and San Francisco', *American Journal of Public Health*, 94.

Reiner, R. (2000) *The Politics of the Police*, 3rd edn, Oxford: Oxford University Press.

Reuter, P. (1984) *Disorganised Crime: Illegal Markets and the Mafia*, Cambridge, MA: MIT Press.

Reuter, P. (1989) *Quantity Illusions and Paradoxes of Drug Interdiction: Federal Intervention into Vice Policy, Note N-2929-USDP*, Santa Monica, CA: RAND.

Reuter, P. and Kleiman, M. (1986) 'Risks and Prices: An Economic Analysis of Drug Enforcement', in M. Tonry and N. Morris (eds), *Crime and Justice, Volume 7*, Chicago: University of Chicago Press.

Reuter, P. and Haaga, J. (1989) *The Organization of High-Level Drug Markets: An Exploratory Study*, Santa Monica, CA: RAND.

Reuter, P. and Stevens, A. (2007) *An Analysis of UK Drug Policy*, London: UK Drug Policy Commission.

Riley, J. (2006) 'Utilitarian liberalism: Between Gray and Mill', *Critical Review of International Social and Political Philosophy*, 9(2): 117–35.

Riley, J., Cassidy, D. and Becker, J. (2009) *Statistics on Race and the Criminal Justice System – 2007/8*, London: Ministry of Justice.

Robertson, L. (2007) 'Taming space: Drug use, HIV, and homemaking in Downtown Eastside Vancouver', *Gender Place and Culture*, 14(5): 527–49.

Rolles, S. (2007) *After the War on Drugs. Tools for the Debate*, Bristol: Transform Drug Policy Foundation.

Room, R., Reuter, P., Lenton, S., Hall, W. and Fischer, B. (2010) *Cannabis Policy: Moving Beyond Stalemate*, Oxford: Oxford University Press.

Rosenbaum, M. (1981) *Women on Heroin*, New Brunswick, NJ: Rutgers University Press.

Rothstein, B. and Uslaner, E.M. (2005) 'All for all. Equality, corruption, and social trust', *World Politics*, 58(October): 41–72.

Rousseau, J.-J. (2004 [1754]) *Discourse on the Origin of Inequality*, Mineola, NY: Dover Publications.

RSA Commission on Illegal Drugs Communities and Public Policy (2007) *Drugs – facing facts*, London: Royal Society for the Encouragement of Arts, Manufactures and Commerce.

Rubinstein, G. and Mukamal, D. (2002) 'Welfare and Housing – Denial of Benefits to Drug Offenders', in M. Mauer and M. Chesney-Lind (eds.), *Invisible Punishment: The Collateral Consequences of Mass Imprisonment*, New York: The New Press.

Runciman, W.G. (1966) *Relative Deprivation and Social Justice. A Study of Attitudes to Social Inequality in Twentieth-Century England*, London: Routledge and Kegan Paul.

Russell, J. (1994) Substance Abuse and Crime (Some Lessons from America), unpublished report to the Commonwealth Fund of New York.

Sabatier, P. and Jenkins-Smith, H. (eds.) (1993) *Policy Change and Learning: An Advocacy Coalition Approach*, Boulder, CO: Westview Press.

Sabet, K.A. (2005) 'Making it happen: The case for compromise in the federal cocaine law debate', *Social Policy & Administration*, 39(2): 181–91.

Sabol, W.J., West, H.C. and Cooper, M. (2009) *Bureau of Justice Statistics Bulletin. Prisoners in 2008*, Washington, DC: US Department of Justice.

SAMHSA (2003) *The DAWN Report*, Rockville, MD: Substance Abuse and Mental Health Administration.

SAMHSA (2009a) *Results from the 2008 National Survey on Drug Use and Health: National Findings*, Washington, DC: SAMHSA, Office of Applied Studies.

SAMHSA (2009b) 'Table 8.1B – Types of Illicit Drug Use in Lifetime among Persons Aged 12 or Older'. Online. Available <http://oas.samhsa.gov/NSDUH/2k8NSDUH/tabs/Sect8peTabs1to43.htm#Tab8.1B> (accessed 29th January 2010)

Sampson, A. (2005) *Who Runs This Place: The Anatomy of Britain in the 21st Century*, 2nd edn, London: John Murray.

Sampson, R.J. and Raudenbush, S.W. (1999) 'Systematic social observations of public spaces: A new look at disorder in urban neighbourhoods', *American Journal of Sociology*, 105(3): 603–51.

SAP (2009) *Sentencing for Drug Offences. Consultation Paper*, London: Sentencing Advisory Panel.

Sapir, J. (2002) *Les économistes contre la démocratie: Pouvoir, mondialisation et démocratie*, Paris: Editions Albin Michel.

Schaub, M., Stevens, A., Berto, D., Hunt, N., Kerschl, V., McSweeney, T., Oeuvray, K., Puppo, I., Santa Maria, A., Trinkl, B., Werdenich, W. and Uchtenhagen, A. (2010) 'Comparing outcomes of "voluntary" and "quasi-compulsory" treatment of substance dependence in Europe', *European Addiction Research*, 16: 53–60.

Schmitt, J. (2009) 'Inequality as policy: The United States since 1979', *Real-world Economics Review*, 51(1): 2–9.

Scruggs, L. and Allan, J. (2006) 'Welfare-state decommodification in 18 OECD countries: A replication and revision', *Journal of European Social Policy*, 16(1): 55–72.

Seddon, T. (2000) 'Explaining the drug-crime link: theoretical, policy and research issues', *Journal of Social Policy*, 29(1): 95–107.

Seddon, T. (2006) 'Drugs, crime and social exclusion: Social context and social theory in British drugs-crime research', *British Journal of Criminology*, 46(4): 680–703.

Seddon, T. (2008) 'Youth, heroin, crack: a review of recent British trends', *Health Education*, 108(3): 237–46.

Seddon, T., Ralphs, R. and Williams, L. (2008) 'Risk, security and the "criminalization" of British drug policy', *British Journal of Criminology*, 48(6): 818–34.

Self, W. (2006) *Junk Mail*, New York, NY: Black Cat.

Semple, D.M., McIntosh, A.M. and Lawrie, S.M. (2005) 'Cannabis as a risk factor for psychosis: Systematic review', *Journal of Psychopharmacology*, 19: 187–94.

Shaw, A., Egan, J. and Gillespie, M. (2007) *Drugs and Poverty: A Literature Review*, Glasgow: Scottish Drugs Forum.

Shepherd, J. (2007) 'The production and management of evidence for public service reform', *Evidence & Policy*, 3(2): 231–51.

Shepherd, J. (2003) 'Explaining feast or famine in randomized field trials – Medical science and criminology compared', *Evaluation Review*, 27(3): 290–315.

Shewan, D. and Dalgarno, P. (2006) 'Evidence for controlled heroin use? Low levels of negative health and social outcomes among non-treatment heroin users in Glasgow (Scotland)', *British Journal of Health Psychology*, 10: 33–48.

Shiner, M. (2009) *Drug Use and Social Change*, London: Palgrave Macmillan.

Shulgin, A. and Shulgin, A. (1991) *PiHKAL: A Chemical Love Story*, Berkeley, CA: Transform Press.

Sim, J. (2009) *Punishment and Prisons: Power and the Carceral State*, London: Sage.

Simon, J. (2007) *Governing through Crime: How the War on Crime Transformed American Democracy and Created a Culture of Fear*, Oxford: Oxford University Press.

Singer, M. (2008) *Drugging the Poor: Legal and Illegal Drugs and Social Inequality*, Long Grove, IL: Waveland Press.

Single, E., Christie, P. and Ali, R. (2000) 'The impact of cannabis decriminalisation in Australia and the United States', *Journal of Public Health Policy*, 21(2): 157–86.

Singleton, N., Meltzer, H., Gatward, R., Coid, J. and Deasy, D. (1997) *Psychiatric morbidity among prisoners: Summary report*, London: National Statistics.

Singleton, N., Bumpstead, R., O'Brien, M., Lee, A. and Meltzer, H. (2001) *Psychiatric morbidity among adults living in private households, 2000*, London: Office for National Statistics.

Skodbo, S., Brown, G., Deacon, S., Cooper, A., Hall, A., Millar, T. Smith, J. and Whitham, K. (2007) *The Drug Interventions Programme (DIP): addressing drug use and offending through 'Tough Choices'*, London: Home Office.

Skorikov, V. and Vondracek, F.W. (2007) 'Positive career orientation as an inhibitor of adolescent problem behaviour', *Journal of Adolescence*, 30(1): 131–46.

Sloman, L. (1998) *Reefer Madness: A History of Marijuana*, New York: St. Martin's Press.

Smith, A. (1970) *The Wealth of Nations*, Harmondsworth: Penguin.

Smith, D. (2009) 'Key Concepts and Theories About Race', in H.S. Bui (ed.), *Race and Criminal Justice*, London: Sage.

Smith, T. and Smith, S.J. (1989) *The Politics of Race and Residence: Citizenship, Segregation and White Supremacy in Britain*, Cambridge: Polity.

Solivetti, L.M. (2001) *Drug Use Criminalization v. Decriminalization: An Analysis in the Light of the Italian Experience*, Rome: Swiss Federal Office of Public Health.

Sommers, I. and Baskin, D.R. (1997) 'Situational or generalized violence in drug dealing networks', *Journal of Drug Issues*, 27(4): 833–49.

South, N. (1998) 'Tackling Drug Control in Britain: From Sir Malcolm Delevigne to the New Drugs Strategy', in R. Coomber (ed.), *The Control of Drugs and Drug Users: Reason or Reaction?* London: CRC Press.

Stevens, A. (2007a) 'When two dark figures collide: Evidence and discourse on drug-related crime', *Critical Social Policy*, 27(1): 77–99.

Stevens, A. (2007b) 'Survival of the ideas that fit: An evolutionary analogy for the use of evidence in policy', *Social Policy and Society*, 6(1): 25–35.

Stevens, A. (2008a) 'Weighing up crime: The estimation of criminal drug-related harm', *Contemporary Drug Problems*, 35(Summer-Fall): 265–90.

Stevens, A. (2008b) 'Quasi-compulsory Treatment in Europe: An Evidence-based Response to Drug-related Crime?', in A. Stevens (ed.), *Crossing Frontiers: International Developments in the Treatment of Drug Dependence*, Brighton: Pavilion Publishing.

Stevens, A. and Reuter, P. (2009) 'Response to: Trends in drug misuse recorded in primary care in the UK from 1998 to 2005', *Journal of Public Health*, doi: 10.1093/pubmed/fdp018.

Stevens, A., Bur, A.-M. and Young, L. (1999) *Include Us In! Participation for Social Inclusion in Europe*. Canterbury: EISS, University of Kent at Canterbury.

Stevens, A., Bur, A.-M. and Young, L. (2003) 'People, jobs, rights and power: The roles of participation in combating social exclusion in Europe', *Community Development Journal*, 38(2): 84–95.

Stevens, A., Trace, M. and Bewley-Taylor, D.R. (2005) *Reducing Drug Related Crime: An Overview of the Global Evidence. Report Five*, Oxford: Beckley Foundation.

Stevens, A., Stöver, H. and Brentari, C. (2010) 'Criminal Justice Approaches to Harm Reduction in Europe', in T. Rhodes (ed.), *Harm Reduction: Evidence, Impacts and Challenges*, Lisbon: European Monitoring Centre on Drugs and Drug Addiction.

Stevens, A., McSweeney, T., van Ooyen, M. and Uchtenhagen, A. (2005) 'On coercion', *International Journal of Drug Policy*, 16: 207–09.

Stevens, A., Radcliffe, P., Hunt, N. and Sanders, M. (2008) 'Early exit: Estimating and explaining early exit from drug treatment', *Harm Reduction Journal*, 5(13): 25 April 2008.

Stevens, A., Radcliffe, P., Pizani-Williams, L., Gladstone, B. and Agar, I. (2009) Offender Management Community Scoping of London Gang Demographics, unpublished report to London Probation Service.

Stevens, A., Berto, D., Heckmann, W., Kerschl, V., Oeuvray, K., van Ooyen, M., Steffan, E. and Uchtenhagen, A. (2005) 'Quasi-compulsory treatment of drug dependent offenders: An international literature review', *Substance Use & Misuse*, 40: 269–83.

Stevens, A., Berto, D., Frick, U., Kerschl, V., McSweeney, T., Schaaf, S., Tartari, M.,

Turnbull, P., Trinkl, B., Uchtenhagen, A., Waidner, G. and Werdenich, W. (2007) 'The victimization of dependent drug users: Findings from a European study', *European Journal of Criminology*, 4(4): 385–408.

Stevens, A., Berto, D., Frick, U., Hunt, N., Kerschl, V., McSweeney, T., Oeuvray, K., Puppo, I., Santa Maria, A., Schaaf, S., Trinkl, B., Uchtenhagen, A. and Werdenich, W. (2006) 'The relationship between legal status, perceived pressure and motivation in treatment for drug dependence: Results from a European study of quasi-compulsory treatment', *European Addiction Research*, 12: 197–209.

Stimpson, J.P., Ju, H., Raji, M.A. and Eschbach, K. (2007) 'Neighborhood deprivation and health risk behaviors in NHANES III', *American Journal of Health Behavior*, 31(2): 215–22.

Stimson, G. Evidence and policy: the use and misuse of drugs statistics, Paper to roundtable on drug policy, London, 2001.

Stimson, G. (1995) 'Aids and injecting drug use in the United Kingdom, 1987–1993: The policy response and the prevention of the epidemic', *Social Science & Medicine*, 41(5): 699–716.

Stockdale, S.E., Wells, K.B., Tang, L., Belin, T.R., Zhang, L. and Sherbourne, C.D. (2007) 'The importance of social context: Neighborhood stressors, stress-buffering mechanisms, and alcohol, drug, and mental health disorders', *Social Science & Medicine*, 65(9): 1867–81.

Stokes, D. (2004) *America's Other War. Terrorizing Colombia*, London: Zed Books.

Stonewall (2003) *Profiles of Prejudice*, London: Stonewall Citizenship 21.

Stöver, H. and Nelles, J. (2003) 'Ten years of experience with needle and syringe exchange programmes in European prisons', *International Journal of Drug Policy*, 14(5–6): 437–44.

Strang, J., Sheridan, J., Hunt, C., Kerr, B., Gerada, C. and Pringle, M. (2005) 'The prescribing of methadone and other opioids to addicts: national survey of GPs in England and Wales', *British Journal of General Practice*, 55(515): 444–51.

Strangleman, T. (2007) 'The nostalgia for permanence at work? The end of work and its commentators', *The Sociological Review*, 55(1): 81–103.

Straw, J. (1996) *Breaking the Vicious Circle: Labour's Proposals to Tackle Drug Related Crime*, London: Labour Party.

Straw, J. and Michael, A. (1996) *Tackling the Causes of Crime: Labour's Proposals to Prevent Crime and Criminality*, London: Labour Party.

Strom, K.J. and MacDonald, J.M. (2007) 'The influence of social and economic disadvantage on racial patterns in youth homicide over time', *Homicide Studies*, 11(1): 50–69.

Sub-Committee On Terrorism, Narcotics and International Operations (1989) *Drugs, Law Enforcement And Foreign Policy: Report By The Sub-Committee On Terrorism, Narcotics and International Operations*, Washington, DC: US Senate, Committee on Foreign Relations.

Sudbury, J. (2005) ' "Mules", "yardies" and other folk devils: mapping cross-border imprisonment in Britain', in J. Sudbury (ed.), *Global Lockdown: Race, Gender and the Prison-Industrial Complex*, London: Routledge.

Summers, D., Jones, S. and Booth, R. (2009) 'David Nutt's sacking causes mass revolt against Alan Johnson', *The Guardian*, 2 November 2009.

Sweney, M. (2009) 'Speedball beer banned', *The Guardian*, 20 January 2009.

Szasz, T. (1975) *Ceremonial Chemistry: the Ritual Persecution of Drugs, Addicts and Pushers*, Woking: Unwin Brothers Limited.

Tauber, J.S. (1993) *The importance of immediate and intensive intervention in a court-ordered drug rehabilitation program. An evaluation of the F.I.R.S.T. diversion project after two years*, Oakland: Oakland-Piedmont-Emeryville Municipal Court.

Taylor, A. (1993) *Women Drug Users: An Ethnography of a Female Injecting Community*, Oxford: Clarendon Press.

Taylor, R., Najafi, E. and Dobson, A. (2007) 'A Meta-analysis of studies of passive smoking and lung cancer', *International Journal of Epidemiology*, 36: 1048–59.

Teague, M. (2009) 'Barack Obama: changing American criminal justice', *Criminal Justice Matters*, 76: 4–5.

Teo, T. (2008) 'From speculation to epistemological violence in psychology – A critical-hermeneutic reconstruction', *Theory & Psychology*, 18(1): 47–67.

The Panel on Fair Access to the Professions (2009) *Unleashing Aspiration: The Final Report of the Panel on Fair Access to the Professions*, London: Cabinet Office.

The Academy of Medical Sciences (2004) *Calling Time. The Nation's drinking as a major health issue*, London: The Academy of Medical Sciences.

The Academy of Medical Sciences (2008) *Brain science, addiction and drugs*, London: The Academy of Medical Sciences.

The Economist (2009) 'Time to come clean', *The Economist*, 5 November 2009.

Therborn, G. (1980) *The Ideology of Power and the Power of Ideology*, London: Verso.

Thompson, J.B. (1990) *Ideology and Modern Culture: Critical Social Theory in the Era of Mass Communication*, Cambridge: Polity Press.

Thornberry, T.P. and Krohn, M.D. (2000) 'The Self-report Method for Measuring Delinquency and Crime', in J.E. Samuels (ed.), *Measurement and Analysis of Crime and Justice. Criminal Justice 2000. Volume 4*, Washington, DC: National Institute of Justice.

Tilly, C. (1998) *Durable Inequality*, Berkeley, CA: University of California Press.

Tilly, C. (2003) 'Changing forms of inequality', *Sociological Theory*, 21(1): 31–36.

Tombs, J. (2003) Evidence in the policymaking process, paper presented at the Department of Criminology, Keele University, 7 May 2003, unpublished.

Tonry, M. (2004) *Punishment and Politics: Evidence and Emulation in the Making of English Crime Control Policy*, Cullompton: Willan Publishing.

Tonry, M. (2009) 'Explanations of American punishment policies. A national history', *Punishment and Society*, 11(3): 377–94.

Tonry, M. and Melewski, M. (2008) 'The malign effects of drug and crime control policies on black Americans', *Crime and Justice*, 37(1): 1–44.

Transform (2006) *After the War on Drugs. Options for Control*, Bristol: Transform Drug Policy Foundation.

Transform (2009a) *After the War on Drugs. Blueprint for Regulation*, Bristol: Transform Drug Policy Foundation.

Transform (2009b) *A Comparison of the Cost-effectiveness of the Prohibition and Regulation of Drugs*, Bristol: Transform Drug Policy Foundation.

Travis, J. (2002) 'Invisible Punishment: An Instrument of Social Exclusion', in M. Mauer and M. Chesney-Lind (eds.), *Invisible Punishment: The Collateral Consequences of Mass Imprisonment*, New York: The New Press.

Turkheimer, E., Haley, A., Waldron, M., D'Onofrio, B. and Gottesman, I.I. (2003)

'Socioeconomic status modifies heritability of IQ in young children', *Psychological Science*, 14(6): 623–28.

Turnbull, P.J., McSweeney, T., Webster, R., Edmunds, M. and Hough, M. (2000) *Drug Treatment and Testing Orders: Final Evaluation Report*, London: Home Office.

Tyrrell, I. (2008) 'The regulation of alcohol and other drugs in a colonial context: United States policy towards the Philippines, c. 1898–1910', *Contemporary Drug Problems*, 35(4): 539–71.

Uchtenhagen, A. (2008) 'Heroin-assisted Treatment in Europe: A Safe and Effective Approach', in A. Stevens (ed.), *Crossing Frontiers: International Developments in the Treatment of Drug Dependence*, Brighton: Pavilion Publishing.

Uchtenhagen, A., Gutzwiller, F., Dobler-Mikola, A. and Stephen, T. (1997) 'Programme for a medical prescription of narcotics: a synthesis of results', *European Addiction Research*, 3(4): 160–63.

Uitermark, J. (2004) 'The origins and future of the Dutch approach towards drugs', *Journal of Drug Issues* (Summer): 511–32.

UN General Assembly (2006) *Resolution 60/262. Political Declaration on HIV/AIDS*, New York: United Nations.

UNAIDS (2001) *Effective Prevention Strategies in Low HIV Prevalence Settings*, Geneva: UNAIDS.

United Nations Economic and Social Council (2009) *Political Declaration and Plan of Action on International Cooperation towards an Integrated and Balanced Strategy to Counter the World Drug Problem*, Vienna: United Nations.

UNODC (2002) *Contemporary Drug Abuse Treatment: A Review of the Evidence Base*, Vienna: United Nations Office on Drugs and Crime.

UNODC (2007) *Sweden's Successful Drug Policy: A Review of the Evidence*, Vienna: United Nations Office on Drugs and Crime.

UNODC (2009) *Press Release: 'Positive Balance Sheet' from Century of Drug Control*, Vienna: United Nations Office on Drugs and Crime.

UNODC and WHO (2008) *Principles of Drug Treatment. Discussion Paper*, Vienna: United Nations Office on Drugs and Crime.

US Department of Justice (2003) *2000 Arrestee Drug Abuse Monitoring: Annual Report*, Washington, DC: US Department of Justice.

Valentine, K. (2009) 'Evidence, values and drug treatment policy', *Critical Social Policy*, 29(3): 443–64.

Valverde, M. (1998) *Diseases of the Will. Alcohol and the Dilemmas of Freedom*, Cambridge: Cambridge University Press.

van 't Land, H., van Duijvenbooden, K., van der Plas, A. and Wolf, J. (2005) *Opgevangen onder dwang procesevaluatie strafrechtelijke opvang verslaafden*, The Hague: WODC, Ministry of Justice.

van den Brink, W., Hendriks, V.M., Blanken, P., Koeter, M.W., van Zwieten, B.J. and van Ree, J.M. (2003) 'Medical prescription of heroin to treatment resistant heroin addicts: two randomised controlled trials', *British Medical Journal*, 327(7410): 310.

van Laar, M. and Ooyen-Houben, M. (2009) '*Evaluation of the Dutch National Drug Policy: Summary*', Utrecht/Den Haag: Trimbos-instituut, WODC. Online. Available <http://english.wodc.nl/onderzoeksdatabase/evaluatie-drugsbeleid.aspx> (accessed 4 January 2010).

van Laar, M., Cruts, G., van Gageldonk, A., van Ooyen-Houben, M., Croes, E.,

Meijer, R. and Ketelaars, T. (2009) *Report on the Drug Situation 2008*, Lisbon: European Monitoring Centre on Drugs and Drug Addiction.
van Ooyen-Houben, M. (2008) 'Quasi-compulsory Treatment in the Netherlands: Promising Theory, Problems in Practice', in A. Stevens (ed.), *Crossing Frontiers: International Developments in the Treatment of Drug Dependence*, Brighton: Pavilion Publishing.
van Swaaningen, R. (2010) 'Louk Hulsman', in K. Hayward, S. Maruna and J. Mooney (eds), *Fifty Key Thinkers in Criminology*, London: Routledge.
Van Zee, A. (2009) 'The promotion and marketing of OxyContin: commercial triumph, public health tragedy', *American Journal of Public Health*, 99(2): 221–27.
von Sydow, K., Lieb, R., Pfister, H., Höfler, M. and Wittchen, H.-U. (2002) 'What predicts incident use of cannabis and progression to abuse and dependence?: A 4-year prospective examination of risk factors in a community sample of adolescents and young adults', *Drug and Alcohol Dependence*, 68(1): 49–64.
Wacquant, L. (2006) *Punishing the Poor: the New Government of Social Insecurity*, Durham, NC: Duke University Press.
Wacquant, L. (2007) *Urban Outcasts: A Comparative Sociology of Advanced Marginality*, Cambridge: Polity Press.
Waddington, P.A.J., Stenson, K. and Don, D. (2004) 'In proportion: Race, and police stop and search', *British Journal of Criminology*, 44(6): 889–914.
Wadsworth, E.J.K., Moss, S.C., Simpson, S.A. and Smith, A.P. (2004) 'Factors associated with recreational drug use', *Journal of Psychopharmacology*, 18(2): 238–48.
WAG (2008) *Working Together to Reduce Harm. The Substance Misuse Strategy for Wales 2008–2018*, Cardiff: Welsh Assembly Government.
WAG (2009) *Substance Misuse in Wales 2008–9*, Cardiff: Welsh Assembly Government.
Walker, A., Flatley, J., Kershaw, C. and Moon, D. (eds) (2009) *Crime in England and Wales, 2008/09. Volume 1. Findings from the British Crime Survey and police recorded crime*, London: Home Office.
Warburton, H., Turnbull, P. and Hough, M. (2005a) *Occasional and Controlled Heroin Use. Not a Problem?*, York: Joseph Rowntree Foundation.
Warburton, H., May, T. and Hough, M. (2005b) 'Looking the other way: the impact of reclassifying cannabis on police warnings, arrests and informal action in England and Wales', *The British Journal of Criminology*, 45: 113–28.
Ward, C. (2009) 'Drugs: Convictions', *Hansard, Written Answers (9 September 2009): Column 1906W*. London: The Stationery Office
Webber, C. (2007) 'Revaluating relative deprivation theory', *Theoretical Criminology*, 11(1): 97–120.
Weber, M. (1920) 'Die Protestantischen Sekten und der Geist des Kapitalismus', *Gesammelte Aufsatze Zur Religionssoziologie*, 1(207–236).
Weiner, M.D., Sussman, S., Sun, P. and Dent, C. (2005) 'Explaining the link between violence perpetration, victimization and drug use', *Addictive Behaviors*, 30(6): 1261–66.
Weiss, C.H. (1977) 'Research for policy's sake: the enlightenment function of social research', *Policy Analysis*, 3: 531–47.
Weiss, C.H. (1999) 'The interface between evaluation and public policy', *Evaluation*, 5(4): 468–86.
Western, B. (2004) 'Politics and social structure in The Culture of Control', *Critical Review of International Social and Political Philosophy*, 7(2): 33–41.

White, M. (2008) THC content of seized cannabis, presentation to the ACMD Cannabis Review Hearing, London.

Whittington, D. (2007) *Beaten Into Violence: Anger, Masculinities, Alcohol, Narcotics*, London: Karnac Books.

WHO (1946) *Preamble to the Constitution of the World Health Organization as adopted by the International Health Conference, New York, 19–22 June, 1946*, Geneva: World Health Organization.

Wilkinson, M. (2008) 'Treatment for all with Hep C.' Presentation to Release Conference on Drugs, Race and Discrimination, London.

Wilkinson, R.G. (1996) *Unhealthy Societies: The Afflictions of Inequality*, London: Routledge.

Wilkinson, R.G. (2005) *The Impact of Inequality: How to Make Sick Societies Healthier*, London: Routledge.

Wilkinson, R.G. and Pickett, K. (2008) *The Spirit Level: Why More Equal Societies Almost Always Do Better*, London: Allen Lane.

Williams, R.J., Zolnar, T., Bertrand, L. and Davis, M. (2004) 'Mental health status of infrequent adolescent substance users', *Journal of Child & Adolescent Substance Abuse*, 14(2): 41–60.

Wilson, J.Q. and Kelling, G.L. (1982) 'Broken windows', *The Atlantic Monthly*, March: 29–38.

Wincup, E., Buckland, G. and Bayliss, R. (2003) *Youth homelessness and substance use: report to the Drugs and Alcohol Research Unit. Findings 191*, London: Home Office.

Wintour, P., Watt, N. and Topping, A. (2008) 'Cameron: absent black fathers must meet responsibilities' *The Guardian*, 16 July 2008.

Wisniewski, A.M., Purdy, C.H. and Blondell, R.D. (2008) 'The epidemiologic association between opioid prescribing, non-medical use, and emergency department visits', *Journal of Addictive Diseases*, 27(1): 1–11.

Woo, S. and Scheck, J. (2009) 'Californians Get a Budget That Leaves Few Happy', *The Wall Street Journal*, 20 February 2009.

Working Group on Inequalities in Health (1988 [1980]) 'The Black Report', in P. Townsend, M. Whitehead and N. Davidson (eds), *Inequalities in Health*, London: Penguin.

Working Party of the Royal College of Psychiatrists and the Royal College of Physicians (2000) *Drugs: Dilemmas and Choices*, London: Gaskell.

Wright, C. (2000) *A Community Manifesto*, London: Earthscan Publications.

Wright, N.M.J. and Tompkins, C.N.E. (2004) 'Supervised injecting centres', *British Medical Journal*, 328: 100–102.

Xu, J., Kochanek, K.D. and Tejada-Vera, B. (2009) 'Deaths: Preliminary Data for 2007', *National Vital Statistics Reports*, 58(1): Table 2.

Yamaguchi, R., Johnston, L.D. and O'Malley, P.M. (2003) *Drug testing in schools: Policies, practices and association with student drug use. Youth, Education & Society Occasional Paper 2*, Ann Arbor: University of Michigan.

Yin, R.K. (1994) *Case Study Research: Design and Methods.* Second edition, London: Sage.

Young, J. (1971) *The Drugtakers: The Social Meaning of Drug Use*, London: Paladin.

Young, J. (1999) *The Exclusive Society*, London: Sage.

Young, J. (2003a) 'Winning the Fight Against Crime? New Labour, Populism and Lost Opportunities', in R. Matthews and J. Young (eds.), *The New Politics of Crime and Punishment*, Cullompton: Willan Publishing.

Young, J. (2003b) 'Merton with energy, Katz with structure: The sociology of vindictiveness and the criminology of transgression', *Theoretical Criminology*, 7(3): 388–414.

Young, J. (2007) *The Vertigo of Late Modernity*, London: Sage.

Young, J. and Matthews, R. (2003) 'New Labour, Crime Control and Social Exclusion', in R. Matthews and J. Young (eds.), *The New Politics of Crime and Punishment*, Cullompton: Willan Publishing.

Young, K., Ashby, D., Boaz, A. and Grayson, L. (2002) 'Social science and the evidence-based policy movement', *Social Policy and Society*, 1(3): 215–24.

Zador, D., Kidd, B., Hutchinson, S., Taylor, A., Hickman, M., Fahey, T., Rome, A. and Baldacchino, A. (2005) *National Investigation into Drug Related Deaths in Scotland, 2003*, Edinburgh: Scottish Executive.

Zinberg, N.E. (1984) *Drug, Set, and Setting: The Basis for Controlled Intoxicant Use*, New Haven, CT: Yale University.

Index

Note: The reference 149n6 refers to note 6 on page 149.